JBTM 18.1 (Spring 2021):1–2

Editorial Introduction

Lloyd A. Harsch, PhD

Lloyd A. Harsch is professor of church history and Baptist studies, occupying the Cooperative Program Chair of SBC Studies; divisional associate dean of the Theological and Historical Studies Division; director of the Institute for Faith and the Public Square; and guest editor, Journal for Baptist Theology and Ministry at New Orleans Baptist Theological Seminary

Dr. Adam Harwood, who normally holds the responsibility of editing this journal is out of the country serving in his additional capacity as Chaplain in the Louisiana Army National Guard. When he was called into active duty, the responsibility of editing the journal came to me. I am happy to fill in for him as he serves both our Lord and our country. On the surface, editing a journal seems so easy until it is your responsibility to do so. I am discovering how much work goes into the process. However, Dr. Harwood did an excellent job of setting things in motion prior to his departure. I am also deeply grateful to my assistant, Gray Clary, for his diligent attention to detail in making this issue a reality.

In the opening article, Ben Hutchison explores Martin Luther's view of death and grieving. For Luther, the Christian's hope from suffering and death was to focus on Christ and his victory over death. He includes contemporary applications of Luther's perspective. The next article examines how writers in the Bible used the literary form of lament as hope in God for a hurting world. Jessica McMillan and Ed Steele trace the use of the lament throughout the Bible and include original musical scores for contemporary use.

Mario Melendez describes how pre- and post-exilic prophets understood the Davidic Covenant, culminating in a messianic message. Rex Butler looks at Early Church writers, with an emphasis on Justin Martyr, as they defend the pre-existence and divinity of Jesus by interpreting Old Testament theophanies as manifestations of Jesus.

Joseph Early traces the impact of Greek philosophy, particularly Aristotlean and Stoic, on the Jewish Philosopher, Philo of Alexandria, in his views of women. Philo's views had significant influence on the allegorically minded Alexandrian school of biblical interpretation and later medieval theology.

The purpose of Christian witness has always been to present the never-changing Gospel, to an ever-changing culture, in a way that makes sense to them. Pete Charpentier examines the hermeneutical implications of Paul utilizing pagan beliefs as starting points for his address to the Areopagus in Athens. Preston Nix concludes with what it means to have boldness in evangelism. He presents a study of the word in Greek and provides his definition of going one step beyond one's comfort level.

As you are encouraged in ministry or challenged in academics, please join me in prayer that Dr. Harwood would have a rich and fruitful ministry to our military personnel and that his family would be well.

Luther's Practical Theology of Dying

Ben Hutchison

PhD., New Orleans Baptist Theological Seminary, 2017

Introduction

What more should God do to persuade you to accept death willingly and not dread but to overcome it? In Christ he offers you the image of life, grace, and of salvation so that you may not be horrified by the images of sin, death, and hell.

Martin Luther, A Sermon of Preparing to Die, 1519

Martin Luther was a theologian who played a crucial role in changing the dynamics of the Christian church and the world. Luther has been given titles such as prophet and hero for his role in the Protestant Reformation.[1] He casts an enormous shadow over church history and the Protestant churches to this day. The day he nailed the *95 Theses* to the door of the Castle Church in Wittenberg, October 31, has been celebrated as Reformation Day. Therefore, to many with only a base knowledge of the Reformation, he is given credit for starting the movement. Luther played a major role in the Protestant Reformation, which should not be minimized. However, his life was not as dramatic as it has been retold in books and film. His passionate writings, defiant struggle with the Roman Catholic Church, and his own struggle of faith have inspired biographies in print and film.

Luther's thought and belief on faith and the Christian life influenced many people of his day and subsequent generations of believers. However, Luther did not systematize his theology but revealed his beliefs in writings, sermons, and lectures.[2] Current

---

[1] Luther was considered a prophet by many during his lifetime and within decades of his death he had been acclaimed a hero of the Reformation in literature. Robert Kolb, *Martin Luther as Prophet, Teacher, Hero* (Grand Rapids: Baker, 1999), 17, 133.

[2] The lack of systemization can be found in a statement by Timothy George asserting that in none of Luther's writings "is there anything remotely resem-

readers of Luther find his theological beliefs in his interpretations of Scripture and treatises along with his correspondences and table talks. Luther produced volumes of work both for the church and the academic realm that can be mined for his thoughts on many subjects of theological or practical concern.

Luther was not only a reformer but a pastor as well. His pastoral role and care of those in his congregation filled much of his time and writings. Luther functioned in a pastoral role to friends and relationships beyond Wittenberg. The pastoral role of Luther was not relegated to preaching and teaching but also to baptizing, observing the Lord's Supper, visiting the sick and dying, and writing letters of counsel.[3] Luther's consolation and encouragement to those facing death is the central feature of Luther as a pastor for the purpose of this study.

Historical and Current Context of Dying

The people of Germany, and the larger continent of Europe, in the early sixteenth century had frequent contact with dying and death. Europe witnessed the Black Plague decimate the population in the middle of the fourteenth century.[4] Deadly diseases remained a constant reality for Luther's generation although the sweeping plague was a becoming a memory as the population grew. Infant mortality was also a factor in Luther's time as part of the general lack of knowledge of disease and care for the sick. Not only infants but young children often succumbed to disease.[5]

Death often occurred in the home with the family and friends present. Luther's home and family were not isolated from painful sickness and death. Two of Luther's daughters died before adulthood. His daughter Elizabeth died in August of 1528, less than a

---

bling a systematic theology." Timothy George, *Theology of the Reformers,* rev. ed. (Nashville: Broadman & Holman, 2013), 57.

[3] Timothy J. Wengert, "Introducing the Pastoral Luther," in *The Pastoral Luther: Essays on Martin Luther's Practical Theology,* ed. Timothy J. Wengert (Grand Rapids: Eerdmans, 2009), 3.

[4] The years of 1347-1350 saw one third of the population of Europe die due to the plague. The plague lowered life expectancy to seventeen years during the most devastating period of the epidemic. Rudolph W. Heinze, *Reform and Conflict,* The Baker History of the Church, Vol. 4 (Grand Rapids: Baker, 2005), 23-25.

[5] Luther wrote multiple letters of consolation to parents of deceased children. One such letter to Conrad Cordatus is examined below.

year old. Another daughter, Magdalene, died at age fourteen in 1542.[6] Thus, Luther was well aware of the pain of his parishioners and friends who grieved.

The distinction between the current western interaction with death that of Luther's day is striking. Dying has largely been moved from the home to hospitals and nursing homes. The talk of death is often relegated to funerals or times of dying. Many of the contrasts are very positive for the current culture. Healthcare has reduced infant mortality and extended the life of many. Children are expected to live to adulthood because of the advances of immunizations and treatments for illness. Diseases of the middle ages have become preventable and treatable. Also, access to treatments is readily available in the West. The current culture speaks of fighting death, yet Luther spoke of accepting death when it came.

The grieving process is also different in the current western setting. People are praised for getting back to their lives quickly after the loss of a friend or relative.[7] However, the Christian church in the West remains an arena for the discussion of death even if the acknowledgement is relegated to occasional sermons and teachings on life after death.

Luther desired to die well and in faith. He also desired to rejoice when those he loved died because they were freed from sin and suffering. The current culture does not often prepare to die well. Death is simply out there for another day but not a close reality of life. Luther's context and teaching offer insights for the contemporary Christian on preparing to die and dying well.

Goal and Scope

The goal of this paper is to examine portions of Luther's writings that pertain to dying, grieving, and approaching death as a Christian. The paper will not develop Luther's understanding of eschatology or life after death. Luther believed there was life after death and hope in a resurrection for Christians. The work below

---

[6] Carl R. Trueman, *Luther on the Christian Life: Cross and Freedom* (Wheaton: Crossway, 2015), 191.

[7] The modern culture approaches death as something to move past with minor acknowledgement. It is almost seen as a virtue to be able to recover quickly from grief. This concept is based on personal observations in the church and my own experiences of death and grief.

assumes this base level of expectation of Luther without fully developing the details of his understanding.[8] The goal is to look at his practical approach to the experience of dying as a Christian. The practices and encouragement of faith in the days and hours of death will form the basis of Luther's practical theology. Emphasis will be given to pastoral works of consolation and encouragement found in the writings and records of Luther. The results of the examination will reveal Luther's implications of his beliefs and practical workings for those he served. The goal is not to systematize, but rather glean themes that are woven through the writings. Based on the theology gleaned, the paper will propose practical applications to the current Christian setting in order to understand dying well as a Christian.

Luther's Pastoral Works on Dying and Death

I am joyful in spirit but I am sad according to the flesh. The flesh doesn't take kindly to this.

-Martin Luther, when his daughter
was placed in the coffin, 1542

Luther's transparent statement above indicates the difficulty of dying and death. Luther was not a man separated from the lives of people. He understood their pain and fear of dying. His writings on death and dying reveal his interaction with Christian death and practical consolation. The writings below are not a systematic understanding of death but pastoral and personal encouragement from Luther based on his view of death. The above quote is the heart of Luther's consolation. He pointed those facing death to God and Christ for perspective and encouragement to endure death or grieve properly the death of another.

---

[8] The first issue that arises with hope after death is the concept of purgatory. Luther's *95 Theses* do not remove the possibility of purgatory, the document combats indulgences. The later letters and writings that will be addressed below indicate that Luther expected believers to be in a positive place after death, rather than punishment in purgatory. Also, Luther's understanding of soul sleep and the resurrection is beyond this work for space. These are not insignificant issues but rather what is needed for Luther's practical understanding of dying as Christian is the fact that faith lies in Christ, who overcame death.

Sermon on Preparing to Die (1519)

Luther published a sermon that was both practical and spiritual encouragement to believers as they face death.[9] The major force that propelled the writing was a request from Georg Spalatin on for a parishioner named Mark Schart. Schart was apparently deeply troubled by thoughts of death and dying.[10] The sermon is very pastoral in nature, preached only a few months after the debate at Leipzig, where Luther "stood in radical opposition to the received doctrines of the Catholic Church."[11] Therefore, the sermon revealed that Luther was able to communicate at an academic level as well as a pastoral level. The focus of the sermon is to aid a believer in preparing for death and the temptation to fear because of sin at the face of death.[12]

Luther's sermon reflects the medieval writings of *ars moriendi*, or art of dying. However, Luther's sermon is in the context of individual, practical encouragement. Other major differences in Luther are the manner of sacraments and the encouragement of saints. The sacrament was to be a reminder of God's gift rather than an extra grace for the dying person. Therefore, the person would forget self and look to Christ. The saints for Luther served as encouragement in that they experienced death before the current dying person. Thus, the Christian was not the first to suffer death and should not feel alone.[13] Luther's work is different from the medieval tradition but relates to the backdrop of pastoral training and practical understanding.

The sermon contains twenty arguments that overlap and build upon each other rather than having twenty distinctly defined

---

[9] Timothy F. Lull and William Russell, ed. *Martin Luther's Basic Theological Writings*, 3rd ed. (Minneapolis: Fortress, 2012), 392.

[10] Dennis Ngien, "The Art of Dying: In Luther's Sermon on Preparing to Die," *Heythrop Journal* 49, no. 1 (January 2008): 1-19, *Academic Search Complete*, EBSCO*host* (accessed October 20, 2016), 1.

[11] Richard Marius, *Martin Luther: The Christian Between God and Death* (Cambridge: Harvard University Press, 1999), 182.

[12] Martin Luther, "A Sermon on Preparing to Die," *Luther's Works Volume 42*, trans. Martin H. Bertram (Philadelphia: Fortress Press, 1969), 98.

[13] The comparative content is based on an article by Jared Wicks, who gives a full analysis and comparison of Luther's Sermon on Preparing to Die and the writings of *ars moriendi*. Jared Wicks, "Applied Theology at the Deathbed: Luther and the Late-Medieval Tradition of the Ars moriendi," *Gregorianum* 79, no. 2 (1998 1998): 345-68, *ATLA Religion Database with ATLASerials*, EBSCO*host* (accessed November 4, 2016), 363-7.

thoughts. The entire sermon is centered on the Christian focusing on three aspects of Christ and the cross. Life, grace, and salvation in the image of Christ are the main encouragement and hope for a Christian to face death without fear.[14] The contrasting evil ideas of death, sin, and hell can lead to doubt and fear. Luther argued for the believer to drive out these three evil thoughts and focus on Christ.[15]

Luther gave his audience practical ways to focus on Christ and combat the three evil thoughts that lead to fear of death. He did not expect an act of human will but of reliance on God and encouragement from the Bible and sacraments. One practical help is that Luther illustrated death with the image of a baby born. The birth is not pleasant but leads to a large and wonderful world beyond the womb. Death for the Christian leads to God, thus past death a new world awaits the Christian.[16] Sacraments formed another practical help for believers in that their signs reminded of the grace and salvation of Christ. Luther called the sacraments beneficial to the faith of Christians facing death as reminders of promises.[17] Luther also encouraged the Christian to become familiar with death before it approaches and is imminent. With a familiarity of death, the Christian would be able to look away from death as it approaches and focus on Christ.[18] Luther also exhorted Christians to pray humbly for God's help in approaching death to remain focused on life, grace, and salvation as death approached.[19]

The sermon also included two practices in preparing for death that relate to family and the community. The first is to make plans for temporal goods, in order to avoid fighting among the ones left behind. The second is to forgive and seek forgiveness in the present life.[20] In the contemporary context the creation of a will seems a bit separate from the rest of Luther's spiritual sermon. However, the focus is unity after death for both practical actions.

---

[14] Wicks, "Applied Theology…", 114.

[15] Wicks, "Applied Theology…", 103.

[16] Wicks, "Applied Theology…", 99-100.

[17] At this time Luther had not fully broken from the Catholic Sacraments in practice but emphasized the work of Christ as the basis for faith, not sacraments. He even mentions the sacrament of Extreme Unction in the sermon. See Wicks, "Applied Theology…", 108.

[18] Wicks, "Applied Theology…", 101-02.

[19] Wicks, "Applied Theology…", 114.

[20] Wicks, "Applied Theology…", 99.

Luther's words emphasize the ultimate hope for a Christian as death approaches is Christ. The image of Christ on the cross pushes back the fear of death. The faithful believer will then praise God for grace at the face of death, rather than doubt in fear. Death is portrayed as difficult but can be filled with assurance by looking to Christ.

Fourteen Consolations

Luther wrote to Fredrick the Wise in 1519 to encourage the Elector during illness. However, the document was revised and a final edition was published in 1536. Luther attempted to restore the document to how it was originally written in 1519.[21] The document is fashioned as an altar screen with fourteen consolations. The first seven are evils experienced in life and the other seven are blessings of God's grace. The work reveals the evils as insignificant in light of the blessings.[22] The document focuses on the suffering of evils but portions center on death. Much of Luther's encouragement in suffering is based on how it could be worse and the comparative situations for those that are not saved. Luther placed suffering of various kinds, even death, in the proper place for believers.[23]

Luther asserted that death is to be preferred over continued living in sin. He did not advocate a disdain of life but rather a reminder that in death sin is ended for the Christian. Luther's argument is in the context of not fearing death because sin in life is a greater evil than death.[24] Luther viewed death as the final evil to endure with patience in light of the grace saving the believer from hell beyond death.[25] The cross is central to the encouragement even in the face of death. Luther noted that the cross makes death a gain for the Christian as is stated by the Apostle Paul.[26] Therefore, death has become a blessing rather than an evil for the believer. The blessing is that death ends the suffering and sins of

---

[21] Martin Luther, "Fourteen Consolations," *Luther's Works Volume 42*, trans. by Martin H. Bertram (Philadelphia: Fortress Press, 1969), 120-21.

[22] Luther, "Fourteen Consolations" 118-21.

[23] Jane E. Strohl, "Luther's Fourteen Consolations," in *The Pastoral Luther: Essays on Martin Luther's Practical Theology,* Edited by Timothy J. Wengert, (Grand Rapids: Eerdmans, 2009), 324.

[24] Luther, "Fourteen Consolations," 130.

[25] Luther, "Fourteen Consolations," 133.

[26] Luther referenced Phil 1:21 and Rom 14:8 for his support from Paul.

life.[27] Luther interacted with death throughout the letter but encouraged endurance of other evils in life as well before the final evil of death.

Luther's encouragement of Fredrick the Wise interacts with his theology of death and dying but does not focus on the subject. However, the letter affirmed much of what Luther wrote in his sermon on preparing for death. Luther wrote "Fourteen Consolations" to "strengthen pious hearts,"[28] not merely those facing death. Therefore, his pastoral communications revealed his understanding of death in light of the cross of Christ as the final evil of the physical life.

Two Funeral Sermons

Luther delivered two funeral sermons for the death of Elector, Duke John of Saxony in August 1532. The first sermon was delivered on Sunday and the second on Thursday. Luther preached from the text of 1 Thessalonians 4:13–18 as encouragement for Christians to experience death and sorrow differently than those who do not believe. Luther asserts that a Christian may grieve the death of a friend or loved one but in moderation. However, the grief of a Christian was to be less bitter because of the hope in Christ.[29]

Luther also encouraged those gathered for the funeral to look to Christ at the time of their deaths so as to not be tempted by the devil. The temptation Luther acknowledged was the same as his sermon on preparing to die, fear and doubt based on a person's sin. The cure for Luther was to look to Christ and remember his death and resurrection.[30]

The ultimate hope in death for Luther was the hope of resurrection in Christ. He encouraged those mourning to remember that God would raise the deceased from the dead because he confessed the gospel.[31] Luther's funeral sermon highlighted future hope for the purpose of comfort in this life. Luther constantly kept the cross of Christ before those who faced death and suffered the loss of loved ones to death.

---

[27] Luther, "Fourteen Consolations," 149–50.

[28] Luther, "Fourteen Consolations," 123.

[29] Martin Luther, "Two Funeral Sermons," *Luther's Works Volume 51*, trans. by John W. Doberstein (Philadelphia: Muhlrnberg Press, 1959), 231–35.

[30] Martin Luther, "Two Funeral Sermons," 242–43.

[31] Martin Luther, "Two Funeral Sermons," 255.

Short Letters of Consolation

Luther wrote many letters to parishioners, friends, and family to encourage them in sickness, suffering, and death. Much of Luther's encouragement was based upon the fact that Christ overcame the world and death. Many of the letters not specifically addressed below at least mention Christ defeating death. Therefore, the majority of comfort was found in the cross.

The letters included below have been selected based on impending death of the recipient or the recent death of a relative of the recipient. The letters were also selected based upon the significance of content to understand Luther's view of death and subsequent pastoral encouragement. Much of the content contributes to understanding Luther's opposition to certain Catholic traditions associated with death or his understanding of Christian death in light of salvation. The letters not only display theological understanding but also the pastoral comfort based on Luther's beliefs about death and dying. The following letters are discussed in chronological order.

Letter to Bartholomew von Staremberg, September 1, 1524

Staremberg was a member of the Austrian nobility with evangelical sympathies and a son who supported the Reformation. The letter was written to comfort Staremberg after the death of his wife. The major focus of the letter was to advise against Masses and vigils and daily prayers for the dead wife's soul. Luther addressed the continual prayers as a lack of trust that God has received the prayer. Luther called the Masses and vigils "unchristian practices which greatly anger God."[32] Luther argued that the Mass was for the living and not the dead. However, Luther's anger is not directed at Staremberg but the clergy that use the Masses and vigils to make money.[33] Therefore, Luther affirmed grief but not in what he considered unchristian practices for the dead who are with God.

---

[32] Martin Luther, "To Bartholomew von Staremberg, September 1, 1524," in *D. Martin Luthers Werke, kritiische Gesammtausgabe, XVIII* (Weimar, 1883–), 1–7, English translation from Theodore G. Tappert, ed. and trans., *Luther: Letters of Spiritual Counsel* (Louisville: John Knox, 1998), 54.

[33] Martin Luther, "To Bartholomew," 55.

To the Widow of a Man Whose Self-Inflicted Injury Led to Death, December 15, 1528

Luther wrote a letter to an unidentified woman whose husband had died shortly after attempting suicide. The circumstances are not fully known but the content of the letter reveals Luther's stance on suicide and damnation. Luther states in the Letter that "Christ finally won the victory" in the struggle of her husband.[34]

Luther attributes the self-inflicted harm to the work of the devil in the members of flesh. This view is further established by a recorded saying of Luther that he did not believe "suicides are to be damned."[35] Luther further compared the suicide to an attack and murder. Thus, Luther attributes the death to the power of the devil at work in a human. Luther further consoled the widow with the fact that her husband was no longer in despair.

Letter to His Father, February 15, 1530

Luther wrote a letter to his father three months before his father died. Due to the illness of Luther's father, Luther wished for his parents to come and live with him. However, this was not possible due to the advanced sickness of his father.[36]

The major thrust of Luther's encouragement is based upon the power of Christ. He encouraged his father to not fear because Christ is the mediator that overcame death. Luther also reminded his father that God would give grace to endure if he was to go on suffering in illness for a lengthy period.[37] Therefore, Luther's encouragement is based on the power of God and work of Christ. Death is not to be feared by the believer.

Letter to Conrad Cordatus, April 2, 1530

Luther wrote to Cordatus, pastor in Zwickau, after the death of his young son. Luther referred to his understanding of the grief of

---

[34] Martin Luther, "To Widow Margret, December, 15, 1528," in *D. Martin Luthers Werke, Briefwechsel,* ed. by Otto Clemen, IV (Weimar, 1930–1948), 624–5, English translation from Theodore G. Tappert, ed. and trans., *Luther: Letters of Spiritual Counsel* (Louisville: John Knox, 1998), 59.

[35] Luther, "Table Talk," 29.

[36] Martin Luther, "To Father John Luther, February, 15, 1530," in *D. Martin Luthers Werke, Briefwechsel,* ed. by Otto Clemen, V (Weimar, 1930–1948), 238–41, English translation from Theodore G. Tappert, ed. and trans., *Luther: Letters of Spiritual Counsel* (Louisville: John Knox, 1998), 29–30.

[37] Martin Luther, "To Father John," 31–32.

the father, as he lost his second child at seven months. Luther encouraged Cordatus with the knowledge that his son was with the best father, God. However, he acknowledged that the pain of child loss is not much comforted at first by this truth.[38] The letter revealed that Luther in the pastoral context affirmed infants that died are with God.

Letter to His Mother, May 20, 1531

Luther wrote to his mother one year after the death of his father. She died on June 30, thirteen months after Luther's father. The letter is longer than the one to his father but contains much of the same basis for encouragement. However, Luther does include direct language against the Roman church such as: "Be thankful that God has brought you to such knowledge and not allowed you to remain in papal error."[39] Luther went on to emphasize that faith was based not in works but in Christ. Such writing reveals the lack of encouragement from the Catholic system in Luther's mind.

Letter to Fredrick Myconius January 9, 1541

Myconius was a pastor and reformer in Gotha suffering with the symptoms of tuberculosis. However, Myconius recovered and outlived Luther by a few weeks. The major significance of this letter is that Luther expresses a desire to be on the deathbed in the place of his friend. Luther desired to "put off [his] useless, outworn, exhausted tabernacle."[40] Luther's desire may have been due to his frequent illness and age but reflects his view of death. Death signaled an end to pain and suffering of life for the believer.

---

[38] Martin Luther, "To Conrad Cordatus, April, 2, 1530," in *D. Martin Luthers Werke, Briefwechsel,* ed. by Otto Clemen, V (Weimar, 1930–1948), 273–74, English translation from Theodore G. Tappert, ed. and trans., *Luther: Letters of Spiritual Counsel* (Louisville: John Knox, 1998), 59–60.

[39] Martin Luther, "To Mrs. John Luther, May, 20 1531," in *D. Martin Luthers Werke, Briefwechsel,* ed. by Otto Clemen, VI (Weimar, 1930–1948), 103–4, English translation from Theodore G. Tappert, ed. and trans., *Luther: Letters of Spiritual Counsel* (Louisville: John Knox, 1998), 35.

[40] Martin Luther, "To Fredrick Myconius, January 9, 1541," in *D. Martin Luthers Werke, Briefwechsel,* ed. by Otto Clemen, IX (Weimar, 1930–1948), 301–3, English translation from Theodore G. Tappert, ed. and trans., *Luther: Letters of Spiritual Counsel* (Louisville: John Knox, 1998), 48.

Table Talk Selections on Dying[41]

Luther's "Table Talk" is a collection of notes taken in conversations with Luther by students and other men who spent time with the reformer. The informal notes recorded Luther's opinions and portions of conversations that interested the recorders. The works went through many editions.[42] The following will be a summary and interaction with several selections that pertain to death and dying.

Luther affirmed a fear of death as a natural expectation in multiple recordings from 1532. The reason for fear is that death is associated with the wrath of God. The connection to God's wrath causes fear in the Christian. However, that fear is related to the flesh and not the spirit because death is a bitter experience of suffering.[43] Ten years later Luther stated "the greatest thing in death is the fear of death."[44] Thus Luther affirms that Christians fear death but the fear is worse than the event of death.

The death of Luther's fourteen-year-old daughter, who died in his arms in 1542, resulted in comments on her death and his interaction with her death.[45] Luther struggled with the sickness of his daughter and her impending death. He stated "I'm unable to rejoice from my heart and be thankful to God."[46] The day she died Luther prayed for God to save her as he held her when she died.[47] Luther knew his daughter was at peace and in heaven yet he deeply grieved the separation. At this death of another child Luther consoled himself in the fact that his daughter was "safely out of [the flesh]."[48] Therefore, Luther's understanding of death impacted his grief in much the same way it impacted his consolation of others.

---

[41] Martin Luther, "Table Talk," *Luther's Works Volume 54*, trans. by Theodore G. Tappert (Philadelphia: Fortress Press, 1967) The volume contains selections from the Weimar edition but not the entire collection of what is known as table talk.

[42] Luther, "Table Talk," xi–xv.

[43] Luther, "Table Talk," 65 and 190.

[44] Luther, "Table Talk," 430.

[45] Roland H. Bainton, *Here I Stand: A Life of Martin Luther* (1950; repr., New York: Meridian, 1995), 237.

[46] Luther, "Table Talk," 430.

[47] Luther, "Table Talk," 431.

[48] Luther, "Table Talk," 433.

Luther's Interpretation of Psalm 90

> For we are brought to an end by your anger;
>   by your wrath we are dismayed.
> You have set our iniquities before you,
>   our secret sins in the light of your presence.
>
> Psalm 90:7–8 ESV

Luther lectured on Psalm 90 in October and November of 1534. The series was completed with a lecture on March and one in May of 1535. The lectures where delivered at Wittenberg and recorded as a manuscript.[49] Paul Althaus notes that "Luther's theology of death is expressed particularly clearly in his powerful interpretation of Psalm 90."[50] This work has been separated from the previous discussion due to the academic setting of the interpretation rather than pastoral encouragement of a sermon or letter. However, the interpretation must be examined in light of the discussion on Luther and death.

Luther contended that Moses places death as part of God's wrath upon sin. Through the focus on wrath, the Psalm terrified the sinner and pointed to God. Luther noted two points of the psalm. "First, Moses here stresses the tyranny of death and of God's wrath, since he shows that human nature is subject to eternal death; he does this for the purpose of terrifying hardened and unbelieving despisers of God. Secondly, Moses prays for a remedy against despair, that men might not succumb to despair."[51] Thus Luther connects the Psalm to the gospel through death as the wrath against sin.

Luther also noted that the psalm highlights the perspective of individual life as short. The believer is reminded in the psalm of the brevity of life as it moves towards death. Luther understands the words of the psalm to indicate that life is "a violent toss which catapults us into death."[52] Therefore, life is short and the seriousness of death was communicated by the psalm to Luther.

The result of death as and expression of God's wrath toward sin implied that man was created in a state with the possibility of

---

[49] Martin Luther, "Psalm 90," *Luther's Works Volume 13,* trans. Paul M. Bretscher (St. Louis: Concordia Press, 1956), xi.

[50] Paul Althaus, *The Theology of Martin Luther,* trans. Robert Schultz (Philadelphia: Fortress, 1966), 405.

[51] Luther, "Psalm 90," 78.

[52] Luther, "Psalm 90," 100.

immortality.[53] Luther thus places God's wrath as the ultimate cause of death in light of Psalm 90. Thus, the emphasis of the psalm is to reveal the seriousness of death in God's wrath.[54] However, Luther gleaned from the psalm that God will comfort those that belong to him. The prayer of Moses was interpreted further by Luther as a hope in the final end of suffering beyond physical life.[55]

Luther's interpretation of Psalm 90 is a theological interpretation derived from what he called "insights which the Lord granted."[56] The interpretation would not fit in the current hermeneutical models which gave Moses credit for using the fear of death to turn people to God. Luther's work on Psalm 90 did give insight to his understanding of death and its relationship to the wrath of God. In Luther's mind death was wrath upon sin but hope is found in the love of God. The Christian was expected to recognize the seriousness of death as wrath and subsequently pray to God in hope.

Luther's Death

Into your hand I commit my spirit;
you have redeemed me, O Lord, faithful God.

-Psalm 31:5 ESV

Luther encouraged and comforted many throughout his life and work as a pastor and reformer. He even faced the loss of two of his children and suffered the grief associated with their deaths. However, Luther's own death merits examination in light of his beliefs and consolations to others.

Luther died during the early morning hours of February 18, 1546, in Eisleben, the town of his birth. Luther had traveled to his home town to settle a dispute between the counts of Mansfield

---

[53] In his "Lectures on Genesis," Luther believed that Adam was created in a state that could have become immortal by sot sinning and moving ultimately without death to glory that was sinless. However, Adam also could fall and thus, be mortal. Therefore, Luther understands the ideal human creation to have not sinned and thus been immortal without suffering death. See Martin Luther, "Lectures on Genesis," *Luther's Works Volume 1,* trans. George V. Schick (St. Louis: Concordia, 1955), 111.

[54] Luther, "Lectures on Genesis," 97–102.

[55] Luther, "Lectures on Genesis," 130–34.

[56] Luther, "Lectures on Genesis," 141.

upon their request.[57] Roland Bainton states that Luther "reconciled the counts, and died on the way home."[58] Luther's death was not as simple Bainton's sentence implies, but he did complete the reconciliation goal of the trip.

Luther had been in good spirits for large portions of the negotiations with the counts but on the 17th he spoke of death. "If I reconcile my dear sovereigns, the counts, and, God willing, carry out the aims of this journey, then I shall return home, lie down to sleep in the coffin, and give the worms a good fat doctor to devour."[59] He slept little that night to awake around one in the morning much worse. Justus Jonas recorded that he spoke a dying prayer of Psalm 31:5, and was ready to die. Then, his companions asked if he confessed Christ, which Luther confirmed with his last word.[60] Heiko Oberman referred to these final moments as a "public test" and "stage" to reveal fortitude in death as a true Christian.[61]

Luther died away from his wife but with friends and after accomplishing a final purpose in reconciling the counts. In light of his encouragement to others, it appeared that Luther did in fact look to Christ in his own death. He did not fight death in fear but trusted that death led to God and out of suffering. Therefore, his words on death and dying impacted his personal death and final hours. Luther was not found to be a hypocrite in this aspect of the Christian life but lived and died based on his view of the cross of Christ.

Luther's Practical Theology Of Dying

Luther as a pastor encountered dying, death, and those grieving the death of a relative or friend. Because of his context, Luther was familiar with death, because he was a pastor and leader of the church, people expected consolation and encouragement. However, Luther needed an underlying belief and understanding of Christian dying to encourage and console. A practical theology of

---

[57] Heinrich Bornkamm, *Luther's World of Thought,* trans. Martin H. Bertram (St. Louis: Concordia, 1958), 284.

[58] Bainton, 300.

[59] The quotation is translated in Bornkamm's work. The original source is the Weimar Edition vol. 55. Borkamm, 285.

[60] Bornkamm, *Luther's World,* 285–86.

[61] Heiko A. Obermann, *Luther: Man Between God and the Devil,* trans. Eileen Walliser-Schwarzbart (New York: Doubleday, 1992), 3.

dying and death for Christians is based upon his writings examined above. The following section notes four major aspects of Luther's belief that encompass his handling of dying and death for practical theology. The theology developed in this section is a reflection of Luther's theology and not necessarily proposed to be held in the same manner by contemporary Christians. Application and proposal for current Christian practices will be given in the conclusion bellow.

All Face Death as a Result of God's Wrath

It is understood that all humans will die and thus face death. A person may live many years or die as an infant less than a year old. The pain associated with death and fear of death that humans share needed to be explained at a level that comforts the Christian. Multiple times Luther associated death with the wrath of God upon sin. However, his strongest address of death as part of God's wrath was in his interpretation of Psalm 90. Luther's understanding is also supported by Romans 5:12 in that death is associated with sin and the fall. Luther clarified that the sin Paul associates with bringing death is the original sin, not individual sins. Therefore, man does not face death in God's wrath for his specific sins but rather the sinful state of humanity.[62] Humans are subject to death as the final suffering of wrath. Therefore, the Christian is right to struggle with death because it is punishment for sin.

Luther's view of death also explained desire for humans to keep on living because God created them for life rather than death. The sins of humanity face the wrath of God in life and death. However, Christ overcame death and thus the Christian may expect death but has hope. The hope for Luther was always centered on the cross of Christ.

The implication of this view is not that a Christian should accept death passively as wrath of an angry God. The Christian is to humbly understand her sin and thus the need for death to end sin. Therefore, the painful suffering in the process of dying and grieving is the ultimate wrath upon sin for the Christian. However, Luther did not understand death itself as an active punishment of God upon the individual. Death as punishment for sin was part of the larger understanding that the consequences of the fall of hu-

---

[62] Martin Luther, *Commentary on the Epistle of Romans*, trans. J. Theodore Mueller (Grand Rapids: Kregel, 1976), 94.

manity. Therefore, dying was associated with God's wrath but for a Christian the experience was not approached as an unbeliever facing God's wrath.

Christ Pushes Back the Fear of Dying

Luther's sermon on preparing to die continually called the listener to look to the image of Christ to drive out fear in the face of death. Luther affirmed the fear of death was natural because he understood death to be a part of God's wrath. Thus, a human who has sinned should fear the wrath of God. The fear of God's judgment was part of Luther's fear of death. He understood the fear in focus upon his sin.[63] Luther feared standing before God because of sin even after his development of justification by faith. However, Luther knew that Christ defeated death and that death was not the end for Christians.

Luther believed that God supplied all a Christian needed to accept and overcome death willingly. The supply is the image of Christ and the trust in God that he will give benefit, help and strength through the dying and grief.[64] The fear of death is real but the grace and salvation in God help the Christian approach death with faith. Luther did not advocate a denial of death in his call to focus on Christ rather than the fear of death. He believed that familiarity with death enabled the Christian to focus on Christ when death approached.

The reality of Christ that Luther emphasized remains the major factor in encouragement of Christians today. Hope of salvation is in Christ and thus fear of death cannot stand up to the truth of Christ and the cross. This truth does not remove all fear because people are still in the flesh, but encouragement is found in the cross. Therefore, the implication for the Christian is to recognize the fear of death but shift her gaze to God and Christ for hope in salvation. Dying is not an easy experience but the Christian should die with faith and confidence in Christ. Confidence in Christ is aided by a familiarity with death. However, familiarity is not a

---

[63] Marius seems to waiver between Luther fearing God's judgment after death or Luther fearing death itself as God's wrath. The research above leans toward Luther fearing the judgement after death because his remedy for fear is to look at what Christ did on the cross. Therefore, Marius' view is somewhat exaggerated in its focus on Luther's fear of the physical death. Marius, 60–1.

[64] Luther, "Sermon on preparing to Die," 114.

morbid fascination but a realistic contemplation on death as a Christian.

The Dead Christian is Better Off Than the Living

The idea that a Christian is better off after death sounds pessimistic and insincere in a conversation with a parent who just lost a child, or a wife who just heard that her husband died in an accident. However, Luther lost two children and witnessed many others get ill and die. Luther believed that the dead Christian was free from suffering and sin. Thus, she was better off than those who remained. After the death of his daughter Luther commented that his daughter was no longer in the flesh and the flesh is where sorrow occurs.[65]

Luther also based this view on being free from a life of sin and not just the suffering of illness and pain. Thus, a Christian is freed from sin after she dies and is better than one continually living in sin. Luther's view and practical application in the area of death being preferred must be approached clearly. Luther does not advocate suicide to leave the world or even denial of enjoyment in life.[66] Rather, the belief is based upon hope beyond death because of Christ.

Luther knew pain and suffering in his life. Multiple sicknesses impacted him along with the mentioned sickness and death of two children. It is not difficult to understand why Luther viewed life after death as an escape from sin and suffering. His view was not a disdain of the flesh but likely a product of his life and times.

Sacraments for the Dying but No Rituals for the Dead

The sacraments were important to Luther as part of the church and life of Christians. For Luther, the sacraments included baptism and the Lord's Supper. These signs were a means of encouragement and practice of faith. Therefore, Luther affirmed that the dying should be able to be encouraged by receiving the sacraments. In his sermon on dying, Luther had not fully departed from the Catholic sacramental system. Later in his ministry, only the two sacraments are affirmed. Luther does not record or encourage the

---

[65] Luther, "Table Talk," 433.

[66] Luther did not believe suicide meant a person was condemned to hell. This was a break with the traditional Catholic view. However, his association of suicide with the work of the devil clearly reveals his negative stance toward the issue.

giving of the Lord's Supper as a last right or in the moments preceding death. However, the Supper serves as a reminder of the promises of God and Luther would have encouraged the sacrament if a person was able.

Luther opposed rituals such as Masses and vigils for the dead. Luther believed the practices to be unchristian. He affirmed that one could pray for the soul of the dead once but repeated prayers showed a lack of faith and trust that God had received the prayer. Luther's rejection is largely based on the practice as unscriptural and an abuse of the church.[67] According to Luther the grieving of a loved one was not easy to Luther but proper mourning of a Christian should not be fixated on rituals for the dead.

The participation in the Lord's Supper or other Christian practices for the dying would serve as encouragement. The practical application is to help dying believers participate and be encouraged by in their faith during the difficulty of dying. The family member or friend could also be encouraged in grief by remembering the dead experiencing the sacrament of faith before he died.

Conclusion

O death, where is your victory?
O death, where is your sting?

-1 Corinthians 15:55

Luther's pastoral role involved practically addressing issues within a congregation and the wider Protestant Reformation. Luther filled the role of comforter to the dying and grieving as many pastors before and since. The writings of Luther shed much light on his understanding of dying and death for practical care. Luther's experiences with death of his children and his own death gave further insight to the reformer who sought to die well as a Christian.

The study above has yielded much in the way of practical advice and perspective on Christian dying and grieving. In light of the current culture of the West that has less interaction with death

---

[67] Luther "To Bartholomew von Staremberg" in *WA*, 58, 1–7, Eng. trans. from Tappert ed. and trans. *Letters of Spiritual Counsel*, 54. It is not clear if Luther later fully rejected the concept of praying for the soul of the dead. This letter was written in 1524. Therefore, it is possible that Luther may have later rejected the notion of praying for the dead completely.

and is not often prepared to die well, two proposals advance a practical theology of dying.

The first proposal is that Christians should become more acquainted with death as they live. In Luther's words, "We should familiarize ourselves with death during our lifetime, inviting death into our presence when it is still at a distance and not on the move."[68] Familiarity with death aids in reducing fear when a person is dying. Humans have greater fear for things they do not understand or with which they are unfamiliar. A child fears the dark because she does not know what is in the darkness. A teenage boy fears asking a girl on a date because he is unfamiliar with the ways in which females think and respond. These examples are light in comparison but the concept remains. Familiarity with death can aid a believer in preparing to face death at the end of his life.

Familiarity with Christian death is not simply about witnessing death or discussing Christians who have died. The Christian must be familiar with the gospel that Jesus overcame death. Therefore, the cross of Christ is essential to a Christian preparing to face death. Once prepared a Christian will not fight death in fear but accept death as Luther in submission to the final suffering of life.

The second proposal is to help those who are dying participate in practices of faith such as the Lord's Supper. The participation will encourage the faith of the one dying. One practice of this application is to read Scripture and sing hymns in the hospital to dying loved ones. Technology has made it possible for many to watch or listen to his church's worship service, even if not physically able to attend. Certain churches will have pastors or ministers bring the elements of the Lord's Supper to a dying or ill person.[69] This practice should not be done as a Last Rights such as in the Catholic Church. The partaker and the minister should recognize that the supper does not convey grace or place one in a better position before God. The participation is for encouragement and reminder of faith in Christ and his work and a continued connec-

---

[68] Luther, "A Sermon on Preparing to Die," 101–2.

[69] The appropriateness of the practice of giving the Lord's Supper to those in hospice or homebound is not agreed upon even in among Baptist circles. Bobby Jamieson gives a recent and clearly articulated argument against individuals or small groups practicing the Lord's Supper apart from the larger local church. See Bobby Jamieson, "One Bread, One Body: The Lord's Supper and the Local Church," *Going Public: Why Baptism is Required for Church Membership* (Nashville: B&H, 2015), 107–35.

tion with the church. The practices suggested could function to encourage in the same manner as Luther's encouragement for his parishioners.

The practices mentioned above occur in the context of contemporary Christians but often only in the final hours or days. However, the dying are often neglected when illness lingers for an extended time. In these cases, it is not the pastor's responsibility to continually supply the Lord's Supper as a means of comfort, but the congregational family's obligation to comfort and encourage the dying one in faith.

The study of Luther's theology of dying has shed much light on the subject of dying and death in contemporary Christian practices. Luther's pastoral encouragement can give aid to current pastors, as well as Christians seeking to die well in faithful confidence. Luther challenged all believers to look to Christ in suffering and death for hope of salvation. The result is that Christians will be able to face death without fear because of Christ and accept death when it draws near.

Selected Bibliography

Primary Sources

Luther, Martin. *Commentary on the Epistle of Romans*, Translated by J. Theodore Mueller. Grand Rapids: Kregel, 1976.

__________. "Fourteen Consolations." *Luther's Works Volume 42.* Translated by Martin H. Bertram. Philadelphia: Fortress Press, 1969.

__________. "Lectures on Genesis." *Luther's Works Volume 1.* Translated by George V. Schick. St. Louis: Concordia, 1955.

__________. "A Sermon on Preparing to Die." *Luther's Works Volume 42.* Translated by Martin H. Bertram. Philadelphia: Fortress Press, 1969.

__________. "Psalm 90." *Luther's Works Volume 13.* Translated by Paul M. Bretscher. St. Louis: Concordia Press, 1956.

__________. "Table Talk." *Luther's Works Volume 54.* Translated by Theodore G. Tappert. Philadelphia: Fortress Press, 1967.

__________. "Two Funeral Sermons." *Luther's Works Volume 51.* Translated by John W. Doberstein. Philadelphia: Muhlrnberg Press, 1959.

Tappert, Theodore G., Editor and Translator. *Luther: Letters of Spiritual Counsel.* Louisville: John Knox, 1998.

Secondary Sources

Althaus, Paul. *The Theology of Martin Luther.* Translated by Robert Schultz. Philadelphia: Fortress, 1966.

Bainton, Roland H. *Here I Stand: A Life of Martin Luther.* 1950. Reprint, New York: Meridian, 1995.

Bornkamm, Heinrich. *Luther's World of Thought,* Translated by Martin H. Bertram. St. Louis: Concordia, 1958.

George, Timothy. *Theology of the Reformers*. Rev. ed. Nashville: Broadman & Holman, 2013.

Kolb, Robert. *Martin Luther as Prophet, Teacher, Hero*. Grand Rapids: Baker, 1999.

Lull, Timothy F. and William Russell, ed. *Martin Luther's Basic Theological Writings*. 3rd ed. Minneapolis: Fortress, 2012.

Marius, Richard. *Martin Luther: The Christian Between God and Death*. Cambridge: Harvard University Press, 1999.

Ngien, Dennis. "The Art of Dying: In Luther's Sermon on Preparing to Die." *Heythrop Journal* 49, no. 1 (January 2008): 1–19. *Academic Search Complete*, EBSCO*host* (accessed October 20, 2016).

Obermann, Heiko A. *Luther: Man Between God and the Devil*. Translated by Eileen Walliser-Schwarzbart. New York: Doubleday, 1992.

Strohl, Jane E. "Luther's Fourteen Consolations." In *The Pastoral Luther: Essays on Martin Luther's Practical Theology,* Edited by Timothy J. Wengert. Grand Rapids: Eerdmans, 2009.

Trueman, Carl R. Luther on the Christian Life: Cross and Freedom. Wheaton: Crossway, 2015.

Wengert, Timothy J. "Introducing the Pastoral Luther," in *The Pastoral Luther: Essays on Martin Luther's Practical Theology,* edited by Timothy J. Wengert. Grand Rapids: Eerdmans, 2009.

Wicks, Jared. "Applied Theology at the Deathbed: Luther and the Late-Medieval Tradition of the Ars moriendi." *Gregorianum* 79, no. 2 (1998 1998): 345–368. *ATLA Religion Database with ATLA Serials*, EBSCO*host* (accessed November 4, 2016).

Lament in Worship in an Evil World

Jessica McMillan, DMA, and Ed Steele, DMA

Jessica McMillan is Director of Doctor of Musical Arts (DMA) at New Orleans Baptist Theological Seminary.

Ed Steele is Professor of Music at Leavell College in New Orleans, Louisiana.

Introduction

The problem of evil transcends all time and has left humanity in the throes of chaos and brokenness since the very beginning. People of all cultures throughout time have experienced suffering and have found methods for expressing their deep pain and overwhelming feelings of despair. Ancient Near Eastern religious expressions were adopted and adapted into other cultural expressions, including the worship of Yahweh. Biblical writers used a recognizable literary form as a basis upon which to share the hope they found in God with the hurting people around them.

Biblical lament and the lament of ancient Near Eastern societies share some strikingly common features, but their functions are remarkably different. The role of ancient ritual lament was to look backward at events and people while biblical lament was (and is) a function of worship which points toward the hope of rescue. Therefore, a proper understanding of the role of lament is important because the truth found in biblical lament is the same truth available for suffering humanity today. The purpose of this paper is to provide an overview of lament from examples found in both Old and New Testament passages as well as to present practical applications for incorporating lament into modern corporate worship gatherings.

Historical Background

Lament in the Old Testament

Throughout the Old Testament, Israel knew Yahweh as the one who could deliver them from affliction. Israel's relationship with him was based on his saving acts when they cried out to him in distress.[1] According to Amos 5:16, mourning was dramatic and loud. Jeremiah 32:9–12 and 41:5–6b allude to some physical aspects, such as the beating of one's breast and the removal one certain types of clothing. The theological significance of the lament genre only can be found in the proper distinction of the lament of *affliction* from that of lament for the *dead*. Funerary laments look backward at the life of someone deceased, and the lament born from affliction gives a voice to suffering while looking forward to the hope of rescue.[2] Although the outward act of weeping is similar for both types of lament, the Hebrew terms for each action should not be mistaken for one another.[3]

Jeremiah

There are many lament passages in the book of Jeremiah, which reveals the presence of Yahweh in the midst of extreme devastation. After the termination of the kingdom of Judah, Nebuchadnezzar's Babylonian empire had captured and/or killed the last of Judah's royalty and decimated the temple. Society was in ruins. Livestock and crops were destroyed. Amid such a catastrophic era, professional mourners received an invitation to sing the dirge found in Jeremiah 9:20.[4]

> Death has climbed in through our windows
> and has entered our fortresses;
> it has removed the children from the streets
> and the young men from the public squares.[5]

Both Baruch and Jeremiah speak as representatives of the community and on behalf of themselves as well, indicating that laments could be both individual and communal.[6]

---

[1] Claus Westermann, "The Role of the Lament in the Theology of the Old Testament," *Interpretation* 28, no. 1 (January 1974): 21.

[2] Westermann, "The Role of the Lament in the Theology of the Old Testament," 22.

[3] Westermann, "The Role of the Lament in the Theology of the Old Testament," 23.

[4] Pamela J. Scalise, "The Logic of Covenant and the Logic of Lament in the Book of Jeremiah," *Perspectives in Religious Studies* 28, no. 4 (Winter 2001): 395.

[5] Spacing reflects poetic reiteration.

[6] Scalise, "The Logic of Covenant and the Logic of Lament in the Book of Jeremiah," 399.

Psalms

There is no doubt that the book of Psalms is full of lament passages, as nearly one third of the psalms found there fit this genre. Hermann Gunkel classifies Psalms 44, 74, 79, 80, and 83 as examples of congregational, or communal lament.[7] The communal lament typically follows a pattern similar to pagan lament practiced in the Ancient Near East and includes the following:

1. Address and introductory cry to God for help
2. Lament, usually political in nature
3. Confession of trust
4. Petition
5. Assurance of being heard
6. Desire for God's intervention
7. Vow of praise
8. Praise of God when petition has been heard[8]

Individual laments, or complaints, found in the book of Psalms are 3; 5; 6; 7; 13; 17; 22; 25; 26; 27:7–14; 28; 31; 35; 38; 39; 42–43; 54–57; 59; 61; 63; 64; 69; 70; 71; 86; 88; 102; 109; 120; 130; 140; 141; 142; 143.[9] Characteristics of the individual lament are (not always in the same order):

1. Summons to Yahweh
2. Complaint (often preceded by a description of the prayer)
3. Considerations inducing Yahweh to intervene
4. Petition

---

[7] Tyler F. Williams, "A Form-critical Classification of the Psalms According to Hermann Gunkel." Used with permission with the stipulation that proper credit be given in this way: Prepared by Tyler F. Williams (10/2006). Sources: Hermann Gunkel, *The Psalms: A Form-Critical Introduction* (Minneapolis, MN: Fortress, 1967; translation of *Die Religion in Geschichte und Gegenwart* [2nd ed.; J. C. B. Mohr (Paul Siebeck), 1930]; and Hermann Gunkel (completed by Joachim Begrich), *Introduction to Psalms: The Genres of the Religious Lyric of Israel* (Macon, GA: Mercer University Press, 1998; translation of *Einleitung in die Psalmen: die Gattungen der religiosn Lyrik Israels* [Vandenhoeck & Ruprecht, 1985], 933); available from http://biblical-studies.ca/blog/2010/05/23/form-critical-classification-of-psalms; Internet.

[8] C. Hassell Bullock, *Encountering the Book of Psalms* (Grand Rapids, MI: Baker Academic, 2001), 136.

[9] Williams, "A Form-critical Classification of the Psalms According to Hermann Gunkel," 2.

5.   Assurance of being heard/vow of praise[10]

The form has other nuances and does not have to contain all of the aforementioned elements to be considered lament.[11]

Lamentations

The entire book of Lamentations expresses the suffering that occurred at the hands of the Babylonians after the destruction of Jerusalem.[12] The writer of the book incorporates many elements of ancient Near Eastern lament into the biblical text. Some of them include subject and mood, structure and poetic technique, the idea of divine abandonment, assignment of responsibility, the divine agent of destruction, the destruction itself, a weeping goddess,[13] lament, and restoration/return of the deities.[14] Various types of Sumerian lament are found in the book. One example includes the use of the female voice, which begins in the first chapter, and is assumed to be taken from the nonliterary performance of laments.[15] Although a male character enters in chapter three, one of the accomplishments of the book is to present an inclusive voice that only can be "accessed through human individuality" which humanity reads through the lens of gender.[16]

Job 3

Sandwiched in the middle of Job's discourse is his lengthy lament. In the beginning of chapter three, Job focuses his lament toward God and toward himself simultaneously as he questions

---

[10] Williams, "A Form-critical Classification of the Psalms According to Hermann Gunkel," 2.

[11] Nancy C. Lee, *Lyrics of Lament: From Tragedy to Transformation* (Minneapolis, MN: Fortress, 2010), 112.

[12] Walter Brueggemann, "Formfulness of Grief," *Interpretation* 31, no. 3 (Jul 1977): 274.

[13] F. W. Dobbs-Allsopp, Weep, O Daughter of Zion: A Study of the City-Lament Genre in the Hebrew Bible (Rome: Pontifical Biblical Institute, 1993), 31.

[14] Since biblical monotheism would not include a goddess, the personified Jerusalem is the Hebrew counterpart to this particular element of Mesopotamian lament. See F. W. Dobbs-Allsopp, "Lamentations," *Interpretation: A Bible Commentary for Teaching and Preaching* (Louisville, KY: John Knox, 2002), 77.

[15] Dobbs-Allsopp, "Lamentations," 107.

[16] Dobbs-Allsopp, "Lamentations," 107.

why he must endure such hardship.[17] After Job's friends speak to comfort him, he responds with lament (against both God and the friends) as he curses the day he was born as well as the days that bring him such woe (Job 3:20–25).

> Why is light given to those in misery, and life to the bitter of soul, to those who long for death that does not come, who search for it more than for hidden treasure, who are filled with gladness and rejoice when they reach the grave? Why is life given to a man whose way is hidden, whom God has hedged in? For sighing has become my daily food; my groans pour out like water. What I feared has come upon me; what I dreaded has happened to me. I have no peace, no quietness; I have no rest, but only turmoil.

In chapter 10:20–23, Job is not consumed by his difficulty as much as he is overwrought with meaninglessness.[18] He wishes again that he had never been born. This lament is similar in structure and form to the individual laments of the Psalms.[19]

Lament in the New Testament

In the New Testament, suffering individuals cry out to Jesus for help. The influence of the Psalter on the New Testament is pervasive as lament psalms are interwoven throughout this portion of scripture.[20] Some elements of lament are only allusions, as in Bartimaus's story in Mark 10:47, while others are outright quotations, as when Jesus quotes the lament found in Psalm 22 from the cross. While lament in the New Testament does not follow the same literary forms as those of the Old Testament, there is no doubt that early believers drew from the practice of lament set before them and adapted it to fit their contemporary setting. Scholars agree that lament regarding the death of Christ is evident in the Synoptic Gospels.[21]

---

[17] Samuel Eugene Balentine, *Prayer in the Hebrew Bible: The Drama of Divine-human Dialogue* (Minneapolis, MN: Fortress, 1993), 169.

[18] Norman C. Habel, *The Book of Job* (Philadelphia: Westminster, 1985), 112.

[19] Raymond B. Dillard and Tremper Longman, *An Introduction to the Old Testament* (Grand Rapids, MI: Zondervan, 1994), 202.

[20] Lee, Lyrics of Lament, 112.

[21] Sean M. McDonough, "Lament in the New Testament," in *A Time for Sorrow: Recovering the Practice of Lament in the Life of the Church*, ed. Scott D. Harrower and Sean M. McDonough (Peabody, MA: Hendrickson, 2019), 53.

John 11:17–32; 12:1–7

Comforting the bereaved was a social and religious duty during the first century AD.[22] In the John 11 passage, most likely a large number of people had visited the grieving family as even those who passed a funeral procession were accustomed to joining it and participating in the lamentation.[23] Slipping out in private to be with Jesus, both Mary and Martha ask "why" even though they think they trust Christ. Their fragmented lament demonstrates that mourning practices that were similar to ancient ones were still common during the early church era and that the sisters' ritual perception of their brother was that he was dead.[24]

Another possible instance of Mary's fragmented lament is John 12:1–7. Lavishing expensive perfumes during funerary activities was not uncommon.[25] Since anointing the corpse and tearing or cutting the hair were also part of the preparation of the body during death rituals, it is possible that Mary's act of worship is a type of lament foreshadowing of Jesus's death that she does not even understand.[26]

Luke 23:26–29

In this preliminary segue to the crucifixion of Christ, the women of Jerusalem were performing their customary ritual of mourning for a victim as he journeyed toward his place of execution. This demonstrates the continued cultural practice of professional feminine mourning. Jesus took the opportunity to redirect the object of their grief as he warns the weeping women that one day they will wish that they had no children because of the terrible fate that awaits them.[27]

---

[22] D. A. Carson, "The Gospel According to John," *The Pillar New Testament Commentary* (Grand Rapids, MI: Eerdmans, 1994), 411.

[23] Craig S. Keener, *The Gospel of John: A Commentary*, Vol. 2 (Peabody, MA: Hendrickson, 2003), 843.

[24] F. F. Bruce, *The Gospel of John* (Grand Rapids, MI: Eerdmans, 1983), 247.

[25] Bruce, *The Gospel of John*, 257.

[26] Angela Standhartinger, "'What Women Were Accustomed to Do for the Dead Beloved by Them' (*Gospel of Peter* 12.50): Traces of Laments and Mourning Rituals in Early Easter, Passion, and Lord's Supper Traditions," *Journal of Biblical Literature* 129, no. 3 (2010): 563.

[27] I. Howard Marshall, *The Gospel of Luke* (Grand Rapids, MI: Eerdmans, 1978), 862.

Matthew 27:45–46

The understanding of Psalm 22 to a pre-Christian audience has been debated for hundreds of years. In the Amoraic period (3rd–5th centuries), the most likely candidate for the suffering individual was Esther as she attempted to save her people and risked her life in doing so. Because the psalm ends in communal lament, some scholars conclude that it must have been "composed for a person with a special relationship to a community, such as a royal figure" who might represent an entire group of people through prayer.[28]

Matthew 27 is just one example in the gospel accounts of Jesus quoting this psalm of lament. In one last beautiful act of worship form the cross, Jesus struggles to quote the words of a well-known lament that, for years, had been associated with suffering. As he comforted his family, friends, and followers as well as his own mother, those in attendance would have known the words well and instinctively recognized that this lament was scripture.[29]

Revelation 18–19

In the consummate biblical lament, Babylon the great has fallen never to rise again. This lament seems to fit into some of the same patterns as the city laments of the Old Testament.[30] Beginning in verses 9–10, a similar pattern as seen in Ezekiel 26:16–18 occurs in response to the fall of Tyre.

> Then all the princes of the coast will step down from their thrones and lay aside their robes and take off their embroidered garments. Clothed with terror, they will sit on the ground, trembling every moment, appalled at you. Then they will take up a lament concerning you and say to you:
>
> "How you are destroyed, city of renown, peopled by men of the sea! You were a power on the seas, you and your citizens; you put your terror on all who lived there. Now the

---

[28] Ester Menn, "No Ordinary Lament: Relecture and the Identity of the Distressed in Psalm 22," *Harvard Theological Review* 93, no. 4 (Oct 2000): 309.

[29] J. Scott Duvall and J. Daniel Hays, *Grasping God's Word: A Hands-on Approach to Reading, Interpreting, and Applying the Bible* (Grand Rapids, MI: Zondervan, 2005), 196.

[30] Of the sources consulted for this paper, none specifically made the comparison (other than fragmentary allusions). Comparing the ancient city lament form with the lament over Babylon might provide an interesting possibility for further research.

coastlands tremble on the day of your fall; the islands in the sea are terrified at your collapse." (Ezekiel 26:16–18)

When the kings of the earth who committed adultery with her and shared her luxury see the smoke of her burning, they will weep and mourn over her. Terrified at her torment, they will stand far off and cry:

"Woe! Woe to you, great city, you mighty city of Babylon! In one hour your doom has come!" (Revelation 18:9–10)

Incorporating Lament in Worship

Lament is a reality of life. In the life of the Hebrew, a *qinah* was sung, the song of lament to mourn the loss of a loved one as was mentioned previously.[31] Deep relationships and deep afflictions call for deep expressions upon their loss. A transparent reflection of these expressions is found in the Psalms, the ebb and flow of praise, lament, gratitude and intercession.[32] While this may be so, the question is, "Should these reflections of life be a part of our corporate worship and if so, how?"

The existence of the book of Psalms in the canon of Scripture with its multitude of laments should be reason enough to incorporate their truths into the liturgy.[33] The sheer number of these laments intermingled with those of praise and thanksgiving indicate that they were natural expressions of the human experience and not exceptions to it. Perhaps the lack of these communal expressions in our worship has inadvertently led to their denial or perceived as just as valid as thanksgiving for blessings received. Rather than a communal "gripe and complain" session disguised as worship, lament can help the believer bridge the gap between grasping the reality and seriousness of evil while looking in hope to the God who cares and is in control.

Believers can hope because God, himself, through his Son has experienced trauma and evil. Scott Harrower summarized how the Apostle Paul understood this idea:

---

[31] Rolf A. Jacobson and Karl N. Jacobson, *Invitation to the Psalms: A Reader's Guide for Discovery and Engagement* (Grand Rapids, MI: Baker Academic, 2013), 36.

[32] John D. Witvliet, *The Biblical Psalms in Christian Worship: A Brief Introduction and Guide to Resources* (Grand Rapids, MI: Eerdmans, 2007), 25.

[33] While all the psalms are Scripture, not all may be appropriate for use in corporate worship, such as 137:9, "Blessed shall he be who takes your little ones and dashes them against the rock!" (CSB).

In a nutshell, for Paul, God the Son's incarnation means that God has general empathy for all who live in a world full of sin, suffering, lament, and trauma. Beyond this, God the Spirit's indwelling within each Christian allows a deeper and person-specific empathy for those who lament. Because God is One, God's general and specific empathy for his people is shared by the Father, Son, and Spirit. In light of this shared Trinitarian knowledge, we will see that God's Spirit in turn shares his concerns for a given individual believer with other members of the Christian community whom he also indwells. When God's empathetic and person-specific knowledge is shared across people, one person whom he indwells may receive specific insights about and gifts of care for another individual or community that is suffering and lamenting. In addition, God may support and strengthen these pastoral efforts by developing an attitude of service and gifted competence in the lives of those who minister alongside those who lament.[34]

Those planning the liturgy must encounter a wealth of expressions covering the gamut of human experience and worthy of use by the congregation. When congregations are limited to only the victory of the Christian life in their expressions of worship, an unintentional message is being communicated: "'If you want to fit in, first get your emotions in order so that you can be positive, and then go to worship.' But the Psalms help show us that bottling up or trying to 'fix' those emotions ourselves is not the right way." He adds, "Fear, anger, confusion, protest – these are all emotions that we can and should bring before our covenant Lord with the psalmists."[35]

How can lament be incorporated into worship? The Lenten season is a natural time to add a service of lament as the church refocuses on the sacrifice and death of Christ. Public recognition of the sin that made the cross necessary can also be a time to recognize other evils present in society. Services of lament could be for special services responding to social injustice, the persecution of believers in some countries, Memorial Day, or 9-11. The diffi-

---

[34] Scott Harrower, "God the Trinity and Christian Care for Those Who Lament," in *A Time for Sorrow*, 71.

[35] J. Todd Billings, *Rejoicing in Lament: Wrestling with Incurable Cancer and Life in Christ* (Grand Rapids, MI: Brazos, 2015), 41.

culty of dealing with evil should not be a reason to avoid grappling with it in worship. Believers must learn to worship in and through all of the experiences of life.

An Order of Service

While the biblical examples of lament vary so that there is no single prescribed order, there are some facets from the examples given that should be included. Praise and thanksgiving aids in reminding those gathered for worship that God is still God even in the midst of evil in the world. Certainly other portions of Scripture that reveal the nature of the human condition and brokenness of the society underscore the great need for God's intervention. Songs can call attention to suffering and hurt and help refocus attention on the God's power to redeem. Prayers of confession and mercy along with expositions of the Word can bring insight during this time of transparency and intimacy with God. The following may be used as an example of what a service of lament might curtail. To give an example of a service of lament, one possible example of an order of worship will conclude this brief study. The more that believers engage in learning how to incorporate lament in corporate worship, better examples and models will arise. The example below should be considered as only one model from which to build and develop others.

Service of Lament

Call to Worship: "Morning Hymn"[36]
Prayer of Thanksgiving
Psalm 73
Responsive Reading:

O God,
Once again we have seen wickedness raise its head,
Thousands of Your children have been martyred simply because they bear Your name;
Countless cry in hunger and pain and precious lives are snuffed out before they can see the light of day, or know the warmth of loving arms.

---

[36] See Appendix A.

Hatred is born from eyes that cannot seen beneath the shades of skin;
Justice is mocked;
The whimpers of huddled masses leak through the thatched roof shanties.
O God,
You are not dead.
Rise up through Your people; Bring glory to Your holy Name by what You do!
Move us from our complacency.
Don't let another sun set until every heart is touched.
Teach us to wipe away the tears streaming down sunken cheeks and shriveled faces.
O God,
You who are eternally Holy, Infinite Love,
Move. Touch. Heal. Convict. Empower. Renew.
We are Your servants, Lord.
We take up the towel and basin.
Remold us into Your image and nature

Prayers of Confession.
Song of Lament[37]
God's Word to God People: A Message
    Matthew 25:35–36
Doxology
Prayer

------

[37] See Appendix B.

Appendix A

Morning Hymn

MUSIC: OLD 100TH Genevan Psalter
WORDS: Ed Steele, Thomas Ken

© Copyright 2019 Ed Steele

14

Appendix B

Lament

Ed Steele © Copyright 2020

15

The Davidic Covenant
as an Interpretational Key

Mario Melendez, PhD

Mario Melendez is the Auguie Henry Chair of Bible and Assistant professor of Old Testament and biblical studies at Oklahoma Baptist University

When studying the Davidic covenant, Walter Brueggemann regarded it as the "dramatic and theological center of the entire Samuel corpus" and as "the most crucial theological statement in the Old Testament."[1] Interestingly, Brueggemann did not layout what he meant by these statements. Thus, the thesis of this article is that the Davidic covenant serves as an interpretational key to understand several subpoints of theology: theology of the temple, theology of peace, and theology of the king/messiah. Several research questions will be asked of the Davidic covenant. 1) What does the covenant entail? 2) How did the prophets understand and utilize the Davidic covenant? 3) What are the possible theological implications of the Davidic covenant? The method in answering these questions will be to survey the original text, prophetic texts and to draw theological conclusions of the two. The hypothesis of this work is that the biblical authors utilized the Davidic covenant to be a theological message to numerous generations culminating with an eternal fulfillment. As such, only when the divine king rules, among the people (in the promised temple), will there be eternal peace.

The Covenant in 2 Samuel

The setting of the covenant, 2 Samuel 7, is the beginning of David's reign. In 2 Samuel 5, David united the kingdom. Shortly thereafter, David took the city of Jerusalem and brought the ark of the covenant into the city. With his capital in control, David began

---

[1] Walter Brueggemann, *First and Second Samuel: Interpretation: A Bible Commentary for Teaching and Preaching*, Reprint edition. (Louisville, KY: Westminster John Knox Press, 2012), 253; Likewise, Anderson notes that this covenant is the theological highlight of Deuteronomistic History. Arnold Albert Anderson, *2 Samuel* (Nashville, TN: T. Nelson, 2000), 112.

constructing the king's palace. At the time of the covenant, David laments that he was living in a grand palace, yet God was relegated to a tent (2 Sam 7:2). Not written into the text is another possible worry of David, his reign. This worry is implicit in the text, for the ancient near eastern tradition was to build a temple for the local deity and sacrifice to him so that the king may have a long ruling dynasty.[2] "The obvious answer to the problem of legitimacy, [a] characteristic of every ruler in the ancient world, is to build a temple. Give God a permanent residence that will solidify the regime."[3] Though this tradition was known to David, God does not permit such a construction. God's reply demonstrates that David was not just worried about honorific patronage, but rather the future of his kingdom, possibly fearing his reign being usurped.[4]

Through a simple understanding of the setting and pericope, one finds the structure of a covenant, though the term *berit* is not within the 2 Samuel text.[5] If David's reign were to be passed on, then what impact would this great covenant have on the subsequent heirs? As William Dumbrell noted, "the purpose of the covenant with David was to engraft the developing monarchy into existing Israelite covenantal structure."[6] As a result, the previous covenants of Abraham, and Moses are extended into the national structure with the Davidic monarchy.

---

[2] William Dumbrell, "The Davidic Covenant," *Reform. Theol. Rev.* 39.2 (1980): 40–41.

[3] Brueggemann, *First and Second Samuel*, 254.

[4] Walter C. Kaiser, *Toward an Old Testament Theology* (Grand Rapids, MI: Zondervan, 1978), 144–49. Like David's divine usurping of Saul, David likewise feared a similar takeover.

[5] Moshe Weinfeld classified the three major covenants into two groups. "The obligatory type is reflected in the Covenant of God with Israel [the Mosaic Covenant] and the promissory type is reflected in the Abrahamic and Davidic covenants." Moshe Weinfeld, "Covenant of Grant in the Old Testament and in the Ancient Near East," *Am. Orient. Soc.* 90 (1970): 185. By placing the Davidic covenant into the historical King Grant form, one has but to look for the fulfillment of the covenant within Scripture, for God himself covenanted to completing the task. Paul R Williamson, *Sealed With An Oath: Covenant in God's Unfolding Purpose* (Downers Grove, IL: Intervarsity Press, 2007), 121.

[6] William Dumbrell, *Covenant and Creation: An Old Testament Covenant Theology* (Milton Keynes: Paternoster, 2013), 127.

The Covenant Keys

A simple reading of 2 Samuel 7 yields the concept of some covenant fulfillments being realized during David's lifetime (2 Sam. 7:8-11a), and some being fulfilled after his death (2 Sam. 7:11b-16). These fulfillments will be termed as "covenant keys," for they will be utilized later to unlock the messages of the prophets. Prior to the phrase, "When your days are fulfilled and you lie down with your fathers" one finds three promises: Great name, Place for the people, and Rest (peace). The first promise answers the previously mentioned concern of David, of his reign, by the Lord's promise of a great name (v. 9). Theologically speaking, this promise of provision of a great name teaches that no king sits on a throne unless granted / led by Yahweh to do such (Dan 2:20-23).

Not only was David concerned for his own reign, but the existence of the empire itself. Thus, the Lord replies with two promises: A Place for the People (v. 10), and Rest from enemies (v. 11). Richard Fuhr and Gary Yates categorizes term these promises as being "far-term fulfillments."[7] Within David's reign, the land of Israel came close to meeting the ideal boundaries promised initially to Abraham (Gen 15:18). Secondly, the promise of rest from enemies (7:1) was undoubtedly welcomed due to the historical setting of David's past. For a season, there is a time of peace which provided David the time to move the ark to Jerusalem and to consider building the temple. Yet, peace was never fully attained during his reign. The peace promised by Yahweh to David is one which is temporary and similar to the type of peace achieved by the judges (2 Sam 7:10b-lla). The theology of Peace during the time of David's reign is temporary and fleeting. Though the first three promises are seen within David's time, they are only partial fulfillments. The theology of Peace during the time of David's reign is temporary and fleeting. This partial fulfillment permits these three to be keys to utilize in future texts. The two primary fulfillments yet to come are an heir and a temple.

Though David is not permitted to build the temple, the permission to move the ark to Jerusalem would have signaled that David's house too, would be one of eternality. The two promises of heir and temple are inseparable. The heir assures that not only the kingdom will last, but that Yahweh will be irrevocably con-

---

[7] Richard Alan Fuhr and Gary E. Yates, *The Message of the Twelve: Hearing The Voice of the Minor Prophets* (Nashville, TN: B&H Academic, 2016), 24.

nected with the Jerusalem rule. David possibly understood these truths as seen in Torah writings: Israel would one day have a king (Gen 17:6, 16; 35:11; Deut 17:14-20) and constitute a kingdom (Num 24:7,19). As a means of not only fulfilling the Davidic covenant, but also Torah passages, the heir of David will not replace the theocracy, but rather be "Yahweh's anointed" (1 Sam 24:6, 2 Sam 19:21).

It is here upon the concept of "Yahweh's anointed" that the Hebrew term Messiah resides. "Anointing set a man apart for the work he was being commissioned to do and was a solemn act declaring God's ordination of them for their task. In the Old Testament, there was anointing unto the priestly office, and anointing unto the kingship as well, both symbolizing the presence and Spirit of Christ upon the man for the work."[8] Due to this concept of anointing (messiah) being the right of crowning a king, the topic of messiah, in this paper is understood to be couched in the topic of the king.

Using the Keys

By tracing the three main promises of the covenant (keys), research will investigate how portions are fulfilled by each generation, yet leave the people with a yearning for the perfect fulfillment. For the purpose of answering how the prophets understand and utilize the Davidic covenant, the Prophets will be divided into four groups: Former Prophets, Pre-Exilic, Exilic, and Post Exilic prophets.

Former Prophets: Solomon

Immediately after David's death, God begins the work of keeping his covenant with David. First, God establishes Solomon as king over all the land (1 Chr 29:23, 1 Kgs 2:12, 45-46). Not only does he establish Solomon as king, but God treats Solomon as a son and perpetuated his kingdom (1 Kgs 11:11-13).[9] Secondly, God permits Solomon to build the temple (1 Kgs 5:5, 8:18-20). Then, due to his reign and political savvy, Solomon saw peace in the land (1 Kgs 4:25). The temple "no doubt reflected the socio-

---

[8] James Williamson, *From the Garden of Eden to the Glory of Heaven* (Greenville, SC: Calvary Press, 2008), 161.

[9] Gregory G Nichols, *Covenant Theology: A Reformed And Baptistic Perspective On God's Covenants* (Birmingham, AL: Solid Ground Christian Bo, 2014), 250.

economic, political innovations under Solomon's royal power. While the temple, of course, was intended to enhance YHWH over competing deities, the stratification and opulence also celebrated and enhanced Solomon's enormous achievements and successes."[10]

Solomon clearly understood his role in the Davidic covenant for at the temple dedication ceremony, Solomon refers to the prophecy that David had told him (I Kgs 8:25).[11] "This ideological utterance is the taproot of the messianic idea in ancient Israel. The promise made to David is for time to come. It explicitly concerns David's son Solomon, but there are always sons to come, generations of David's yet unborn, each of which is the carrier of this unconditional gospel."[12] In 1 Kgs 9:4-8 God reminds Solomon of the covenant with David.

> [4] And as for you, if you will walk before me, as David your father walked, with integrity of heart and uprightness, doing according to all that I have commanded you, and keeping my statutes and my rules, [5] then I will establish your royal throne over Israel forever, as I promised David your father, saying, 'You shall not lack a man on the throne of Israel.' [6] But if you turn aside from following me, you or your children, and do not keep my commandments and my statutes that I have set before you, but go and serve other gods and worship them, [7] then I will cut off Israel from the land that I have given them, and the house that I have consecrated for my name I will cast out of my sight, and Israel will become a proverb and a byword among all peoples. [8] And this house will become a heap of ruins. (1 Kgs 9:4-8)

Avraham Giladi wrote, "the covenant's unconditional aspect – that of an enduring dynasty – left open the possibility of YHWH's appointment of a loyal Davidic monarch in the event of a disloyal monarch's default."[13] During the time of Zedekiah, God will fulfill this portion of the warning for the monarchy and the temple will

---

[10] Walter Brueggemann, *Reverberations of Faith: A Theological Handbook of Old Testament Themes* (Louisville, KY: Westminster/John Knox Press, 2003), 207.

[11] When Abijam (I Kgs. 15:4) and Joram (II Kgs 8:19) are crowned there comes a similar recitation and remembrance of the Davidic covenant.

[12] Brueggemann, First and Second Samuel, 257.

[13] Avrāhām Gil'ādî and Roland K Harrison, *Israel's Apostasy and Restoration: Essays in Honor of Roland K. Harrison* (Grand Rapids, MI: Baker, 1988), 159.

both fall, but will one day be renewed again (I Kgs 9:42).[14] Thus the reader of 2 Samuel 7 is right in utilizing the Davidic covenant keys to understand the Solomonic reign, but Solomon cannot be the ultimate fulfillment of the Davidic covenant. The statement concerning the eternality of the Davidic rule (vv. 13, 16) point beyond the time frame of Solomon.

The period of Solomon can be concluded as such, though Solomon may have fulfilled the covenant as described in above section, the prophets thought it yet to be fulfilled.[15] The Davidic covenant thus served as a theological tutor instructing Solomon on his reign, and responsibility as a constructor of the Temple. However, it also should be seen that it was a message to Solomon concerning the future fulfillment, for Solomon himself was not an eternal king. "Out of this oracle there emerges the hope held by Israel in every season that there is a coming David who will right wrong and establish a good governance."[16]

Pre-Exilic Prophets[17]

The second prophetic group to examine is the Pre-Exilic prophets. The question to prove the thesis is, "how did the prophets understand and utilize the Davidic covenant?" Within the Pre-Exilic prophets, five prophets utilize the Davidic Covenant as a means of conveying a message: Isaiah, Jeremiah, Hosea, Amos, and Micah. The process of determining the use of the covenant will be to evaluate the three main keys and the focus in context.

Since the covenant is most obviously mentioned when David is listed, the heir to the covenant will be considered first. There are three ways that the pre-exilic prophets refer to the Davidic heir: current heir on the throne, nation as heir and divine heir to come.

First, concerning the current heirs, Isaiah addresses Hezekiah to remind him that Yahweh is the God of David who is your father (Isa 38:5). Jeremiah utilizes the Davidic covenant to be a

---

[14] Hayyim Angel, "The Eternal Davidic Covenant in II Samuel Chapter 7 and Its Later Manifestations in the Bible," *Jew. Bible Q.* 44.2 (2016): 84.

[15] Williamson, *Sealed with an Oath*, 141.

[16] Brueggemann, *First and Second Samuel*, 257.

[17] It is the contention of this writer that Isaiah (750-695 BC) and Jeremiah (628-588 BC) wrote in the pre-exilic periods. Through Yahweh's revelation to these authors they were able to look into the exilic and post-exilic period, thus providing future prophecy.

means by which he can judge the current ruling Davidic kings (Jer 13:13-14; 22:2-5, 30). As a message to the current Davidic rulers, the Davidic covenant also serves as a theological tutor, reminding them who anoints and removes kings.

A second pre-exilic use of the Davidic Covenant is often applied to the people of Israel. For many, Otto "Eissfeldt argued persuasively that in Isa 55:3 – 5 the promises to David are transferred to the people of Israel as a whole and his conclusions have been widely received."[18] Likewise, Gerhard Von Rad noted, "He [author of Isaiah] does not, however, interpret Jahweh's promises concerning the throne of David and the anointed one of Israel in the traditional way, for he understands them to have been made not to David but to the whole nation."[19] As the heirs of the covenant, the people are to embody the role of servant, who glorifies God in their lifes. As such, many scholars believe that the Davidic king and messianic hope is abandoned in the exilic period.[20]

Third, and most common, the Davidic heir is utilized as a means of understanding one who is to come. Though many may jump directly into messianic implications, the overtones of these passages can be seen also as earthly messages of coming Davidic rulers. Isaiah hails him as the "Prince of peace" Isa 9:6-7, Stump of Jesse (Isa 11:1-2, 10) and one who receives the "everlasting covenant" (Isa 55:3-5). Isaiah is most known for his use of the

---

[18] Kenneth E. Pomykala, *The Davidic Dynasty Tradition in Early Judaism: Its History and Significance for Messianism* (Atlanta, GA: Scholars Press, 1995), 39; Original Otto Eissfeldt, "Promises of Grace to David in Isaiah 55" in James Muilenburg, Bernhard W Anderson, and Walter J Harrelson, *Israel's Prophetic Heritage: Essays in Honor of James Muilenburg* (Eugene, OR: Wipf & Stock Publishers, 2010), 206–7.

[19] Gerhard von Rad, *Old Testament Theology: The Theology of Israel's Prophetic Traditions*, trans. D. M. G. Stalker (New York, NY: Harper & Row, 1965), 2:240.

[20] Christopher R North, *The Suffering Servant in Deutero-Isaiah; an Historical and Critical Study*. (Eugene, OR: Wipf and Stock, 2005); Robert D Bell, *The Theological Messages of the Old Testament Books* (Greenville, SC: Bob Jones University Press, 2010), 297. North's work delves primarily into the suffering servant passages of Isaiah. His work chronologically shows that many in varying generations did not believe the suffering servant to be the savior, but rather a prediction of the suffering to happen in the exilic period. The North's deduction, therefore, is that many believed the messianic hope to be abandoned in exile. Other scholars, like Bell, have contested such a concept, for the suffering servant suffers on behalf of the people.

Davidic covenant in this role in Isa 9:6-7 where the heir sits on the throne of David.

Kenneth Pomykala recognizes this Davidic quotation as an enthronement hymn. As such the names attributed to the coming heir are based "on the model of Egyptian practice, highlighting his role as a wise leader, military hero, protector of the people and guarantor of peace and prosperity."[21] In a similar structure, Jeremiah confronts the current heir, then proclaims the raising of a righteous branch of David (Jer 23:5-6; 33:15). For Jeremiah, when he comes, David will "never lack a man to sit on the throne of the house of Israel" (Jer 33:17, 20-26). The David who sits upon the throne is named Yahweh our Righteousness, indicating that the Messiah would be God himself.[22] Likewise, Hosea confronts the people of Israel through his earthly marriage to Gomer. After such a difficult marriage and life in ministry, Hosea proclaims that David will be their king (Hos 3:5).

Amos' message concerning the Davidic heir utilizes the phrase "booth of David" (Amos 9:11). "The allusion to David in Amos 6:5 is as a liturgical figure and has no messianic coloring. The rebuilt 'booth of David' (Amos 9:11) refers to Jerusalem as the site of the temple, and the final prophecy of hope democratizes Davidic promises."[23] Pomykala asserts that if the temple were the point of reference in Amos 9:11 one would expect that either the phrase "the booth of Solomon" or "the booth of the Lord" would be used.[24] Micah reverberates and claims that this coming Davidic King will be born in Bethlehem (Mic 5:2) and he will rightly shepherd God's flock (Mic 5:4).

Continuing the use of Davidic covenant keys one finds three means by which the pre-exilic prophets utilize the temple motif: earthly, eternally, and rebuilt. As previously mentioned concerning the heir, Amos utilized the motif of "booth of David." Many have surmised this to be an allusion to not only the kingly lineage but

---

[21] Pomykala, *The Davidic Dynasty Tradition in Early Judaism*, 19.

[22] Bell, *The Theological Messages of the Old Testament Books*, 319.

[23] Greg Goswell, "David in the Prophecy of Amos," *Vetus Testam.* 61.2 (2011): 243.

[24] Kenneth Pomykala, "Jerusalem as the Fallen Booth of David" (pp.275-293), in Simon John De Vries et al., *God's Word for Our World: Biblical Studies in Honor of Simon John De Vries* (Edinburgh: T & T Clark International, 2004), 257.

also the temple itself.[25] The other terms utilized in 9:11 ("repair, breaches, ruins") alludes to much more than a familial line. Thus, with the divine heir, comes the Temple. The book of the Twelve carries this motif of heir and temple in that they envision a coming removal, purification, and restoration of the land with people worshipping in a new Temple in Jerusalem.[26] Likewise, the pre-exilic Hosea argued for a restored land with people worshipping Yahweh in the temple of Jerusalem (Hos 1-3). "The period of cultic and political deprivation is balanced by a future cultic (seeking the Lord) and political (seeking David their king) restoration."[27]

The prophetic message of Amos is that there will be a defeat of enemies (Amos 2:13-16) and a destruction of the high places (Amos 7:9).

> The people had been religious enough but in only a pro forma way, so much so that the Lord said he hated their festivals, assemblies, and sacrifices (Amos 5:21-23). What he wanted was not a religious charade but the display of authentic justice and righteousness (v. 24). Only then would the glorious promises of the restoration of the house of David become a reality.[28]

Thus, Hosea summarizes by stating that *hesed* (covenant faithfulness) and a living knowledge of God are more important than sacrifice (Hos 6:6). God's response is to betroth Israel and covenant with them in righteousness, justice, love, compassion and faithfulness.[29] Connected with this personal focus of Hosea is Jeremiah's caution concerning the temple. The prophet warns the people against trusting in the "temple of Yahweh, temple of Yahweh, temple of Yahweh" (Jer 7:4). "The triple repetition conveys the deterioration of a theology of God's presence in the temple to a

---

[25] According to Andersen and Freedman, "[the booth of David] could stand for one or more of the buildings of the capital city that had symbolic significance", and they opt for the tent housing the ark "because that is the one structure presumably erected by David for which we do not have a name." Francis I. Andersen and David Noel Freedman, *Amos: a new translation with introduction and commentary* (New York, NY: Doubleday, 1997), 914.

[26] David M Morgan, "Ezekiel and the Twelve: Similar Concerns as an Indication of a Shared Tradition?," *Bull. Biblic. Res.* 20.3 (2010): 385.

[27] Pomykala, *The Davidic Dynasty Tradition in Early Judaism*, 17.

[28] Eugene H. Merrill, *Everlasting Dominion: A Theology of the Old Testament* (Nashville, TN: B&H Academic, 2006), 496.

[29] Merrill, *Everlasting Dominion*, 497.

meaningless mantra"[30] Thus the absence of explicit references to a new temple suggests to some that Jeremiah did not regard the temple as necessary.

The final Davidic covenant key to consider within the pre-exilic prophets is peace and rest. What is most interesting about peace in the pre-exilic prophets is their declaration of peace, yet the reality of pending invasion.

> Peace and rest are closely interconnected ideas in the Prophetic books. When depicting current social and political realities, they refer to a state of existence characterized by security and prosperity. They also play an important role in the prophetic description of the future. In such passages rest and peace are an integral part of Yahweh's eschatological gift of salvation.[31]

Therefore, Isaiah and Jeremiah speak of peace, though it is not to be found. Peace for Isaiah and Jeremiah is the absence of war and bondage (Isa 39:8; Jer 14:13). The result of such peace is the state of health and prosperity (Jer 29:7)

As Isaiah looked to the future exile, the Babylonian exile, he found the message of peace to be much more treasured by God's people (Isa 49-55). These chapters transcend their original historical situation and points toward "a new exodus, a fundamental new salvific event described in the categories of creation."[32] The result of such exilic peace is not just peace for Israel, but for the world. In essence, it is a picture of universal peace (Isa 2:2-4). Peace, however, is unachievable without righteousness. Ultimately the heir to the throne, the servant of God who is righteous, will hail the period of righteous. As such, peace is explicitly described as the result of righteousness dwelling among the community (Isa 32:17).

In sum, the pre-exilic prophets utilized the Davidic covenant for several reasons. First, the theology of the king is mentioned as a word of caution to current reigning Davidic heirs, to be a word of guidance to coming heirs, and to be a word of hope of a divine final heir. In the Pre-exilic prophets, the theology of the temple and peace are likewise directly connected with the monarchy. The

---

[30] Mark J. Boda and J. Gordon McConville, eds., *Dictionary of the Old Testament: Prophets* (Downers Grove, IL: IVP Academic, 2012), 769.

[31] Boda and McConville, *Dictionary of the Old Testament*, 574.

[32] Boda and McConville, *Dictionary of the Old Testament*, 575.

temple and peace will soon be destroyed with the pending invasion, but like the hope of a divine final heir, there is hope placed upon the heir who will reconstruct the temple and dwell among the people in righteousness, thus resulting in peace.

Exilic Prophets

When Babylon invades in 586 B.C., God's people begin to question whether or not God has abandoned them, and whether or not God has abandoned the covenant.[33] The Lord responds concerning the Davidic covenant through two exilic prophets: Ezekiel and Daniel.

The exilic hope of an heir is summarized in Ezekiel's understanding of God's servant being the shepherd to God's people (Ezek 34:23-24; 37:24-25). In chapter 34 of Ezekiel, the Lord condemns the shepherds (alluding to kings) for they have led the sheep astray. He follows the condemnation with a promise that his Davidic heir will be a good shepherd who will not only rid of the former shepherds but segregate the sheep. As such, the people hearing the message of Ezekiel undoubtedly understood the time of the exile to be not an abandonment of God, but rather a time of sifting by God. Furthermore, "The Lord decided to bring about renewal because His own reputation was at stake" (Ezek 20:44).[34]

Though the exilic message of the Davidic heir seems straightforward, the exilic picture of the Temple is not. Within the message of Daniel and Ezekiel one finds a temple which is empty of the Lord's presence (on earth), and an eternal / future one which is grander and gloriously filled with the presence of the Lord.

Indeed, the central theme of Ezekiel 1-24 is the loss of God's presence in the temple and the associated judgment on Jerusalem. In Ezekiel 8-11 the prophet watches as God actually leaves the temple. This is a devastating even for Israel, yet very important for our understanding of the temple and our theological understanding of God's presence in the Old Testament. At the end of Ezekiel (chaps. 40-48), however, the prophet describes a new future temple, complete

---

[33] The opening to Habakkuk's book is a biblical attestation to this questioning of God's presence.

[34] Bell, *The Theological Messages of the Old Testament Books*, 347.

with the restoration of God's presence once again with his people.[35]

As J. Daniel Hays noted, "the presence of God in the temple is the source of life, blessing, forgiveness, and protection."[36] Therefore when Ezekiel sees the presence of God leave the temple, he sees the protection, blessings, and forgiveness of sins vacate as well. This reality heavily shapes Ezekiel's focus on a restored land and people with the Davidic her. Matthew Lynch directly connects the fleeing presence of the Lord to a failing covenant. "While on the one hand, YHWH gave Solomon and his descendants permanent responsibility for his house and kingdom, the benefits and power of Yahweh's kingdom were only realized in conjunction with a faithful cult."[37] These religious understandings of the Lord's presence in the temple are the backdrop and precursors for the cosmic temple seen in Yahweh's Jerusalem.

Though Ezekiel sees the earthly temple vacated by the Lord and then defiled by invaders, he moves the concept of the Lord's presence from being contained in the temple to being wherever God's people are. Ezekiel 11:16 "Therefore say, 'Thus says the Lord GOD: Though I removed them far off among the nations, and though I scattered them among the countries, yet I have been a sanctuary to them for a while in the countries where they have gone." "YHWH's permanent dwelling among his people constituted, in effect, the sign of the Davidic covenant."[38] The phrase "Sanctuary for a while" minimizes the need for the Jerusalem temple and also hints to its eventual restoration. Even in light of the reconstructed temple, Ezekiel's message of the coming temple is that it will be a sanctuary in the midst of the people (Ezek 37:26,28). This dramatic theology of God's presence becomes the basis for the new temple in Ezekiel 40-48.[39]

During the time of the exile was peace to be known among the prophets? The hope of the exiles comes in the form of Ezekiel

---

[35] J. Daniel Hays, *The Temple and the Tabernacle: A Study of God's Dwelling Places from Genesis to Revelation* (Ada, MI: Baker Books, 2016), 104–5.

[36] Boda and McConville, *Dictionary of the Old Testament*, 769.

[37] Matthew Lynch, "The Davidic Covenant and Institutional Integration in Chronicles," in Nathan MacDonald, *Covenant and Election in Exilic and Post-Exilic Judaism* (Tubingen, Germany: Mohr Siebeck, 2015), 184.

[38] Gil'ādî and Harrison, *Israel's Apostasy and Restoration*, 160.

[39] Merrill, *Everlasting Dominion*, 546.

proclaiming safety (Ezek 34:25,27,28).[40] The promise of a life of security and peace becomes prominent in prophetic texts during and after exile. Peace and Temple meet in the Ezekiel message of a new covenant of peace (Ezek 37:26).

The conclusion of exilic use and understanding of the Davidic Covenant is one of assurance for the future, and comfort in exile. "What is somewhat surprising in all this is the infrequency of direct reference to any form of pre-exilic royal ideology."[41] What is clear concerning the theology of the King is Ezekiel's criticism. Ezekiel criticized the shepherds for leading the people astray, but he assures the exiles that the heir of David will be a faithful shepherd. Concerning the theology of the Temple and God's peace, Ezekiel sees God's presence leave the temple in Jerusalem, but sees the presence of God remaining with and in the midst of the people. As such, it is by recognizing God's presence that one finds peace in exile.

Post-Exilic Prophets

In the aftermath of the exile, the Davidic covenant becomes even more necessary for encouragement.[42] When the older priests who remembered the first temple saw the second, they wept (Ezra 3). Zechariah's message concerning the Davidic covenant directly answers this sorrow, for David is the king who will build up an eschatological temple (Zech 3:8-10; 6:9-15). Likewise, replying to the sorrow of Ezra 3, Haggai prophesies that Yahweh is with them (Hag 1:13) emphasizing that the temple does not give sole assurance that the presence of God is with them. Haggai prophesies a shaking of the universe and the nations (Hag 2:5-6) which will fill the temple with a greater glory. "Thus, the temple focuses the returnees' dreams and hopes of a God-given better life, which is anticipated even now in a promise of blessing (Hag 2:19)."[43] Some have noted that the Haggai quotation of the Davidic heir is

---

[40] Boda and McConville, *Dictionary of the Old Testament*, 574.

[41] Pomykala, *The Davidic Dynasty Tradition in Early Judaism*, 41.

[42] Lynch contends that the book of Chronicles is post-exilic and written to aid the task of reigniting the Davidic hope. "Because Chronicles positions the Davidic and Solomonic kingdom within the wider context of the Divine kingdom, some contend that divine kingship is the book's true concern." MacDonald, *Covenant and Election in Exilic and Post-Exilic Judaism*, 171.

[43] Boda and McConville, *Dictionary of the Old Testament*, 773.

reliant upon the identification of Zerubbabel in Chronicles.[44] Von Rad stated, "It is common to point out that Haggai here differs radically from pre-exilic prophets by naming a living member of the house of David as the coming anointed one."[45] However, if one were to identify the Haggai prophecy with the divine David, then the identification of Zerubbabel does not negate the efficacy of Haggai's message.

Not only does the post-exile find the Davidic king to be a faithful constructor of the temple, but also a priest. The postexilic prophets confirm the perpetual nature of God's covenant when Zechariah anticipates a messianic time when a priest will be on the throne of David (Zech 6:9-15). As temple studies of post-exilic prophets continues one finds a concern for constructing Yahweh's temple. "Although Joel and Jonah probably have a postexilic composition, it is in these last books of the Twelve, Haggai-Zechariah, and Malachi, where the rebuilding of YHWH'S sanctuary is the chief concern."[46] This connection with the temple and the Davidic heir directly flows into the concept that true peace is not the outcome of human efforts but rather stems from God's presence dwelling among people. Zechariah calls the temple a holy dwelling in heaven (Zech 2:13), but he looks to the rebuilding of the earthly temple (Zech 1:16; 4:8-10). Joel's vision of the eschatological future includes a temple that will be the source of a fountain of water for the land, a physical and symbolic sign of blessing (Joel 3:18). Focus upon the eternal temple is partnered with criticism of earthly temple worship. Interestingly, this post-exilic criticism parallels pre-exilic worship criticism. Malachi, like the pre-exilic prophets, condemns the priest for imperfect sacrifices (Mal 1:6-10), and wrong attitudes (Mal 1:10).

It is within the post-exilic prophets that one finds a similar use of the Davidic covenant as found in the pre-exilic prophets. The theology of the king focuses upon a divine heir who gladdens the sad hearts with a grand temple. The presence of the Lord will reside there and among the people. Peace will be a result of the king, temple, and presence.

The point of the tabernacle and the temple, after all, is to provide a residence for God, who comes and actually dwells

---

[44] Pomykala, *The Davidic Dynasty Tradition in Early Judaism*, 50.

[45] Rad, *Old Testament Theology Vol. 2*, 2:284.

[46] Morgan, "Ezekiel and the Twelve," 393.

in their midst in a very literal sense. Yet, that simply does not happen in the second temple, and this signals that a very significant change has taken place. God still promises his presence (Hag. 2:4-5), but he shifts to focusing on the presence of his Spirit among them, rather than his actual residence in the most holy place of the temple. He promises that his glory will come and fill this temple (Hag 2:6-9), but he leaves the time of this event as an unspecified time in the future.[47]

In sum, the post-exilic prophets quoted the Davidic covenant to point toward a unified (Israel & Judah) independent eternal nation (eternal king) without enemies (peace). Much like the Babylonians, peace cannot be known without a defeat of certain enemies. Therefore, in the final stage of prophetic use, David is a warrior king who wins the battle and provides peace.[48]

Implications of Prophetic Uses

The implications of the Davidic covenant come in two parts: for it is pro-Davidic, and pro-monarchial. As a pro-Davidic document, the Davidic covenant directly confronts the Sauline era which preceded David. Every time the Davidic covenant is quoted, one can understand it to be a support of the Davidic throne, over any other kingship. Furthermore, it is a document to support an eternal Davidic throne. Yahweh not only chose David and raised him up to be king, but he will raise up a Davidic heir to be eternally king. As a pro-monarchial document, it supports the concept of kingship in Israel. As mentioned previously the anointing of a Davidic king is not to undermine the reality of the theocracy, for God is still the one in control of all things. As such, the implication of this kingship document is that there is an eternal monarch, who presumably is God himself.

---

[47] Hays, *The Temple and the Tabernacle*, 130. Much of the messianic overtones of the post-exilic prophets possibly relates to the missing ark of the covenant. "Nowhere in the accounts of the second temple (Ezra, Haggai, Josephus) is the ark of the covenant ever mentioned."

[48] Boda and McConville, *Dictionary of the Old Testament*, 575.

Interpreting Theological Implications

There is no clear statement in the biblical text that makes known the implications of the Davidic covenant upon theology. As such, interpretations must be gleaned from the text. The themes to be gleaned are theology of the temple, theology of peace, theology of the king / messiah. As theological topics, these subjects do indeed have more passages of supporting data, however, due to the focus of this work, only passages concerning the Davidic Covenant or books that utilize the Davidic covenant will be considered.

Theology of the Temple

What is termed in this paper as the theology of the temple, has surrounded the topic of the Lord's Presence. As one progresses through the former prophets and into the later prophets, they will find that the theology of the Lord's presence is always taught with the theology of the temple. Thus, the theology progresses in a unique manner, concerning the Davidic covenant. At first, the theology of the temple is not needed, for Yahweh responds to David that he has lived in a tent and doesn't need a temple (2 Sam 7:5-7). However, David's desire for a temple in the capital underlines the theology that if there is a brick and mortar place of worship, then God will not leave or abandon the people. Later prophetic work has shown that the temple, with the presence of God therein, is the source of life, blessing, forgiveness, and protection for the people. Thus, the temple theology is not only one of presence, but provision. Such a theological understanding unlocks the messages of the prophets, for many point to an eternal / divine temple as being the real temple. Ezekiel's vision of Yahweh leaving the Jerusalem temple is connected with the last theological reality of the Davidic temple, God dwells among his people. (Ezek 37:26,28). This dramatic theology of God's presence becomes the basis for the new temple in Ezekiel 40-48.[49] In sum, the theology of the temple, couched within the Davidic covenant, is one of the Lord's presence being eternally with his people. Furthermore, the actual temple was only to be a temporary means of grasping what

---

[49] Christian theologians, such as dispensationalists and Covenantalists, look to this theological truth and rightfully make much of the incarnation.

it means to have the Lord's presence and provision within a particular kingdom.[50]

Theology of Peace

The theology of Peace during the time of David's reign is temporary and fleeting. Yet, the Davidic covenant promises peace and rest form enemies in the land. As the prophets handled the Davidic covenant they found that peace will not be fully achieved until the people of God are in the presence of the divine heir who will bring an end to their enemies and provide enteral peace. This connection with the temple and the Davidic heir directly flows into the concept that true peace is not the outcome of human efforts but rather stems from God's presence dwelling among people.

Theology of the King-Messiah

The last and most pertinent theological point is the theology of the king. Directly connected to this is the theology of the messiah, for many of the heir passages have eternal language. The first note within the theology of the king is that the recitation of David's past with Yahweh teaches that no king sits on a throne unless granted / led by Yahweh to do such. The harsh tone of the later prophets, toward the Davidic heirs, is one of reminding that Yahweh crowned David and he can uncrown you. Secondly, the theology of the king does not undermine the reality of the theocracy. Here the kingdom meets the messianic terms, for a messiah is one who is anointed, as are all of the Davidic kings. The king, therefore, should be one who humbly works within his anointing and rightly shepherds God's people. As such, Ezekiel 34 reminds the people that the divine Davidic heir is one who will confront earthly rulers. Most of the Davidic restoration prophecies come with oracles of judgement. Thus, the heir will even rid of bad sheep, but he will remain as a faithful shepherd to his people. The third theological point of the king is that he oversees building a temple. Though many solely take this to be a reality of the earthly temple, one should understand that the King / Messiah is one who ushers

---

[50] Williamson contends that the church becomes the fulfillment of the Davidic temple, for the presence of God dwells within the believers. James Williamson, *From the Garden of Eden to the Glory of Heaven*, 2 edition. (Greenville, SC: Calvary Press, 2008), 178–79.

the people of God into the presence of God. In Zechariah and Ezekiel, this point is pictured as an actual temple, but the presence is the primary focus of these passages. Lastly, if the theology of the king is primarily about pointing toward the Lord's rulership and presence, then the divine heir will be one who is a priest, for that is the requirement to operate within such proximity to Yahweh.

Conclusion

Walter Brueggemann regarded the Davidic covenant as the "dramatic and theological center of the entire Samuel corpus" and as "the most crucial theological statement in the Old Testament."[51] Through the accomplished research, the Davidic covenant has been shown to be an interpretational key to several points of theology; theology of the temple, theology of peace, theology of the king, and theology of the messiah. These points come from the covenant promises: name, peace, heir, and temple. The direct implication of the Davidic covenant can be found in the life and reign of Solomon. However, his reign does not perfectly fulfill the covenant, for the covenant, has eternal language. As such, the prophetic writers utilized the Davidic covenant to teach subsequent Davidic rulers theology of the king, temple, and peace. Finally, the prophetic writers utilized the Davidic covenant to provide hope to many people, for the eternal impact of the Davidic covenant was never missed in their interpretations. From these historical and biblical studies, the thesis has been further proven by summarizing the different points of theology taught in relation to the Davidic covenant. The results of this research yields the reality that God covenanted with David, and promised more than he could fathom. One day in Christ, God's covenantal plan will be achieved. As Sandra Richter stated, "this was God's perfect plan: the **people** of God in the **place** of God dwelling in the **presence** of God."[52]

---

[51] Walter Brueggemann, *First and Second Samuel: Interpretation: A Bible Commentary for Teaching and Preaching*, Reprint edition. (Louisville, Ky.: Westminster John Knox Press, 2012), 253; Likewise, Anderson noted that this covenant is the theological highlight of Deuteronomistic History. Arnold Albert Anderson, *2 Samuel* (Nashville: T. Nelson, 2000), 112.

[52] Sandra L. Richter, *The Epic of Eden: A Christian Entry into the Old Testament* (Downers Grove, IL: IVP Academic, 2008), 104.

Selected Bibliography

Andersen, Francis I., and David Noel Freedman. *Amos: a new translation with introduction and commentary*. New York, NY: Doubleday, 1997.

Anderson, Arnold Albert. *2 Samuel*. Nashville, TN: T. Nelson, 2000.

Anderson, Bernhard, and Walter Harrelson, eds. *Israel's Prophetic Heritage: Essays in Honor of James Muilenburg*. Eugene, OR: Wipf & Stock, 2010.

Angel, Hayyim. "The Eternal Davidic Covenant in II Samuel Chapter 7 and Its Later Manifestations in the Bible." *Jew. Bible Q.* 44.2 (2016): 83–90.

Bell, Robert D. *The Theological Messages of the Old Testament Books*. Greenville, S.C.: Bob Jones University Press, 2010.

Boda, Mark J., and J. Gordon McConville, eds. *Dictionary of the Old Testament: Prophets*. Downers Grove, IL: IVP Academic, 2012.

Brueggemann, Walter. *First and Second Samuel: Interpretation: A Bible Commentary for Teaching and Preaching*. Reprint edition. Louisville, KY: Westminster John Knox Press, 2012.

———. *Reverberations of Faith: A Theological Handbook of Old Testament Themes*. Louisville, KY: Westminster/John Knox Press, 2003.

Dumbrell, William. *Covenant and Creation: An Old Testament Covenant Theology*. Milton Keynes: Paternoster, 2013.

———. "The Davidic Covenant." *Reform. Theol. Rev.* 39.2 (1980): 40–47.

Fuhr, Richard Alan, and Gary E. Yates. *The Message of the Twelve: Hearing The Voice of the Minor Prophets*. Nashville, TN: B&H Academic, 2016.

Gilʿādî, Avrāhām, and Roland K Harrison. *Israel's Apostasy and Restoration: Essays in Honor of Roland K. Harrison*. Grand Rapids, MI: Baker, 1988.

Goswell, Greg. "David in the Prophecy of Amos." *Vetus Testam.* 61.2 (2011): 243–57.

Hays, J. Daniel. *The Temple and the Tabernacle: A Study of God's Dwelling Places from Genesis to Revelation*. Baker Books, 2016.

Kaiser, Walter C. *Toward an Old Testament Theology*. Grand Rapids, MI: Zondervan, 1978.

MacDonald, Nathan. *Covenant and Election in Exilic and Post-Exilic Judaism*. Tubingen, Germany: Mohr Siebeck, 2015.

Merrill, Eugene H. *Everlasting Dominion: A Theology of the Old Testament*. Nashville, TN: B&H Academic, 2006.

Morgan, David M. "Ezekiel and the Twelve: Similar Concerns as an Indication of a Shared Tradition?" *Bull. Biblic. Res.* 20.3 (2010): 377–96.

Nichols, Gregory G. *Covenant Theology: A Reformed And Baptistic Perspective On God's Covenants*. Birmingham, AL: Solid Ground Christian Bo, 2014.

North, Christopher R. *The Suffering Servant in Deutero-Isaiah; an Historical and Critical Study*. Eugene, OR: Wipf and Stock, 2005.

Pomykala, Kenneth E. *The Davidic Dynasty Tradition in Early Judaism: Its History and Significance for Messianism*. Atlanta, Ga: Scholars Press, 1995.

Rad, Gerhard von. *Old Testament Theology: The Theology of Israel's Prophetic Traditions*. Translated by D. M. G. Stalker. Vol. 2. New York, NY: Harper & Row, 1965.

Richter, Sandra L. *The Epic of Eden: A Christian Entry into the Old Testament*. Downers Grove, IL: IVP Academic, 2008.

Vries, Simon John De, J. Harold Ellens, Deborah L. Ellens, Rolf P. Knierim, and Isaac Kalimi. *God's Word for Our World: Biblical Studies in Honor of Simon John De Vries*. T & T Clark International, 2004.

Weinfeld, Moshe. "Covenant of Grant in the Old Testament and in the Ancient Near East." *Am. Orient. Soc.* 90 (1970): 184–203.

Williamson, James. *From the Garden of Eden to the Glory of Heaven*. Greenville, SC: Calvary Press, 2008.

Williamson, Paul R. *Sealed With An Oath: Covenant in God's Unfolding Purpose*. Downers Grove, IL: Intervarsity Press, 2007.

"The Son of God Appeared to Prophets and Patriarchs": Ante-Nicene Views of Christophanies

Rex D. Butler

New Orleans Baptist Theological Seminary

Introduction

In searching for "Christ in All Scriptures," some scholars look for Christ in his alleged Old Testament appearances, often called "Christophanies." In 1978, James Borland published his dissertation under the title, *Christ in the Old Testament*, which he described as a "Study of Old Testament Appearances of Christ in Human Form." In his comprehensive monograph in favor of Christophanies, Borland argued: "The thesis of this work is that all Old Testament theophanies that involved the manifestation of God in human form were appearances of the second person of the Trinity, and as such their purpose was not only to provide immediate revelation but also to prepare mankind for the incarnation of Christ."[1] Walter Kaiser registered his support of Borland in his foreword, in which he insisted that a biblical theology of Christophanies is an urgent need and more than a mere academic exercise.[2]

More recently, Michael Bird in his *Evangelical Theology* affirmed that divine appearances in the Old Testament were Christophanies, manifestations of the pre-incarnate Son of God.[3] In this assertion,

---

[1] James A. Borland, *Christ in the Old Testament: A Comprehensive Study of Old Testament Appearances of Christ in Human Form* (Chicago: Moody Press, 1978), 3-4.

[2] Walter Kaiser, "Foreword," in James A. Borland, *Christ in the Old Testament*, vii-viii.

[3] Michael Bird, *Evangelical Theology: A Biblical and Systematic Introduction* (Grand Rapids, MI: Zondervan, 2013), 103, 360-361. See also John Macartney Wilson, "Angel," in *International Standard Bible Encyclopedia* (Grand Rapids, MI: Eerdmans, 1979), 125; and Wayne Grudem, *Systematic Theology: An Introduction to Biblical Doctrine* (Grand Rapids, MI: Zondervan, 1994), 401. For popular presentations of Christophanies, see Mark Driscoll and Gerry Breshears, *Doctrine: What Christians Should Believe* (Wheaton, IL: Crossway, 2010), 44-45; and David Murray, *Jesus on Every Page: 10 Simple Ways to Seek and Find Christ in the Old Testament* (Nashville, TN: Thomas Nelson, 2013), 73-85.

Bird included appearances by the "Angel of the LORD," who "speaks with immediate divine authority."[4]

In counterpoint to these views, Andrew Malone stated flatly that "Michael Bird is wrong!"[5] Fred Sanders just said, "No to Christophanies."[6] In 1975, William MacDonald anticipated the controversy with his essay, "Christology and the 'Angel of the Lord,'" in which he expressed concerns that acceptance of Christophanies in the Old Testament would compromise the doctrine of Christ's incarnation in the New Testament.[7]

During the early centuries of Christian thought, the Ante-Nicene fathers had much to say regarding divine appearances in the Old Testament, which they attributed to the second person of the Godhead. The apologists Justin Martyr and Theophilus of Antioch pointed to Christophanies as proof of Christ's divinity. Later church fathers, including Irenaeus, Clement of Alexandria, Tertullian, and Novatian, drew from a wide selection of Christophanies to prove to pagans and heretics correct theologies of the person of Christ and personal distinctions in the Trinity.

Definitions of Terms

The broader term for a divine appearance in the Old Testament is "theophany," a transliteration of the Greek noun θεοφάνεια. In the fifth century B.C., the Greek historian Herodotus used this term to describe the Feast of the Divine Appearance at Delphi.[8] Early Christians then appropriated the term as a refer-

---

[4] Bird added in a footnote: "On Jesus and angels, I would point out that in Revelation Jesus is portrayed with angelic characteristics, he sends his 'angel' as a messenger, and yet it is basically himself who speaks (Rev 1:1; 22:16)." Bird, *Evangelical Theology*, 361 n. 48.

[5] Andrew Malone, *Knowing Jesus in the Old Testament?: A Fresh Look at Christophanies* (Nottingham, England: InterVarsity Press, 2015), 15. Malone described Bird as "a prolific young scholar" and "orthodox," but Malone holds Bird up as a typical, contemporary proponent of Christophanies, with whom he disagrees.

[6] Fred Sanders, *The Triune God* (Grand Rapids, MI: Zondervan, 2016), 224. Sanders' rejected Christophanies within his broader discussion of Trinitarian theology and his more particular presentation of prosoponic exegesis.

[7] William Graham MacDonald, "Christology and the 'Angel of the Lord,'" in *Current Issues in Biblical and Patristic Interpretation*, ed. Gerald F. Hawthorne (Grand Rapids, MI: Eerdmans, 1975), 324-335.

[8] Herodotus, *The Histories* 1.51, cited in Borland, *Christ in the Old Testament*, 6.

ence to "the manifestations of God under the Old Covenant."[9] This latter idea, however, is quite broad, for it incorporates not only the temporary, bodily appearances of God but also the more permanent, phenomenal manifestations, such as the Shekinah and the pillars of cloud and fire. For this reason, Borland preferred to discuss human-form theophanies as "Christophanies."[10]

Borland formulated a concise definition of "Christophany":

> The term *Christophany* … will denote those unsought, intermittent and temporary, visible and audible manifestations of God the Son in human form, by which God communicated something to certain conscious human beings on earth prior to the birth of Jesus Christ.[11]

He further distinguished Christophanies from dreams and visions[12] and from anthropomorphic metaphors.[13] Borland summarized his definition of Christophanies with a list of nine characteristics:

- Christophanies were actual occurrences, not imaginary experiences.
- Christophanies could be initiated only by the sovereign God.
- Christophanies had immediate purposes of issuing promises, warnings, or instructions.
- Christophanies were intended for individuals, not multitudes.
- Christophanies were intermittent, unpredictable occurrences.
- Christophanies were temporal and transitory.
- Christophanies were audible and visible.
- Christophanies were always human, but otherwise they varied in form.

---

[9] Bernard Pick, "Theophany," in *Cyclopaedia of Biblical, Theological, and Ecclesiastical Literature*, ed. John McClintock and James Strong, 10 vols. (1869-91); reprint ed., Grand Rapids: Baker, 1970), cited in Borland, *Christ in the Old Testament*, 6.

[10] Borland, *Christ in the Old Testament*, 10.

[11] Borland, *Christ in the Old Testament*, 10.

[12] Gen. 15:1; 20:3, 6; 28:12; 31:10-11, 24; 37:5; 40:5; 41:17, 22; and 46:2. "God Himself distinguished these from His more personal, physical manifestations to Moses (Num. 12:12:6-8)." Borland, *Christ in the Old Testament*, 11.

[13] For example, Judg. 5:4-5. Borland, *Christ in the Old Testament*, 11.

- Christophanies were confined to the Old Testament era; after the incarnation, such Christophanies were no longer necessary.[14]

These Christophanies included, but were not limited to: the LORD, who appeared to Moses at the oaks of Mamre (Gen. 18:1-33) and rained down fire upon Sodom and Gomorrah (Gen. 19:24); the God who sees and hears, who cares for Hagar and her son (Gen. 16:7-14; 21:17-19); God, who wrestled with Jacob (Gen. 32:24-32); the burning bush (Exod. 3:2-4:17); the commander of the LORD's army, who instructed Joshua (Josh. 5:13-6:5); and the fourth man in the fiery furnace (Dan. 3:25).

Justin Martyr

During the Ante-Nicene era, the Apostolic Fathers wrote about the pre-existence of Christ but did not have occasion to discuss Christophanies in the Old Testament. During the second and third centuries, however, as apologists and other church fathers took up the cause of Christ against opponents without and heretics within the church, they found in the Christophanies effective proofs of Christ's deity and pre-existence as well as the plurality of Persons in the Godhead.[15] Borland observed that the Ante-Nicene Fathers "are especially helpful in their comments regarding the theophanies in human form. In most cases, these early writers merely argued that Christ was the one who appeared in these theophanies. They did not attempt to develop a regular theology regarding such occurrences."[16]

The earliest and most prolific church father to explain the divine appearances in the Old Testament as Christophanies was the second-century apologist, Justin Martyr (c. 110-165). In doing so, he advanced his own defense of the Christian faith aimed at pagan intellectuals and Jews and also prepared the way for later apologists.[17] At the same time, however, he promoted some ideas that became questionable in Post-Nicene times.

---

[14] Borland, *Christ in the Old Testament.*, 32-33.

[15] MacDonald, "Christology and the 'Angel of the Lord,'" 325. See also Benedict Kominiak, *The Theophanies of the Old Testament in the Writings of St. Justin* (Washington, DC: Catholic University of America Press: 1948), 3.

[16] Borland, *Christ in the Old Testament*, 146-7.

[17] MacDonald, "Christology and the 'Angel of the Lord,'" 325.

In his *First Apology*, Justin set out on his initial foray into the subject of Christophanies. As Benedict Kominiak observed, Justin's approach to his pagan audience differed from his dealings with the Jews in his later *Dialogue with Trypho*: "Unlike the Jews, the polytheistic pagans would have no scruples about admitting the existence of another Divine Person. However, they would have to be convinced that Jesus Christ is such a person."[18] One proof that Justin offered was the pre-existence of Jesus as the Son of God and the Word as testified by Moses in the account of the burning bush: "[O]ur Christ conversed with [Moses] under the appearance of fire from a bush, and said, 'Put off thy shoes, and draw near and hear.' ... And he received mighty power from Christ, who spoke to him in the appearance of fire ...."[19] Later, Justin continued the story:

> Now the Word of God is His Son, as we have before said. And He is called Angel and Apostle; for He declares whatever we ought to know and is sent forth to declare whatever is revealed .... From the writings of Moses also this will be manifest; for thus it is written in them, "And the Angel of God spake to Moses, in a flame of fire out of the bush, and said, I am that I am, the God of Abraham, the God of Isaac, the God of Jacob, the God of thy fathers ...." And if you wish to learn what follows, you can do so from the same writings .... But so much is written for the sake of proving that Jesus the Christ is the Son of God and His Apostle, being of old the Word, and appearing sometimes in the form of fire, and sometimes in the likeness of angels ....[20]

To begin his argument, Justin simply asserted that Christ appeared to Moses in the burning bush (Exod. 3:2-4) and then supported his assertion with various proofs. He listed the titles accorded to Jesus: the Word of God, God's Son, Angel and Apostle. The application of the term *Logos*, or Word, to Jesus bore serious implications in a conversation with a pagan audience. Justin's

---

[18] Kominiak, *The Theophanies of the Old Testament in the Writings of St. Justin*, 55.

[19] Justin Martyr, *First Apology* 62, trans. Marcus Dods and George Reith, in *Ante-Nicene Fathers*, ed. Alexander Roberts and James Donaldson, vol. 1 (Christian Literature Publishing Company, 1885; reprint edition, Peabody, MA: Hendrickson Publishers, 2012), 184. Future references to *Ante-Nicene Fathers* will be abbreviated *ANF*.

[20] Justin Martyr, *First Apology* 63, *ANF* 1:184.

readers would be familiar with the philosophical concept of *Logos* as a mediator between God and creation. In the biblical sense, therefore, the term *Logos* communicated this truth: "For there is one God and one mediator between God and humanity, the man Christ Jesus" (1 Tim. 2:5 CSB). There were, on the other hand, inherent dangers in the Platonic origin of the concept, which conveyed the false idea that the Logos was not God but a lesser, created entity that mediated between a transcendent deity and creation. Justin, however, took care to identify the *Logos* with the Son of God, thereby preserving his deity. Kominiak clarified that "Justin did not adopt, nor was he teaching, the pagan *logos* doctrine, but he adopted and taught a Christian doctrine expressed in philosophical terminology."[21]

Justin furthered his argument by identifying Jesus as Angel and Apostle. The Greek text clearly connected the executor of the office with the duties executed by him. Christ is called Angel (ἄγγελος), and he declared (ἀπαγγέλλει) what is revealed by the Father. He is called Apostle (ἀπόστολος), and he was sent (ἀποστέλλεται) to us from the Father.[22]

Having identified Jesus as Angel, Justin declared him also to be God, citing the account of the burning bush. The Angel of God, who spoke to Moses, announced himself as the God of Abraham, Isaac, and Jacob, the God of Moses's fathers. Finally, Justin concluded his argument about the Christophany at the burning bush with the assertion that "the Father of the universe has a Son; who also, being the first-begotten Word of God, is even God."[23]

In his *Dialogue with Trypho*, an apologetic treatise addressed to Jews,[24] Justin also utilized Christophanies as arguments for Jesus's divinity, his pre-existence, and the plurality of the Persons of the Godhead. He intended "to show the Jews that Scripture admits

---

[21] Kominiak, *The Theophanies of the Old Testament in the Writings of St. Justin*, 56-7.

[22] Kominiak, *The Theophanies.*, 57.

[23] Justin Martyr, *First Apology* 63, *ANF* 1:184.

[24] According to Kominiak, *The Theophanies of the Old Testament in the Writings of St. Justin*, 25, most scholars consider the *Dialogue* to be the record of a genuine conversation. But even among scholars who disagree with that assessment, there is general agreement that in the character of Trypho, Justin has created a "faithful exponent of Jewish doctrine and a true representative of Palestinian Judaism."

another Divine Person distinct from the Father."[25] Compared to the Apology, however, he approached this argument differently as would be expected in a controversy with Jews, who have a background in the Scriptures and a monotheistic presupposition.[26] Again, Justin included the episode of the burning bush, but he led off with the extended story of the divine appearance to Abraham by the oak of Mamre and the destruction of Sodom and Gomorrah (Genesis 18-19). Then he followed up these two accounts with the divine appearances to Jacob and Joshua.

Justin sought to prove from the theophany at Mamre the plurality of Divine Persons:

> Moses, then, the blessed and faithful servant of God, declares that He who appeared to Abraham under the oak in Mamre is God, sent with the two angels in His company to judge Sodom by Another (ὑπὸ ἄλλου) who remains ever in the supercelestial (ὑπερουρανίοις) places, invisible to all men, holding personal intercourse with none, who we believe to be Maker and Father of all things.[27]

Thus, Justin contended that God, who appeared to Abraham, was Christ, while "Another" God, the Father and Creator and Judge, remained unseen in heaven.

In response to Trypho's objection that this passage did not indicate a plurality of Divine Persons, Justin replied:

> I shall attempt to persuade you, since you have understood the Scriptures, [of the truth] of what I say, that there is, and there is said to be, another (ἕτερος) God and Lord subject to (ὑπὸ) the Maker of all things; who is also called an Angel, because He announces to men whatsoever the Maker of all things — above whom there is no other God — wishes to announce to them.[28]

Post-Nicene readers might be suspicious of Justin's statement that "there is ... another God and Lord *subject to* the Maker of all things." Dods and Reith acknowledged that some translators inserted "besides" instead of "subject to," but they stood by their translation even with its tendency toward subordination.[29] Komin-

---

[25] Kominiak, *The Theophanies of the Old Testament in the Writings of St. Justin*, 27.
[26] Kominiak, *The Theophanies.*, 58.
[27] Justin Martyr, *Dialogue with Trypho* 56, *ANF* 1:223.
[28] Justin Martyr, *Dialogue* 56, *ANF* 1:223.
[29] Marcus Dods and George Reith, *ANF* 1:223, n. 3.

iak used the word "beneath" in his translation but admitted that the concept "might easily lead one to suspect a subordinationist trend in the apologist's theology."[30] William Trollope, in his Greek edition of the *Dialogue*, explained: "It is proper to remark that the *subordination* here indicated does not imply inequality of *essence*, but of *person*. In the *infinite* perfections of the Godhead, there can be no idea of *more* or *less*; but in respect of *person*, the Father, who *begat*, must be superior to the Son, who *was begotten*; and upon this inequality the subordination in question rests."[31]

Elsewhere in the *Dialogue*, Justin implied a subordinationist understanding of the Son when he introduced his exposition of the divine appearance to Joshua (Josh. 5:13-15):

> I shall give you another testimony, my friends ... from the Scriptures, that God begat before all creatures a Beginning, [who was] a certain rational power [proceeding] from Himself, who is called by the Holy Spirit, now the Glory of the Lord, now the Son, again Wisdom, again an Angel, then God, and then Lord and Logos; and on another occasion He calls Himself Captain, when He appeared in human form to Joshua the son of Nave (Nun). For He can be called by all those names,[32] since He ministers to the Father's will, and since He was begotten of the Father by an act of will.[33]

Trollope, recognizing the harshness of the term "Beginning" (ἀρχήν), explained: "Justin seems here to speak in accordance with the opinion very prevalent in his time, which, assigning to the Logos an eternal generation and pre-existence, maintained also that he came forth from God as the *creative principle* of the universe, shortly before the worlds were made."[34] Kominiak made a similar point that "the doctrine of the Trinity was not yet part of the faith revealed to all." He further observed that if the apologist had intended to communicate subordinationism, he would have done so

---

[30] Kominiak, *The Theophanies of the Old Testament in the Writings of St. Justin*, 29.

[31] William Trollope, *Justin Martyr's Dialogue with Trypho: Greek Text with Notes*, vol. 1 (Cambridge: G. Bell, J. Hall & Son, 1846), 111 n. 21.

[32] God the Father, on the other hand, is nameless. See Justin Martyr, *First Apology* 10, *ANF* 1:165: "God who is called by no proper name." William Trollope, *Justin Martyr's Dialogue with Trypho*, 124 n. 7.

[33] Justin Martyr, *Dialogue with Trypho* 61, *ANF* 1:227.

[34] William Trollope, *Justin Martyr's Dialogue with Trypho*, 123 n. 2.

more explicitly in order to make his arguments more agreeable to the Jews. But instead of emphasizing a subordinate character of the Son, he insisted upon his full divinity.[35]

When Justin claimed that the Son "was begotten of the Father," he intended his teaching on the divine generation to maintain a balance between the unity of God and the plurality of the Godhead. In so doing, he explained "the perfect agreement or union of thought which exists between the Father and the Son as the total submission of the Son in respect to the Father."[36] Post-Nicene readers, therefore, must not equate Justin with Arius: "For the heresiarch, the Word is a creature of God; for Justin, He is the Son of God."[37]

In Justin's exposition of the episode at Mamre, he asserted that the Divine Person who appeared to Abraham was called Angel. Again, Justin's intention was not to imply subordination or inferiority by this title. Instead, Kominiak insisted, "By the name *Angel*, not nature but office is signified …. This second Divine Person is not inferior by nature to the Creator, for He is God, ἐστὶ Θεὸς, but is merely called Angel, ἄγγελος καλεῖται."[38]

Having maintained the plurality of the Godhead, namely the invisible Creator, who remained in heaven, and the present Angel, who made the announcement to Abraham, Justin next explained the distinction between these two Divine Persons:

> Reverting to the Scriptures, I shall endeavor to persuade you, that He who is said to have appeared to Abraham, and to Jacob, and to Moses, and who is called God, is distinct from Him who made all things, – numerically, I mean, not [distinct] in will. For I affirm that He has never at any time done anything which He who made the world – above whom there is no other God – has not wished Him both to do and to engage Himself with.[39]

The plurality and the distinctions among the Persons of the Godhead as well as the divinity of Jesus Christ are at the crux of

---

[35] Kominiak, *The Theophanies of the Old Testament in the Writings of St. Justin*, 65-6.

[36] Kominiak, *The Theophanies.*, 68.

[37] Kominiak, *The Theophanies.*, 67.

[38] Kominiak, *The Theophanies of the Old Testament in the Writings of St. Justin*, 29; Borland, *Christ in the Old Testament*, 147-8.

[39] Justin Martyr, *Dialogue with Trypho* 56, *ANF* 1:223-4.

Justin's arguments at this point in the *Dialogue*. And Justin's attempt to prove these claims solely from the Hebrew Scriptures would provide him with an apologetic advantage. Kominiak noted that "with these doctrines Christianity rises or falls, Judaism is proved to be true or false."[40]

As the narrative of the Divine Appearance to Abraham at Mamre continued to the next scene, the destruction of Sodom and Gomorrah, Justin found the proof that he needed for the distinction of the Divine Persons:[41]

> And now have you not perceived, my friends, that one of the three, who is both God and Lord, and ministers to Him who is in the heavens, is Lord of the two angels? For when [the angels] proceeded to Sodom, He remained behind, and communed with Abraham in the words recorded by Moses; and when He departed after the conversation, Abraham went back to his place. And when he came [to Sodom], the two angels no longer conversed with Lot, but Himself, as the Scripture makes evident;[42] and he is the Lord who received commission from the Lord who [remains] in the heavens, i.e., the Maker of all things, to inflict upon Sodom and Gomorrah the [judgments] which the Scripture describes in these terms: "The Lord rained down upon Sodom and Gomorrah sulphur and fire from the Lord out of heaven."[43]

---

[40] Kominiak, *The Theophanies of the Old Testament in the Writings of St. Justin*, 34.

[41] Henry Parry Liddon, *The Divinity of Our Lord and Saviour Jesus Christ*, 18th ed. (London: Longmans & Green, 1897; reprint, Minneapolis, MN: Klock & Klock Christian Publishers, 1978), 56.

[42] The Septuagint, which Justin was reading, made it evident that Lot spoke to the Lord (Κύριε). Most English translations read: "No, my lords …." (Gen. 19:18 CSB), indicating that Lot continued to speak to the angels. For Justin, however, the reading in the Septuagint was necessary for the point he needed to make. See also Cyril of Alexandria, *Catena on Genesis* 3.1139: "It seems that now, after the exodus from Sodom, the conversation is no longer with angels but with the Lord." *Ancient Christian Commentary on Scripture*, Old Testament, vol. 2, Genesis 12-50, ed. Mark Sheridan, gen. ed. Thomas C. Oden (Downers Grove, IL: InterVarsity Press, 2002), 78.

[43] Justin Martyr, *Dialogue with Trypho* 56, *ANF* 1:225.

For Justin, this passage from Gen. 19:24 was the capstone of his arguments for the plurality of the Godhead.[44] Later, as he repeated this assertion in a summary of his arguments:

> When Scripture says, "The Lord rained fire from the Lord out of heaven," the prophetic word indicates that there were two in number: One upon the earth, who, it says, descended to behold the cry of Sodom; Another in heaven, who also is Lord of the Lord on earth, as He is Father and God; the cause of His power and of His being Lord and God.[45]

Kominiak outlined Justin's arguments in five concise points:
- According to Scripture, the Lord who appeared to Abraham is God.
- This Lord who appeared to Abraham is the same Lord who destroyed Sodom.
- Therefore, the Lord who destroyed Sodom is the God who appeared to Abraham.
- But the Lord who destroyed Sodom is distinct from God the Creator in heaven.
- Therefore, the God who appeared to Abraham is distinct from God the Creator in heaven.[46]

The bottom line, then, was that the Divine Being who appeared to Abraham and then destroyed Sodom is distinct from God the Creator in heaven.

Trypho and his companions attended carefully to Justin's arguments because he "referred everything to the Scriptures."[47] In spite of his intention to remain within the confines of the Hebrew Scriptures, however, Justin occasionally showed influence from his philosophical background. One example appeared early in his discussion of the divine appearance at Mamre, in which he described the Father as "ever in the supercelestial places, invisible to all men, holding personal intercourse with none."[48]

Justin continued this line of thinking in his exposition of the burning bush. First, he asserted from Exod. 3:2-4 "how this same

---

44 Will Rutherford, "*Altercatio Jasonis et Papisci* as a Testimony Source for Justin's "Second God" Argument?" in *Justin Martyr and His Worlds*, ed. Sara Purvis and Paul Foster (Minneapolis, MN: Fortress Press, 2007), 138.

45 Justin Martyr, *Dialogue with Trypho* 129, *ANF* 1:264.

46 Kominiak, *The Theophanies of the Old Testament in the Writings of St. Justin*, 41.

47 Justin Martyr, *Dialogue with Trypho* 56, *ANF* 1:224.

48 Justin Martyr, *Dialogue with Trypho* 56, *ANF* 1:223.

One, who is both Angel, and God, and Lord, and man, and who appeared in human form to Abraham and Isaac,[49] appeared in a flame of fire from the bush, and conversed with Moses."[50] Trypho objected that "it was an angel who appeared in the flame of fire, but God who conversed with Moses; so that there were really two persons in company with each other, an angel and God, that appeared in that vision." Justin conceded the possibility of two persons seen by Moses, but he insisted that "it will not be the Creator of all things what is the God" that spoke to Moses, "but it will be He who has been proved to you to have appeared to Abraham, ministering to the will of the Maker of all things." Then Justin persisted with his philosophical understanding of the transcendence of God the Father, maintaining that "he who has but the smallest intelligence will not venture to assert that the Maker and Father of all things, having left all supercelestial matters, was visible of a little portion of the earth."[51]

Justin's contention for the invisibility and transcendence of God the Father was not a passing thought in the *Dialogue*. In his extensive summary of Christophanies, he recounted many divine appearances that could not be God the Father:

> I suppose that I have stated sufficiently, that wherever God says, 'God went up from Abraham,' or, 'The Lord spake to Moses,' and 'The Lord came down to behold the tower which the sons of men had built,' or when 'God shut Noah into the ark,' you must not imagine that the unbegotten God Himself came down or went up from any place. For the ineffable Father and Lord of all neither has come to any place, nor walks, nor sleeps, nor rises up, but remains in His own place, wherever that is, quick to behold and quick to hear, having neither eyes nor ears, but being of indescribably might; and He sees all things, and knows all things, and none of us escapes His observation; and He is not moved or confined to a spot in the whole world, for He existed before the world was made. How, then, could He talk with any one, or be seen by any one, or appear on the smallest por-

---

[49] The Greek text in William Trollope, *Justin Martyr's Dialogue with Trypho*, reads καὶ Ἰακώβ. Perhaps a scribe omitted "and Isaac" because Justin never mention God's appearance to the second patriarch, but see Gen. 26:2, 24.

[50] Justin Martyr, *Dialogue with Trypho* 59, *ANF* 1:226.

[51] Justin Martyr, *Dialogue with Trypho* 60, *ANF* 1:227.

tion of the earth, when the people at Sinai were not able to look even on the glory of Him who was sent from Him; and Moses himself could not enter into the tabernacle which he had erected, when it was filled with the glory of God; and the priest could not endure to stand before the temple when Solomon conveyed the ark into the house in Jerusalem which he had built for it? Therefore, neither Abraham, nor Isaac, nor Jacob, nor any other man, saw the Father and ineffable Lord of all, and also of Christ, but [saw] Him who was according to His will His Son, being God, and the Angel because He ministered to His will; whom also it pleased Him to be born man by the Virgin.[52]

Justin ascribed to the Father/Creator alone the attribute of transcendence along with the negative qualities of invisibility and immutability. The Son, however, left his abode in heaven, appeared on earth, and conversed with men and women. The Son was called Angel and fulfilled the role of messenger, subject to the Father's will.[53]

Justin drew upon his philosophical expertise for these concepts, seeking to connect his arguments with current intellectual reasoning, such as, for example, the idea of *Logos*, which he cultivated elsewhere and has already been discussed. The Christian philosopher, however, had another source for such a thought: the writings of the Apostle John. In the prologue to the Gospel of John,[54] Justin found one inspiration for his use of *Logos* as Mediator and Revealer of God to humanity: "In the beginning was the Word (λόγος), and the Word was with God, and the Word was God. He was with God in the beginning…. No one has ever seen God. The one and only Son, who is himself God and is at the Father's side — he has revealed him" (John 1:1-2, 18 CSB).

To summarize, Justin relied chiefly upon the Hebrew Scriptures, including various Christophanies, for his arguments in favor of Christ's pre-existence and divinity and the plurality of the Godhead. The antiquity of the ancient writings would impress the pa-

---

[52] Justin Martyr, *Dialogue with Trypho* 127, *ANF* 1:263.

[53] Kominiak, *The Theophanies of the Old Testament in the Writings of St. Justin*, 44.

[54] C.E. Hill, "Was John's Gospel among Justin's Apostolic Memoirs?" in *Justin Martyr and His Worlds*, ed. Sara Purvis and Paul Foster (Minneapolis, MN: Fortress Press, 2007), 88, suggests that John's prologue influenced Justin's Logos Christology and argues that "certain of John's statements in the Prologue were foundational to Justin's Christology."

gans while the sacred writings would be the decisive factors in convincing the Jews. Justin drew also, however, upon his philosophical expertise for concepts such as the Father's transcendence and invisibility. Christian doctrine allied with philosophical reasoning would be more acceptable to the intellectuals and would impress even the Jews. In both the *First Apology* and the *Dialogue with Trypho*, "nothing is left undone by the apologist to proclaim the faith of the Christians in the Almighty God and in Jesus Christ His only Son."[55] Later church fathers drew inspiration from Justin as they, too, presented Christophanies as apologetic proofs for the Christian faith.

Other Ante-Nicene Fathers

A contemporary of Justin Martyr and also an apologist, Theophilus of Antioch (c. 115-188), wrote his treatise *To Autolycus*, a pagan friend, in order to convince him of the truth of the Christian faith.[56] In the second book of his treatise, Theophilus gave much attention to the creation story, including the account of God's walking in the garden with Adam and Eve. Anticipating Autolycus's objections against the idea that the transcendent God could be contained in a location on earth, Theophilus explained the divine appearance of the Word of God, His Son:

> His Word, through whom He made all things, being His power and His wisdom, assuming the person of the Father and Lord of all, went to the garden in the person of God, and conversed with Adam. For the divine writing itself teaches us that Adam said that he had heard the voice. But what else is this voice but the Word of God, who is also His Son? ... The Word, then, being God, and being naturally produced from God, whenever the Father of the universe wills, He sends Him to any place; and He, coming, is both heard and seen, being sent by Him, and is found in a place.[57]

Theophilus chose to explicate God's communion with Adam and Eve, a divine appearance not discussed by Justin, but he approached the Christophany similarly. First, he attributed the appearance to the Word of God, the Son. Second, he described the

---

[55] C.E. Hill, "Was John's Gospel"., 47.

[56] Borland, *Christ in the Old Testament*, 148.

[57] Theophilus, *To Autolycus* 2.22, trans. Marcus Dods, 2:103.

Word as power and wisdom. Third, he viewed the Word as subject to God the Father, who sent the Word to any location according to his will. And finally, God the Father is transcendent and, therefore, cannot be found in a place on earth.

The next three church fathers, who ministered at the turn of the third century, were vitally concerned to establish Jesus Christ's divinity. To address this concern, Irenaeus, Clement of Alexandria, and Tertullian drew upon a wide variety of Christophanies.[58]

One Christophany cited by Irenaeus, Bishop of Lyons (c. 130-c. 202), was the Son's appearance at Mamre and Sodom: "The Son, who had also been talking with Abraham, had received power to judge the Sodomites for their wickedness."[59] Then, Irenaeus called his readers' attention to Christ's presence in the burning bush: "When the Son speaks to Moses, He says, 'I am come down to deliver this people'" (Exod. 3:8). Later, the Gallic father put forward these two Christophanic appearances as evidence of Christ's pre-incarnate appearances:[60] "Therefore have the Jews departed from God, in not receiving His Word, but imagining that they could know the Father [apart] by Himself, without he Word, that is, without the Son; they being ignorant of that God who spake in human shape to Abraham, and again to Moses .... For the Son, who is the Word of God, arranged these things beforehand from the beginning."[61]

Elsewhere, Irenaeus put forward that the visible Word was in the fiery furnace: "He was seen with those who were around Ananias, Azarias, Misael, as present with them in the furnace of fire, in the burning, and preserving them from [the effects of] fire: 'And the appearance of the fourth,' it is said, 'was like to the Son of God'" (Dan. 3.26).[62] For Irenaeus, the divine appearances of Christ in the Old Testament were proofs of his pre-existence: "As it has been clearly demonstrated that the Word, who existed in the beginning with God, ... was also always present with mankind."[63]

Clement of Alexandria (c. 150-c. 215), teacher at the great catechetical school, wrote a treatise regarding *The Instructor*, whom he

---

[58] Borland, *Christ in the Old Testament*, 148.

[59] Irenaeus, *Against Heresies* 3.6.1, trans. Alexander Roberts and William Rambaut, *ANF* 1:418-19.

[60] Borland, *Christ in the Old Testament*, 149.

[61] Irenaeus, *Against Heresies* 4.7.4, *ANF* 1:470.

[62] Irenaeus, *Against Heresies* 4.20.11, *ANF* 1:491.

[63] Irenaeus, *Against Heresies* 3.18.1, *ANF* 1:445-6.

identified as "the holy God Jesus, the Word, who is the guide of all humanity." According to Clement, the Instructor led the people through the Exodus and provided for them, saying "I am the Lord thy God, who brought thee out of the land of Egypt" (Exod. 20:2). The Instructor appeared to Abraham and affirmed: "I am thy God, be accepted before Me" (Gen. 17:1-2). And the Instructor wrestled with Jacob, who "called the name of the place, 'Face of God.' 'For I have seen,' he says, 'God face to face; and my life is preserved' (Gen. 32:24, 30). The face of God is the Word by whom God is manifested and made known."[64]

The Carthaginian theologian, Tertullian (c. 155-c. 225), utilized Christophanies in his polemical treatises. He endeavored to convince heretics of their errors by demonstrating that the pre-existent Christ appeared in the Old Testament. Writing *Against Praxeas*, Tertullian made the distinction that God "is invisible as the Father, and visible as the Son."[65] Therefore, "it was the Son whom certain Old Testament saints saw in the human-form theophanies."[66] For example, in his polemic *Against Marcion*, Tertullian provided yet one more reference to Christ's appearance at Mamre: "He did Himself appear with the angels to Abraham in the verity of the flesh."[67] Finally, in his treatise *On Prescription against Heretics*, Tertullian affirmed: "This Word is called His Son, and, under the name of God, was seen 'in diverse manners' by the patriarchs, heard at all times in the prophets, at last brought down by the Spirit and Power of the Father into the Virgin Mary, was made flesh in her womb, and, being born of her, went forth as Jesus Christ."[68]

Novatian (c. 200-258), the Roman presbyter, was a schismatic but also a theologian, who composed a *Treatise Concerning the Trinity*. One argument followed a familiar line of thought that the transcendent God the Father is "infinite and without end, not as being enclosed in any place, but as one who includes every place ... so that with reason He can neither descend nor ascend, because He Himself both contains and fills all things." How then, Novatian

---

[64] Clement of Alexandria, *The Instructor* 1.7, trans. William Wilson, *ANF* 2:223-4.

[65] Tertullian, *Against Praxeas* 14, trans. Peter Holmes, *ANF* 3:609.

[66] Borland, *Christ in the Old Testament*, 149-50.

[67] Tertullian, *Against Marcion* 3.9, trans. Peter Holmes, *ANF* 3:329.

[68] Tertullian, *On Prescription against Heretics* 13, trans. Peter Holmes, *ANF* 3:249.

asked, did God the Father descend to the Tower of Babel? "Neither, therefore, did the Father descend .... Then it remains that He must have descended, of whom the Apostle says, 'He who descended is the same who ascended above all the heavens, that He might fill all things' (Eph. 4:10), that is, the Son of God, the Word of God."[69]

Next, Novatian turned his attention to God the Father's invisibility: "If God cannot be seen, how was God seen?" The answer to the question is that the Son "is the image of the invisible God." Novatian illustrated this concept with the "sudden light of the sun after darkness, with its too great splendor," which "will not make manifest the light of day to unaccustomed eyes, but will rather strike them with blindness. And lest this should occur to the injury of human eyes, the darkness is broken up and scattered by degrees; and the rising of that luminary, mounting by small and unperceived increments, gently accustoms men's eyes to bear its full orb by the gentle increase of its rays." In the same way, Christ "is looked upon by men, inasmuch as He could be seen ....And thus the weakness and imperfection of the human destiny is nourished, led up, and educated by Him; so that, being accustomed to look upon the Son, it may one day be able to see God the Father Himself."[70]

Novatian continued this lesson with discussions of the divine appearances to Hagar (Gen. 21:17-19), to Abraham at Mamre, and to Lot at Sodom. He concluded that the Angel of the Lord was the Son of God, the Announcer of the Father's will, the Angel of Great Counsel. "Assuredly Christ is not only man, but angel also; and not only angel, but He is shown by the Scriptures to be God also."[71]

The Constitutions of the Holy Apostles were compiled, probably in Syria, late in the Ante-Nicene era. The unknown author listed several divine appearances throughout the Old Testament and connected them to "the Christ of God":

To Him did Moses bear witness and said: "The Lord received fire from the Lord, and rained it down" (Gen. 19:24).
Him did Jacob see as a man, and said: "I have seen God

---

[69] Novatian, *Treatise Concerning the Trinity* 17, trans. Robert Ernest Wallis, *ANF* 5:627.

[70] Novatian, *Treatise Concerning the Trinity* 18, ANF 5:627-8.

[71] Novatian, *Treatise Concerning the Trinity* 18, ANF 5:629.

face to face, and my soul is preserved" (Gen. 32:30). Him did Abraham entertain, and acknowledge to be the Judge, and his Lord (Gen. 18:25, 27). Him did Moses see in the bush (Exod. 3:2) …. Him did Joshua the son of Nun see, as the captain of the Lord's host, in armour, for their assistance against Jericho; to whom he fell down and worshipped, as a servant does to his master (Josh. 5.14).[72]

As H.P. Liddon once observed, "It is unnecessary to multiply quotations in proof of a fact which is beyond dispute."[73]From the examples presented here as well as an abundance of others,[74] clearly "the Ante-Nicene period … was one in which the Christians believed that the Lord Jesus Christ was the one who appeared in the Old Testament Christophanies."[75]

Conclusion

The Ante-Nicene Fathers saw "Christ in All Scriptures," particularly from the viewpoint of Christophanies in the Old Testament. Their Christophanic interpretations of the divine appearances served apologetic and polemical purposes. Christophanies demonstrated the pre-existence of Christ and, therefore, his divinity as well as the plurality of the Godhead and the distinctiveness of the Divine Persons. Moreover, as Andrew Malone admitted, "Discovering Jesus more patently in the Old Testament is a winning scenario by any Christian measure."[76]

The positive outcomes of Christophanies, however, often were accompanied by problematic concepts such as the extreme transcendence of God the Father and the subordination of God the Son.[77] In the fourth century and beyond, the Arian heresy called into question previous views of divine appearances in the Old Testament. The Arians argued that "if the Father was invisible, while the Son had been seen in the Old Testament … the Father

---

[72] *Constitutions of the Holy Apostles* 5.20, trans. William Whiston, ed. James Donaldson, *ANF* 7:448.

[73] Liddon, *The Divinity of Our Lord and Saviour Jesus Christ*, 57.

[74] For an extensive list of references, see Liddon, *The Divinity of Our Lord and Saviour Jesus Christ*, 57 footnote a.

[75] Borland, *Christ in the Old Testament*, 150.

[76] Malone, *Knowing Jesus in the Old Testament*, 28.

[77] Sanders, *The Triune God*, 225.

thus possessed a distinct and higher nature than the Son."[78] For this reason, Post-Nicene fathers departed from their predecessors' positions, which seemed to diminish rather than to enhance Christ's divinity.[79] Furthermore, Fred Sanders, a modern commentator rejected the notion of Christ's appearances in the Old Testament because such a concept denies the uniqueness of the Incarnation.[80]

A fresh investigation of the Ante-Nicene fathers' interpretation of Christophanies could inform the contemporary discussion of Christ in the Old Testament. Necessarily, the ancient tendencies toward subordinationism and the extreme transcendence of God must be excised. What remains from such a Christophanic study would be a great help toward discovering "Christ in All Scripture."

---

[78] Borland, *Christ in the Old Testament*, 151.
[79] Borland, *Christ in the Old Testament*, 154.
[80] Sanders, *The Triune God*, 226.

Selected Bibliography

Bird, Michael. *Evangelical Theology: A Biblical and Systematic Introduction.* Grand Rapids, MI: Zondervan, 2013.

Borland, James A. *Christ in the Old Testament: A Comprehensive Study of Old Testament Appearances of Christ in Human Form.* Chicago: Moody Press, 1978.

Brandeis, Don. *The Gospel in the Old Testament.* Grand Rapids, MI: Baker Book House, 1960.

Driscoll, Mark and Gerry Breshears. *Doctrine: What Christians Should Believe.* Wheaton, IL: Crossway, 2010.

Hanson, Anthony Tyrell. *Jesus Christ in the Old Testament.* London: S.P.C.K., 1965.

Hill, C.E. "Was John's Gospel among Justin's *Apostolic Memoirs?*" in *Justin Martyr and His Worlds*, ed. Sara Purvis and Paul Foster, 88-94. Minneapolis, MN: Fortress Press, 2007

Kominiak, Benedict. *The Theophanies of the Old Testament in the Writings of St. Justin.* Washington, DC: Catholic University of America Press: 1948.

Kuntz, J. Kenneth. *The Self-Revelation of God.* Philadelphia: The Westminster Press, 1967.

Liddon, Henry Parry. *The Divinity of Our Lord and Saviour Jesus Christ*, 18th ed. London: Longmans & Green, 1897; reprint, Minneapolis, MN: Klock & Klock Christian Publishers, 1978.

MacDonald, William Graham. "Christology and the 'Angel of the Lord,'" in *Current Issues in Biblical and Patristic Interpretation*, ed. Gerald F. Hawthorne, 324-335. Grand Rapids, MI: Eerdmans, 1975.

Malone, Andrew. *Knowing Jesus in the Old Testament?: A Fresh Look at Christophanies.* Nottingham, England: InterVarsity Press, 2015.

Murray, David. *Jesus on Every Page: 10 Simple Ways to Seek and Find Christ in the Old Testament.* Nashville, TN: Thomas Nelson, 2013.

O'Collins, Gerald. *The Tripersonal God: Understanding and Interpreting the Trinity.* New York: Paulist Press, 1999.

Rutherford, Will. "*Altercatio Jasonis et Papisci* as a Testimony Source for Justin's "Second God" Argument?" in *Justin Martyr and His Worlds*, ed. Sara Purvis and Paul Foster, 137-144. Minneapolis, MN: Fortress Press, 2007.

Sanders, Fred. *The Triune God.* Grand Rapids, MI: Zondervan, 2016.

Savran, George W. *Encountering the Divine: Theophany in Biblical Narrative.* London: T&T Clark International, 2005.

Trollope, William. *Justin Martyr's Dialogue with Trypho: Greek Text with Notes*, vol. 1. Cambridge: G. Bell, J. Hall & Son, 1846. https://archive.org/details/sjustiniphilosop01just

Wright, Christopher J.H. *Knowing Jesus through the Old Testament.* Downers Grove, IL: IVP Academic, 2014.

Philo of Alexandria's Concept of Woman

Joseph E. Early Jr., PhD

Joseph E. Early Jr. is Professor of Church History at Campbellsville University in Campbellsville, Kentucky.

Philo (20 BCE–50 CE) was a Hellenized Jewish philosopher active in Alexandria in the first half of the first century of the Common Era. His system demonstrates that he was influenced by the *Septuagint*, and drew frequently from concepts found in Pythagoreanism, Stoicism, Platonism, and Aristotelianism. Philo's most noted contribution to philosophy was his use of allegory in his attempt to synthesize the *Septuagint* and Greek philosophy. He often applied this exegesis when attempting to uncover the deeper or hidden meanings of the actions, roles, and nature of Old Testament women. His hermeneutic and depiction of women's nature influenced many of the Patristic era's greatest theologians and their understandings of the nature, role, and purpose of women.

Philo's similarities to earlier philosophers are evident in his views on human regeneration. His concept of reproduction and Aristotle's are nearly identical.[1] He held that in reproduction the man provides the active cause via semen which acts on the passive material provided by the woman. Man provided the soul, and woman provided the body. Philo stated that "the material of the female is supplied to the son from what remains over the eruption of blood, while the immediate maker and cause of the son is the male."[2] Women served as little more than the providers of raw material and incubators.

Philo held that within each person's mind there are masculine and feminine thoughts. Masculine thoughts are in a higher realm and include aspects such as wisdom, virtue, self-control, and things that are good in general. Philo's God was asexual, and mas-

---

[1] Sister Prudence Allen, *The Concept of Women: The Early Humanist Reformation, 1250–1500*, Vol. 2 (Grand Rapids: Eerdmans, 2016), 93.

[2] Philo, *Questions and Answers in Genesis* 3:47, in *The Works of Philo: Complete and Unabridged*, trans. C. D. Yonge (Peabody, MA: Hendrickson, 1993), 857. Unless otherwise noted, all of Philo's works are cited from the Yonge text.

culine thoughts were thus also asexual.[3] Feminine thoughts were of a lower realm, softer, lacking self-control, emotionally passionate, and devoid of reason. His reliance on Stoicism can be seen in the importance he places on the mind in relation to self-control and overcoming emotional passion. A person could alter their nature by striving to change their thoughts and thus their nature. A woman could become more masculine by dwelling on the more masculine aspects of thought and eliminating those that were more emotionally passionate and feminine. Men, however, were in danger of being drawn into emotional thoughts and becoming more feminine.[4] Having a penis did not necessarily make one male and the lack of one did not necessarily make one female.[5] "Manhood was not a state to be definitively achieved but something always under construction and constantly open to scrutiny."[6] One's manhood had to always be protected. Men, therefore, should never wear feminine clothes and they should also protect other men's masculinity when necessary. In this regard, Philo believed Lot acted properly at Sodom by offering to surrender his daughters to the mob to keep his male guest's masculinity unharmed.[7]

Philo understood the soul in a platonic manner. He held that men and women differ sharply in manner of soul. Man identified with the higher aspects of the soul which he calls the *nous*. The *nous* was patterned after God. Philo states,

> Moses says that man was made in the image and likeness of God. And he says well; for nothing that is born on the earth is more resembling God than man. And let no one think that he is able to judge of this likeness from the characters of the body: for neither is God a being with the form of a man, nor is the human body like the form of God; but the

---

[3] Richard A. Baer, *Philo's Use of the Categories Male and Female* (Leiden: Brill, 1970), 21.

[4] Philo, *Questions and Answers in Genesis* 2:49 (trans. Yonge, 830).

[5] D. M. Halperin, J. J. Winkler, and F. I. Zeitlin, *Before Sexuality: The Construction of Erotic Experience in the Ancient Greek World* (Princeton: Princeton University Press, 1990), 478.

[6] Maud Gleason, *Making Men: Sophists and Self-Presentation in Ancient Rome* (Princeton: Princeton University Press, 1995), 22.

[7] William Loader, *Philo, Josephus, and the Testaments on Sexuality: Attitudes Towards Sexuality in the Writings of Philo and Josephus and in the Testaments of the Twelve Patriarchs* (Grand Rapids: Eerdmans, 2011), 37.

resemblance is spoken of with reference to the most important part of the soul, namely, the mind: for the mind which exists in each individual has been created after the likeness of that one mind which is in the universe as its primitive model, being in some sort the God of that body which carries it about and bears its image within it.[8]

Woman had lower reasoning and had no part in the *nous*. Philo used living quarters as an example to describe women's souls. "The woman's quarters are a place where womanly opinions go about and dwell, being followers of the female sex. And the female sex is irrational and akin to bestial passions, fear, sorrow, pleasure, and desire."[9] This irrational quality of the soul was the reason why women entice sexual desire in men.[10] The rational *nous* allowed man to ignore woman's sexual temptations. Philo listed Potiphar's wife[11] and the Midianite women[12] of Numbers 25 as examples of irrational women with uncontrolled sexual passions. Within the masculine and feminine categories there could be subcategories. For instance, Philo placed Sarah and Leah in the higher part of the feminine soul and Hagar and Rachel in the lower. In men, the soul was more rational or sensible.[13] Philo believed that Moses was the perfect example of the highest masculine soul. He kept control of his passions; he was masculine, and he displayed a manly spirit. If a man had an effeminate mind, he believed that he would produce female children. Philo states,

> And no unjust man at any time implants a masculine generation in the soul, but such, being unmanly, and broken, and effeminate in their minds, do naturally become the parents of female children; having planted no tree of virtue, the fruit of which must of necessity have been beautiful and salutary, but only trees of wickedness and of the passions, the shoots of which are womanlike. On account of which fact these men are said to have become the fathers of

---

[8] Philo, *On the Creation of the World* 69 (trans. Yonge, 10).

[9] Philo, *Questions and Answers in Genesis* 4:15, trans. Ralph Marcus (Cambridge: Harvard University Press, 1953), 288.

[10] Judith R. Wegner, "The image of Woman in Philo," *Society of Biblical Literature 1982 Seminar Papers*, ed. Kent Harold Richards (Chico, CA: Scholars, 1982), 552.

[11] Philo, *On Joseph* 41 (trans. Yonge, 438–39).

[12] Philo, *Allegorical Interpretations* 241 (trans. Yonge, 78).

[13] Philo, *On Mating with the Preliminary Studies* 26–28 (trans. Yonge, 306).

daughters, and that no one of them is said to have begotten a son.[14]

The opposite was also true. A masculine mind always produced male children. He used Noah as an example. "Noah, was; for since the just Noah had male children, as being a man who followed reason, perfect, and upright, and masculine, so by this very fact the injustice of the multitude is proved to be altogether the parent of female children. For it is impossible that the same things should be born of opposite parents; but they must necessarily have an opposite offspring."[15]

Philo applied Stoicism to his explanation of how virtue applied to the difference in the activity and passivity of the two sexes.[16] He believed that virtue was active as displayed in noble deeds, words, self-control, and actions. These attributes belonged to a masculine mind. Female thought lacked self-control and was too passive to be virtuous.[17] Women could be virtuous, but it was quite rare. Because virtue is important in public affairs, he held that only men should be involved in state matters. Women should tend to the household, rarely leave it, and virgins should be secluded.[18] In *On the Special Laws*, Philo stated, "Market places, and council chambers, and courts of justice, and large companies and assemblies of numerous crowds, and a life in the open air full of arguments and actions relating to war and peace, are suited to men; but taking care of the house and remaining at home are the proper duties of women; the virgins having their apartments in the center of the house within the innermost doors, and the full-grown women not going beyond the vestibule and outer courts."[19] She should also seek a life of seclusion and not be a busybody and meddle with affairs outside the home.

Philo was ambivalent concerning marriage and sparingly discussed it. When he discussed the positive aspects of marriage, his comments were patronizing. His comments concerning the disadvantages of marriage can be described as nothing short of misogynistic. Philo held that marriage brought both elements of the

---

14 Philo, *On the Giants* 1:4–5 (trans. Yonge, 152).
15 Philo, *On the Giants* 1:4–5 (trans. Yonge, 152).
16 Allen, *The Concept of Women*, 96.
17 Philo, *On Abraham* 102 (trans. Yonge, 420).
18 Philo, *Questions and Answers in Genesis* 1:26 (trans. Yonge, 796).
19 Philo, *On the Special Laws* 3:169 (trans. Yonge, 611).

soul back together. Without each other they are imperfect. Man functions better when with a woman. A good wife will always remember that she must be in servitude to her husband and obedient to him in all things.[20] If done properly, marriage accords both with a sense of responsibility, balance, and order. Men should handle the outside world, and women should oversee the home. He saw home management as an important duty. In *Questions and Answers in Genesis*, he stated that,

> The union and the plentitude of concord formed by the man and woman is symbolically called a house; but everything is altogether imperfect and destitute of a home, which is deserted by a woman; for to the man the public affairs of the state are committed, but the particular affairs of the house belong to the woman; and a want of the women will be the destruction of the house; but the actual presence of the woman show the regulation of the house.[21]

Philo also made harsh statements about the nature of wives. In praising the Essenes for not taking wives, he stated that "a woman is a selfish creature and one addicted to jealousy in an immoderate degree, and terribly calculated to agitate and overturn the natural inclinations of the man, and to mislead him by her continual tricks."[22] The husband must always be on guard and prepared for the irrational nature of his wife.

Philo held that there were three phases of a woman's life. Menstruation, childbearing, and menopause.[23] It appears that Philo believed females were asexual beings prior to menstruation. Menstruation makes a woman more sexual. At this point she has the choice to remain a physical virgin or get married. If virginity was chosen, she put aside her female nature and became something akin to an asexual third sex. Giving up this aspect of her sex allowed her to become more male in mind and soul. If a virgin marries, she becomes a woman and aspects such as irrationality, lower reason, and emotionality dominate her soul.[24] Sex was only for procreation and not for pleasure. Sex pursued for pleasure only

---

20 Philo, *Hypothetica* 7.3 (trans. Yonge, 743).

21 Philo, *Questions in Genesis* 1:26 (trans. Yonge, 796).

22 Philo, *Hypothetica* 11:14–17 (trans. Yonge, 746).

23 Dorothy Isabel Sly, "The Perception of Women in the Writing of Philo of Alexandria" (PhD diss., McMaster University, 1987), 90.

24 Philo, *On the Cherubim* 50 (trans. Yonge, 85).

becomes the enemy.[25] Sexual passion can also overtake men. He believed that circumcision was meant to keep men from loving sexual intercourse too much.[26] Once a woman bore children and reached menopause, her feminine passions disappeared and she would be more inclined to seek a union with God that would make her once again a virgin in matters of soul. Philo explained, "But when God begins to associate with the soul, he makes that which was previously woman now again virgin. Since banishing and destroying all the degenerate appetites unbecoming a human being, by which it had been made effeminate, he introduces in their stead genuine, and perfect, and unadulterated virtues." [27] Spiritually, a virgin is the equivalent to a man.[28]

Philo believed that some women who the Bible stated were married and had children were soul virgins. Because the scriptures make no reference to them "knowing" their husbands, he maintained that God was their father. According to Dorothy Sly, Philo does not transfer their allegorical virginity to the literal stories. Sly maintains that Philo's reason might be that he saw these women as different on an allegorical level and they could serve as models for women.[29] Sarah was the prime example. Philo stated that is why God did not use her (Gen 18:11) to bear Isaac until after menopause so that she had time to overcome her femaleness and be ranked as a virgin.[30] Other married women who bore children but were deemed soul virgins include Zipporah, Rachel, and Leah.[31] Eve was not included among their ranks.

A woman could also become an ascetic and practice virginity. The Therapeutae were aged virgins whom Philo admired. These virgins resembled the first Christian monks. They did not own private property and practiced chastity, fasting, and lived solitary lives. He admired them because "they are indifferent to the pleasures of the body, desiring not a mortal but immortal offspring,

---

[25] Loader, *Philo, Josephus, and the Testaments on Sexuality*, 25.

[26] Philo, *Questions and Answers in Genesis* 3:48 (trans. Yonge, 857–58).

[27] Philo, *On the Cherubim* 50 (trans. Yonge, 85).

[28] Sly, "The Perception of Women in the Writing of Philo of Alexandria," 109.

[29] Sly, "The Perception of Women in the Writing of Philo of Alexandria," 89.

[30] Philo, *On the Cherubim* 50 (trans. Yonge, 85).

[31] Philo, *On the Cherubim* 40 (trans. Yonge, 84).

which the soul that is attached to God, is alone able to produce by itself and from itself."[32]

Philo had much to say about Eve. He believed that Adam and Eve were mythical characters that should be understood in an allegorical manner. They were prototypes of man/husband and woman/wife. He began his exposition with the creation accounts. Philo had no trouble with Genesis having two creation accounts because he believed there were two creations. He maintained that the first account (Gen 1:1–2:3) depicted humanity's spiritual birth in the image of an asexual God. This image was the Mind of God. The rational aspect, the Mind, related to the body, as does God to the world.[33] Adam in this account was androgynous containing both the male and female components of humanity.[34] The second account (Gen 2:2–25) depicted the physical creation of Adam. By God breathing life into him, Adam received the higher, masculine part of the soul.[35] The dust represented the bodily realm with its senses, emotions, and sexual passions. God then removed the female, material aspects to create the woman while Adam retained the Mind. Both souls were mortal but "the man who came into existence after the image of God is what one might call an idea, or a genus, or a seal, an object of thought, incorporeal, neither male nor female, but incorruptible."[36] Philo further clarified women's inferior status by explaining why God created woman from man's rib. "This was so ordained in the first place, in order that the woman might not be of equal dignity with the man."[37] Women, therefore, have a secondary ontological status to man. Man was created in the image of God and thus had a rational mind. Being made from the material aspects of man, the woman cannot have a rational mind. Philo maintained that man being first in creation, having superior reason, and superior dignity meant that the or-

---

[32] Philo, *On the Contemplative Life* 68 (trans. Yonge, 704).

[33] Loader, *Philo, Josephus, and the Testaments on Sexuality*, 12. See also Baer, *Philo's Use of the Categories Male and Female*, 21.

[34] Philo, *On the Creation of the World* 76 (trans. Yonge, 11); Sharon Lea Mattila, "Wisdom, Sense Perception, Nature, and Philo's Gender Gradient," *The Harvard Theological Review* 89, no. 2 (April 1996): 104; Loader, *Philo, Josephus, and the Testaments on Sexuality*, 15.

[35] Philo, *Who is the Heir* 56–58 (trans. Yonge, 280–81); Loader, *Philo, Josephus, and the Testaments on Sexuality*, 14.

[36] Philo, *On the Creation* 134 (trans. Yonge, 19).

[37] Philo, *Questions and Answers in Genesis* 1:27 (trans. Yonge, 796).

dered world should be hierarchal with the man in the superior position.[38]

Philo believed that Adam was initially happy as one being. Adam's mind was in tune with creation and God. It was not until after the creation of woman from Adam that problems began. In his *On the Creation,* Philo noted that the two immediately recognized their similarities, and they had a desire to procreate creatures like themselves. "And this desire caused likewise pleasure to their bodies, which is the beginning of iniquities and transgressions, and it is owing to this that men have exchanged their previously immortal and happy existence for one which is mortal and full of misfortune."[39] With the creation of the material woman came sexual awareness and mortality. The woman, therefore, was the reason death entered the world. Philo also found it ironic that Adam chose the name Eve for the first woman. Eve means life, but instead she brought death.[40] Philo found this fitting as life and every good thing come from men and death and all bad things come from women.

Philo also explained why the serpent approached Eve rather than Adam. "The woman was more accustomed to be deceived than the man. For his counsels as well as his body are of a masculine sort, and competent to disentangle the notions of seduction; but the mind of the woman is more effeminate, so that through her softness she easily yields and is easily caught by the persuasions of falsehood, which imitate the resemblance of truth."[41] Because she held none of the masculine virtues, the serpent approached her because she would more easily be deceived. The feminine mind does not have a strong aptitude to deduce whether something is true or false. The serpent chose the easier rather than the harder target.

Philo also explained how the woman's mind could be cajoled by the serpent. He writes in *Questions on Genesis,*

> Why the woman first touched the tree and ate of its fruit, and the man afterwards, receiving it from her? The words used first of all, by their own intrinsic force, assert that it was suitable that immortality and every good thing should

---

[38] Philo, *On the Creation* 165 (trans. Yonge, 23).

[39] Philo, *On the Creation* 151 (trans. Yonge, 21).

[40] Philo, *Who is the Heir?* 52 (trans. Yonge, 280).

[41] Philo, *Questions and Answers in Genesis* 1:33 (trans. Yonge, 798).

be represented as under the power of the man, and death and every evil under that of the woman. But with reference to the mind, the woman, when understood symbolically, is sense, and the man is intellect. Moreover, the outward senses do of necessity touch those things which are perceptible by them; but it is through the medium of the outward senses that things are transmitted to the mind. For the outward senses are influenced by the objects which are presented to them; and the intellect by the outward senses.[42]

The woman surrendered to the serpent's deceit and could not resist experiencing the sensory pleasures of the tree. She could not overcome her desire that comes from lower reasoning and sense experience. She desired to understand it and the only way she could was through her outward senses.[43]

Like Plato's tripartite soul, Philo believed Genesis 1–3 allegorically presented all three elements of the individual soul. Adam represented mind and rationality. Eve characterized sense perception and irrationality. The serpent symbolized pleasure. Sense perception is valuable, but it needs supervision from the rational, masculine mind.[44] Sly notes that Adam bears some responsibility for the Fall. Eve did not have the capacity to discern what was occurring. Adam was blessed with the higher mind and did nothing to stop it. She was his responsibility. Adam's fault was in his infatuation with Eve and following her direction.[45] He chose to follow passion rather than God. The arousal of passion is a danger that women pose to all men.

Philo had an impact on Alexandrian Christianity's understanding of women and his writings appear to have been accessible at its catechetical school.[46] His interpretation of the Old Testament by allegorical means appealed to this city's earliest Christian theologians. These philosophically minded theologians found answers and a hermeneutic in Philo's writings that allowed them to move

---

[42] Philo, *Questions and Answers in Genesis* 1:37 (trans. Yonge, 798–99).

[43] Philo, *On the Creation* 156 (trans. Yonge, 22).

[44] Kristen E. Kvam, Linda S. Schearing, and Valerie H. Ziegler, ed. *Eve & Adam: Jewish, Christian, and Muslim Readings on Genesis and Gender* (Bloomington: University of Indiana Press, 1999), 42.

[45] Sly, "The Perception of Women in the Writing of Philo of Alexandria," 125.

[46] James Nelson Novoa, "The Appropriation of Jewish Thought by Christianity," *Science et Espirit* 55, no. 3 (2003): 289.

beyond the constraining literal interpretation of scripture and find a deeper meaning. Philo's thought concerning women are perceptible in the writings of Clement of Alexandria (150–215),[47] Origen (184–253),[48] Didymus the Blind (313–398),[49] Ambrose of Milan (337–397),[50] Gregory of Nyssa (335–398),[51] and Augustine (354–430).[52] Through the influence of these theologians and others, Philo's thoughts on the nature, purpose, and role of women spread throughout much of the Patristic world and into theological acceptance by the early Middle Ages.

---

[47] Clement of Alexandria, *Stromateis*, 1:28–32. Elizabeth Castelli, "Virginity and Its Meaning for Woman's Sexuality in Early Christianity," *Journal of Feminist Studies in Religion* 2, no. 1 (Spring 1986): 73.

[48] Origen, "Homily I," trans. Ronald E. Heine, in *Homilies on Genesis and Exodus*, The Fathers of the Church, vol. 71 (Washington, DC: Catholic University of America Press, 1982), 67–68.

[49] David T. Runia, *Philo in Early Christian Literature: A Survey* (Minneapolis: Fortress, 1993), 199, 202–3.

[50] Ambrose, "Paradise," trans. John J. Savage, in *Hexameron, Paradise, and Cain and Abel*, The Fathers of the Church, vol. 42 (Washington, DC: Fathers of the Church, 1961), 336–37; Runia, *Philo in Early Christian Literature*, 51; A. Kent Hieatt, "Eve as Reason in a Tradition of Allegorical Interpretation of the Fall," *Journal of the Warburg and Courtland Institutes* 43 (1980): 221.

[51] Gregory of Nyssa, "Life of Macrina," in *Ascetical Works*, The Fathers of the Church, vol. 58 (Washington, DC: Catholic University of America Press, 1967), 66–67. Runia, *Philo in Early Christian Literature*, 254–55. M. Poorthuis, "Who is to Blame: Adam or Eve? A Possible Jewish Source for Ambrose's 'De paradiso' 12,56," *Vigiliae Christianae* 50, no. 2 (1996): 128.

[52] Hieatt, "Eve as Reason in a Tradition of Allegorical Interpretation of the Fall," 221.

What Does Evangelical Preaching in a Pluralistic Culture Look Like?

Exploring Homiletical Implications from the Content and Rhetorical Strategies of Paul's Sermon in Acts 17 for Contemporary Evangelical Preaching

Pete Charpentier, DMin

Pete Charpentier is associate professor of theology and pastoral ministry at Grand Canyon Theological Seminary in Phoenix, Arizona.

Abstract

Paul's sermon in Acts 17:22–31 has been evaluated in diverse ways. This article contends that both its content and rhetorical strategies represent a positive model for evangelical preaching. In Acts 17:22–31, Paul communicated the gospel within the biblical narrative of redemption as he creatively connected with his audience and boldly challenged their core philosophical presuppositions. The above understanding yields implications for appropriate approaches to argumentation from a posture of humility in contemporary evangelical preaching.

Introduction

One of the challenges facing contemporary evangelical preaching is how to defend the gospel to a culture awash in pluralism.[1] To meet this challenge, preachers must engage in effective argumentation[2] even when many in their audiences may bristle at the

---

[1] The word "pluralism" is being used here to make an important distinction others have made between pluralism as a descriptive term and pluralism as a reference to a prescriptive philosophical presupposition. For brief discussions of this distinction, see D. A. Carson, "The Challenge from Pluralism to the Preaching of the Gospel," *Criswell Theological Review* 7, no. 1 (1993): 100–109; and Alister E. McGrath, "The Challenge of Pluralism for the Contemporary Christian Church," *Journal of the Evangelical Theological Society* 35, no. 3 (September 1992): 361–63.

[2] The word "argumentation" is used in a broad sense in this article since any particular approach to argumentation should take into account the general mindset of its specific audiences. For example, for audiences with a more modern worldview, effective types of argumentation may be those presented by

exclusive claims of Scripture. Yet, argumentation in preaching is not optional. Although it is difficult to navigate the tricky currents of postmodernism,[3] the biblical text repeatedly confronts preachers with exhortations to communicate the gospel persuasively (see, for example, 1 Pet 3:15 and Jude 3).[4] Specifically, Paul's sermon in Acts 17:22–31 functions as a model for offering an effective strategy of argumentation before a pluralistic audience.[5] Of course, Paul's sermon in Athens has been the focus of much scholarly attention.[6] In light of this, the following article will limit its analysis of Acts 17:16–34 to relevant homiletical implications for contemporary evangelical preaching in a pluralistic culture.

Diverse Approaches Paul's Preaching Ministry in Acts 17

Assessments of Paul's sermon in Athens have run the gamut of colossal failure to unbridled praise. For instance, some have read Paul's words in 1 Cor 2:1–5 as evidence that the apostle himself viewed his approach in Athens as an egregious error that needed radical correction.[7] While Martin Dibelius rejected this proposal as

---

John A. Broadus, *On Preparation and Delivery of Sermons*, 4th ed., rev. Vernon L. Stanfield (San Francisco: Harper, 1979), 141–64. However, for audiences with a more postmodern worldview, persuasive approaches to argumentation may be those similar to the overall ideas presented by John G. Stackhouse, Jr., *Humble Apologetics: Defending the Faith Today* (Oxford: Oxford University Press, 2002).

[3] For some recent treatments of this particular subject, see Zack Eswine, *Preaching to a Post-Everything World: Crafting Biblical Sermons that Connect with Our Culture* (Grand Rapids, MI: Baker, 2008); Timothy Keller, *Preaching: Communicating Faith in an Age of Skepticism* (New York: Viking, 2015); and Craig A. Loscalzo, *Apologetic Preaching: Proclaiming Christ to a Postmodern World* (Downers Grove, IL: IVP Academic, 2000).

[4] Tony Merida, *Faithful Preaching: Declaring Scripture with Responsibility, Passion, and Authenticity* (Nashville, TN: Broadman and Holman, 2009), 185–87.

[5] For a discussion on the issue of pluralism in the first century, see Bruce W. Winter, "In Public and in Private: Early Christians and Religious Pluralism," in *One God, One Lord: Christianity in a World of Religious Pluralism*, ed. Andrew D. Clarke and Bruce W. Winter (Grand Rapids, MI: Baker, 1992), 125–48.

[6] Ben Witherington, III, *The Acts of the Apostles: A Socio-Rhetorical Commentary* (Grand Rapids, MI: Eerdmans, 1998), 511. For brief lists of key resources for further research on Paul's preaching ministry in Athens, see Ibid.; and John B. Polhill, *Acts*, The New American Commentary, vol. 26, ed. David S. Dockery (Nashville, TN: Broadman, 1992), 369–70.

[7] David Smith, *The Life and Letters of St. Paul* (New York: George H. Doran, n.d.), 148–49. For a more recent expression of this view, see Joseph Pathrapankal, "From Areopagus to Corinth (Acts 17:22–31; 1 Cor 2:1–5) A

"sheer fantasy ... [without] a shred of evidence,"[8] he nevertheless held a dim view of Paul's sermon in Acts 17:22–31 as an example of pure Christian proclamation.[9] Similarly, Hanz Conzelmann asserted that "[Luke did not want to sketch a model sermon for handy use by a missionary.... . This address was not meant to be a general pattern to be repeated everywhere."[10]

Others, however, have had an opposite approach to Paul's preaching ministry in Athens. For example, some have noted that Paul was an experienced missionary by the time he entered Athens and, consequently, was not experimenting with different evangelistic methodologies.[11] Also, others have observed that when Paul's pagan audience is factored into the equation,[12] the contents of his message align well with his overall theology on similar themes in his Epistles.[13] In light of his positive assessment of Paul's preaching ministry on this occasion, John Polhill concludes, "Luke presented the Areopagus speech as a model of Paul's preaching *to the pagan world*."[14]

Study on the Transition from the Power of Knowledge to the Power of the Spirit," *Mission Studies* 23, no. 1 (2006): 61–80.

[8] Martin Dibelius, *Studies in the Acts of the Apostles* (Mifflintown, PA: Sigler, 1999), 73.

[9] Dibelius, *Studies*, 57–58.

[10] Hanz Conzelmann, "The Address of Paul on the Areopagus," in *Studies in Luke-Acts*, ed. Leander E. Keck and J. Louis Martyn (Mifflintown, PA: Sigler, 1999), 226.

[11] F. F. Bruce, *Paul: Apostle of the Heart Set Free* (Grand Rapids, MI: Eerdmans, 1977), 246.

[12] Bruce, *Paul*, 244.

[13] John B. Polhill, *Paul and His Letters* (Nashville, TN: B&H, 1999), 212; Conrad Gempf, "Athens, Paul at," in *Dictionary of Paul and His Letters*, ed. Gerald F. Hawthorne and Ralph P. Martin (Downers Grove, IL: InterVarsity, 1993), 53–54; Bertil Gärtner, *The Areopagus Speech and Natural Revelation*, Acta Seminarii Neotestamentici Upsaliensis, XXI, trans. Carolyn Hannay King (Ejnar Munksgaard, Copenhagen: C. W. K Gleerup, 1955), 249–250; and Colin J. Hemer, "The Speeches of Acts II. The Areopagus Address," *Trinity Bulletin* 40 (1989): 248–55.

[14] Polhill, *Paul and His Letters*, 212. Emphasis in the original.

Acts 17 and the Ministry Strategy and Teachings
of the Historical Paul

While some scholars have questioned the historicity of Luke's depiction of Paul and his preaching in Acts 17,[15] other aspects of the Lukan narrative and Paul's Epistles do not warrant such an assessment.[16] It may be noted how Paul's ministry activity outlined in Acts 17:17 fits well with his overall missionary strategy in other parts of Acts.[17] Also, Paul's reaction to the idolatrous worship that saturated Athens fits his overall profile in the New Testament. For instance, Polhill comments, "For Paul, Jew that he was with his strong monotheism and distaste for graven images, the scene [in Athens] was most unappealing."[18] Of course, Paul's strong reaction against the idolatry in Athens is not surprising given his repeated exhortations against idols in his Epistles (see, for example, 1 Cor 5:11; 6:9–11; 10:6–7, 14; 12:1–3; 2 Cor 6:14–18; Gal 5:19–21; Eph 5:5; Col 3:5; and 1 Thess 1:9).

The Content and Rhetorical Strategies of Acts 17:22–31

A rhetorical analysis of Acts 17:22–31 is inextricably linked to its setting. While Luke could have geography in focus in Acts 17:22a,[19] some type of court session seems more likely,[20] although a strict formal hearing is not required.[21] In light of this, the rhetorical makeup of Acts 17:22–31 does not appear to be monolithic. Of the major rhetorical classification options,[22] elements of both

---

[15] Conzelmann, 218; and Dibelius, 64–66.

[16] Bruce, *Paul*, 245.

[17] Eckhard J. Schnabel, "Contextualising Paul in Athens: The Proclamation of the Gospel before Pagan Audiences in the Graeco-Roman World," *Religion and Theology* 12, no. 2 (2005): 172; and F. F. Bruce, *The Acts of the Apostles: The Greek Text with Introduction and Commentary*, 3rd rev. and enlarged ed. (Eugene, OR: Wipf & Stock, 2000), 376.

[18] Polhill, *Acts*, 366.

[19] Bruce, *The Acts of the Apostles*, 377.

[20] Witherington, *The Acts of the Apostles*, 515; Hemer, 239–41; and Polhill, *Acts*, 367–69.

[21] Polhill, *Acts*, 368.

[22] Burton L. Mack, *Rhetoric and the New Testament*, Guides to Biblical Scholarship: New Testament Series, ed. Dan O. Via, Jr. (Minneapolis, MN: Fortress, 1990), 34–35.

judicial and deliberative orations surface in the address.[23] However, the combination of diverse rhetorical elements in a speech was not an anomaly.[24] Also, given the convergence of Paul's missionary zeal and the general court setting for the speech, the apostle would understandably offer a defense for teaching the gospel in Athens to persuade his audience to turn from the folly of idolatry to faith in the one, true God.[25]

Although a detailed rhetorical analysis of Acts 17:22–31 is beyond the scope of this paper, the following four observations are pertinent for gleaning homiletical implications from this text. First, Paul sought to establish immediate rapport with his audience in the *exordium* of his address.[26] Yet, it is important to note that his opening thoughts, while respectful in tone, still allowed him to challenge his audience's overall spiritual blindness.[27] Second, Paul used a point of contact with his audience to segue seamlessly into a proclamation of the redemptive storyline of Scripture.[28] As with the previous observation, the nuances of the apostle's language in Acts 17:23 both commended and critiqued the core religious tenets of his audience.[29] Third, Paul packaged biblical themes in ways his pagan listeners could more readily understand them. For instance, he interacted with ideas and sources familiar to his audience.[30] Of course, this observation does not mean that Paul's speech was void of biblical allusions and perhaps even quotations.[31] Fourth, Paul proclaimed the heart of the kerygma in Acts

---

[23] For discussions on the rhetorical nature of Acts 17:22–31, see Dean Zweck, "The *Exordium* of the Areopagus Speech, Acts 17.22, 23," *New Testament Studies* 35 (1989): 94–95; and Witherington, *The Acts of the Apostles*, 518.

[24] Mack, *Rhetoric*, 34–35

[25] Witherington, *The Acts of the Apostles*, 517–18.

[26] J. Daryl Charles, "Engaging the (Neo)Pagan Mind: Paul's Encounter with Athenian Culture as a Model for Cultural Apologetics (Acts 17:16–34)," *Trinity Journal* 16 (1995): 54.

[27] Witherington, *The Acts of the Apostles*, 520.

[28] Polhill, *Acts*, 371.

[29] Charles, "Engaging," 54–55.

[30] For the view that two quotations from Greek sources surface in Paul's message here, see F. F. Bruce, *The Book of Acts*, The New International Commentary on the New Testament, rev. ed., ed. F. F. Bruce (Grand Rapids, MI: Eerdmans, 1988), 338–39. For the view that only one direct quotation from a Greek source is mentioned by Paul in Acts 17:28, see Polhill, *Acts*, 375–76.

[31] I. Howard Marshall, "Acts," in *Commentary on the New Testament Use of the Old Testament*, ed. G. K. Beale and D. A. Carson (Grand Rapids, MI: Baker Academic, 2007), 594. For a more detailed argument of how Paul's message in

17:22–31.[32] When the contents of Paul's proclamation are coupled with Luke's summary of the apostle's teaching in Acts 17:20, the heart of the kerygma emerges.

Acts 17:22–31 and the Biblical Narrative of Redemption

Not only did Paul's message in Acts 17 convey biblical themes in general, but these themes followed the broad storyline of redemption in Scripture. After his *exordium*, Paul presents God as the Creator, who is distinct from creation in Acts 17:24a. This dovetails with Gen 1–2 and simultaneously cuts across the pantheistic grain of the beliefs of the apostle's Stoic listeners.[33] Paul also expanded his portrait of God in Acts 17:24b–25 to emphasize his infinite and self-sufficient nature. Erickson connects these particular theological themes with an understanding of God's "immateriality and spirituality."[34] This view of God challenged the materialism of the Epicureans' belief system.[35] Thus, Paul began where Scripture begins its story of redemption.

Next, Paul narrowed his focus to God's redemptive work among humanity in Acts 17:26–29. Of course, this also follows the biblical storyline of redemption. The apostle affirmed that all of humanity originated with Adam and Eve (Acts 17:26). This notion of common ancestry, however, was a rejection of the Greek claims of superiority over others.[36] Moreover, the fall of humanity is implied in Paul's declaration that human beings "should seek God, in the hope that they might feel their way toward him and find him" (Acts 17:27 ESV). Although this language may appear to affirm the salvific potential of natural revelation alone, Moore

---

Acts 17:22–31 is connected with various Old Testament themes, see Kenneth D. Litwak, "Israel's Prophets Meet Athens' Philosophers: Scriptural Echoes in Acts 17,22–31," *Biblica* 85, no. 2 (2004): 199–216.

[32] For a discussion on how elaborate or streamlined the kerygma was in apostolic preaching, see John R. W. Stott, "The Preacher's Portrait: Some New Testament Word Studies," in *Biblical Preaching Today* (Grand Rapids, MI: Eerdmans, 1961), 38–39.

[33] Schnabel, "Contextualising," 179.

[34] Millard J. Erickson, *Christian Theology*, 2nd ed. (Grand Rapids, MI: Baker Academic, 1998), 298–99.

[35] Everett Ferguson, *Backgrounds of Early Christianity*, 2nd ed. (Grand Rapids, MI: Eerdmans, 1993), 351.

[36] Kenneth O. Gangel, "Paul's Areopagus Speech," *Bibliotheca Sacra* 127, no. 508 (October–December 1970): 310.

notes that this "is not a note of optimism but an indictment of Athenian paganism."[37]

The above point provides a climax to Paul's message in Acts 17:30–31. Here, Paul boldly issued God's call to universal repentance in light of Christ's redemptive work because of impending judgment. Clearly, if natural revelation alone was sufficient for salvation, then the call to repentance was unnecessary. However, if natural revelation was only supplementary in the equation of salvation, then Paul would build upon this knowledge to declare God's redemption in Christ.

Thus, Paul's Areopagus address followed the general storyline of redemption in Scripture. It began with a presentation of God as Creator, who is distinct from creation. It then moved to focus on humanity and its desperate need for redemption. Finally, it culminated with a call to repentance in view of Christ's finished salvific work and the reality of impending judgment.

Homiletical Implications for Evangelical Preaching from Acts 17

The above discussions yield the following homiletical implications for evangelical preaching in a contemporary pluralistic culture. First, a dichotomy does not necessarily exist between an unwavering commitment to biblical truth and a respectful tone in communication. Sire contends, "the Christian faith is best promoted when the Christian character of Christianity is demonstrated in the very rhetorical style of its presentation."[38] Navigating this balance is crucial, and it is possible through the wisdom and enabling power of God's Spirit.[39]

Paul was not dispassionate when he delivered his Areopagus address. He was deeply disturbed in his spirit by the idolatry of Athens (Acts 17:16). Also, some in his audience were suspicious of him and his teachings (Acts 17:18).[40] Although these factors

---

[37] Russell D. Moore, "Natural Revelation," in *A Theology for the Church*, ed. Daniel L. Akin (Nashville, TN: B&H Academic, 2007), 82–83.

[38] James W. Sire, *Why Good Arguments Often Fail: Making a More Persuasive Case for Christ* (Downers Grove, IL: IVP, 2006), 78.

[39] C. H. Spurgeon, *Lectures to My Students*, complete and unabridged (Grand Rapids, MI: Zondervan, 1954), 189–90.

[40] Duane Litfin, *Paul's Theology of Preaching: The Apostle's Challenge to the Art of Persuasion in Ancient Corinth* (Downers Grove, IL: IVP Academic, 2015), 329.

precipitated Paul's defense before the Areopagus, they did not preclude him from preaching with conviction and rhetorical decorum. He began his message with respect, while he also presented a biblical portrait of God and his redemptive work in Christ.[41] Thus, contemporary evangelical preachers should proclaim the gospel passionately, faithfully, *and* respectfully (1 Pet 3:15).[42]

Second, the heart of the gospel should be homiletically packaged with an understanding and appreciation of the culture's core philosophical presuppositions from a posture of humility. This implication is supported in Acts 17:22–31 by how Paul affirmed and challenged his audience's belief systems.[43] The apostle's message reveals that he did not splice his message together from disparate tenets of diverse philosophical systems and ideas.[44] Instead, he demonstrated familiarity, understanding, and appreciation for the views of his listeners. For example, Paul interacted with one of their poets (Acts 17:28–29b). So, he identified their God-given longings and challenged them to look to Christ as the only one who could fulfill their yearnings.[45]

Timothy Keller conveys this aspect of Paul's preaching in Acts 17 as follows: "By affirming people's better impulses, by granting insights where he finds them, by adopting concepts and ways of reasoning that they understood, Paul is not merely seeking to refute them, but also to respect them."[46] Of course, Keller also notes that this rhetorical strategy was not confined to Paul. He argues that John adopted a similar approach.[47] Thus, he concludes, "The early Christian communicators … reframed the culture's questions, reshaped its concerns, and redirected its hopes."[48]

This homiletical implication does not only impact one's approach to argumentation in general; it also speaks specifically to the tones of appreciation and humility in preaching. With a tone

---

[41] D. A. Carson, *The Gagging of God: Christianity Confronts Pluralism* (Grand Rapids, MI: Zondervan, 1996), 498–99.

[42] Jerry Vines and Jim Shaddix, *Power in the Pulpit: How to Prepare and Deliver Expository Sermons* (Chicago: Moody, 1999), 179.

[43] Charles, 60; Sire, 133–38.

[44] Polhill, *Acts*, 367.

[45] Timothy Keller, *Center Church: Doing Balanced, Gospel-Centered Ministry in Your City* (Grand Rapids, MI: Zondervan, 2012), 112–14.

[46] Keller, *Preaching*, 101.

[47] Keller, *Preaching*, 98.

[48] Keller, *Preaching*, 99.

of appreciation in preaching, evangelicals can affirm some core longings of the culture, and then they can challenge where the culture tries to go with these longings.[49] With a tone of humility in preaching, evangelicals should dialogue with others rather than presume to know their beliefs. This dialogue can then help evangelicals to share the gospel with more clarity.[50]

Third, rhetorical strategies should be employed in conjunction with a dependence on the power of the Spirit to transform lives. Paul acknowledged that spiritual transformation only comes by the power of God's Spirit rather than by human rhetoric (1 Cor 2:1–5; 3:5–9). However, this does not mean that the apostle disparaged the importance of effective communication.[51] Any cursory perusal of Paul's speeches in Acts and his Epistles refutes this idea.[52] Paul affirmed an appropriate place for rhetorical strategies coupled with a dependence on God's Spirit.

Of course, various homileticians have affirmed the need for preachers to depend on the power of God's Spirit while also working to improve their communication skills as well. For example, Charles Spurgeon's *Lectures to My Students* addressed the multifaceted aspects of a preacher's need to depend on the Holy Spirit's power among a host of other topics related to effective preaching.[53] Bryan Chapell succinctly summarizes this point well when he cautions that "Great gifts do not necessarily make for great preaching. The technical excellence of a message may rest on your

---

[49] For a recent example of this approach, see Ravi Zacharias and Vince Vitale, *Jesus Among the Secular Gods: The Countercultural Claims of Christ* (New York: Hachette, 2017), 93–135.

[50] I. Howard Marshall, "Dialogue with Non-Christians in the New Testament," *Evangelical Review of Theology* 16 (1992): 28–47.

[51] Jason Meyer, *Preaching: A Biblical Theology* (Wheaton, IL: Crossway, 2013), 214.

[52] D. A. Carson, *The Cross and Christian Ministry: Leadership Lessons from 1 Corinthians* (Grand Rapids, MI: Baker, 1993), 34–35; G. W. Hansen, "Rhetorical Criticism," in *Dictionary of Paul and His Letters*, ed. Gerald F. Hawthorne and Ralph P. Martin (Downers Grove, IL: InterVarsity, 1993), 822–26; and S. Greidanus, "Preaching from Paul Today," in *Dictionary of Paul and His Letters*, ed. Gerald F. Hawthorne and Ralph P. Martin (Downers Grove, IL: InterVarsity, 1993), 737–43.

[53] Spurgeon, *Lectures to My Students*, 185–204.

skills, but the spiritual efficacy of your message resides with God."[54]

As with the first homiletical implication, preachers should avoid forcing a false dichotomy between effective communication skills and the need to depend upon the power of the Spirit.[55] The reality is that one or the other is not needed. Instead, *both* are important.[56]

Conclusion

Preachers in every age have been and will be challenged concerning how to proclaim the gospel faithfully and persuasively.[57] While each generation poses different obstacles, Scripture provides God's timeless truths and examples for how to navigate these challenges well.[58] Paul's message in Acts 17:22–31 is one such model, and it is particularly relevant because of the currents of pluralism pulsating throughout contemporary culture.[59] Those committed to evangelical preaching can effectively present the heart of the gospel within the biblical storyline of redemption in ways that both connect with and confront today's cultural climate as Paul did in Athens.

---

[54] Bryan Chapell, *Christ-Centered Preaching: Redeeming the Expository Sermon* (Grand Rapids, MI: Baker Academic, 2005), 33. For a similar thought, consider the following distinction between bad, good, and great preaching: "the difference between a bad sermon and a good sermon is largely located in the preachers – in their gifts and skills and in their preparation for any particular message. . . . However, while the difference between a bad sermon and a good sermon is mainly the responsibility of the preacher, the difference between good preaching and *great* preaching lies mainly in the work of the Holy Spirit in the heart of the listener as well as the preacher." Keller, *Preaching*, 10–11.

[55] Stephen F. Olford and David L. Olford, *Anointed Expository Preaching* (Nashville, TN: B&H, 1998), 183–87.

[56] Daniel L. Akin, Bill Curtis, and Stephen Rummage, *Engaging Exposition* (Nashville, TN: B&H Academic, 2011), 252.

[57] John R. W. Stott, "Between Two Worlds: The Art of Preaching in the Twentieth Century," in *Biblical Preaching Today* (Grand Rapids, MI: Eerdmans, 1961), 147–50.

[58] Christoph Stenschke, "The Challenges and Opportunities for Preaching from the Acts of the Apostles," in *Preaching the New Testament*, ed. Ian Paul and David Wenham (Downers Grove, IL: IVP Academic, 2013), 87.

[59] Carson, *The Gagging of God*, 496–501.

JBTM 18.1 (Spring 2021): 105–18

Boldness in Personal Evangelism

Preston L. Nix

Toward the end of the personal evangelism class that I teach each semester at New Orleans Baptist Theological Seminary, I ask my students to share with me the "biggest takeaway" they have gleaned from the course including all lecture material, textbook readings, writing assignments, and class discussions, as well as the personal witnessing they have been required to do with their evangelism teams. Every semester without fail the largest percentage of my students indicate to me that the "biggest takeaway" they receive from my class is the practical definition of boldness in personal evangelism that I share with them in my initial lecture for the semester. In that particular lecture on the subject of Intentional Evangelism that sets the tone for the class for the semester, I encourage my students to be bold witnesses for Christ and share with them my practical definition of boldness in personal evangelism. Repeatedly, students have told me that remembering this definition of boldness has helped to counteract the fear they have had to overcome in sharing their faith with others. Further, they have shared with me that recalling this definition of boldness has assisted them in their actual witnessing encounters to communicate confidently the content of the Gospel and to call for a personal response from those with whom they have shared their faith. Certainly seeing my definition of boldness in witnessing impact my students as they have indicated has been extremely rewarding for me as an evangelism professor in my attempts to instill in my students a passion for personal evangelism as well as to equip them to be more effective in sharing their faith with those around them who need Christ.

The fact that my practical definition of boldness in personal evangelism has encouraged and assisted my students in sharing their faith with others has provided the primary motivation for me to write this article to define what boldness in evangelism actually is and how any believer can be a bold witness for Christ. My hope is that the content of this article not only will inform believers outside of the seminary classroom as to my definition of boldness in personal evangelism but also will inspire as well as equip them to be bold witnesses for the Lord Jesus Christ to those who desperately need to hear the saving message of the Gospel in today's world.

Several other important reasons can be enumerated for the need of a serious treatment of the subject of boldness in personal evangelism. First and foremost, the Bible calls for boldness in evangelism, illustrates boldness in evangelism, and describes the effectual results of boldness in evangelism. Although the Scripture advocates bold witnessing by the church and individual believers to the lost, very little has been written specifically on the subject of boldness in evangelism. Books in the field of evangelism as well as evangelism training programs and resource materials may contain a sentence or two concerning the need for boldness in evangelism but very little else is mentioned about the subject.[1] The lack of biblical teaching on boldness in evangelism and the lack of practical application as to how to be a bold witness for Christ

---

[1] The writer located one book in which the author covered the subject of boldness in the New Testament but the content was focused on pulpit proclamation rather than personal evangelism. However, the word study on boldness in the work proved to be helpful and as a result, the resource is utilized later in the article. See Stanley B. Marrow, *Speaking the Word Fearlessly: Boldness in the New Testament* (Ramsey, NJ: Paulist Press, 1982). Another book appeared to be promising on the subject with the word "boldness" in the title and the term "evangelistic lifestyle" in the subtitle. Regrettably, the author promoted the social gospel and social activism rather than authentic New Testament evangelism. See Paul R. Dekar, *Holy Boldness: Practices of an Evangelistic Lifestyle* (Macon, GA: Smyth & Helwys Publishing, 2004). Another book on witnessing contained a chapter titled "Being Bold" but the focus of the entire chapter was on boldly living for Christ and "preaching the Gospel" through actions and not about verbally presenting the Gospel. See Tim Baker, *Witnessing 101* (Nashville: W Publishing Group, 2003). The writer found two other books with chapters covering the subject of boldness in personal evangelism. One book included a chapter by Scott Dawson titled "Don't Be Afraid! Becoming a Bold Witness" which consisted primarily of personal testimonies of witnessing and encouragement to overcome fear in witnessing in *The Complete Evangelism Handbook: Expert Advice for Reaching Others for Christ* ed. Scott Dawson (Grand Rapids: Baker Books, 2006), 99-103. The longest and most helpful discussion of boldness in evangelism located was a ten page chapter titled "Be Bold: Slaying the Fear Factor When Sharing Our Faith" in the book *Marks of the Messenger*. See J. Mack Stiles, *Marks of the Messenger: Knowing, Living and Speaking the Gospel* (Downers Grove, IL: InterVarsity Press, 2010), 81-90. Finally, a booklet produced by the Billy Graham Evangelistic Association included a somewhat brief but very biblical and practical reflection on boldness in evangelism in the context of overcoming fear in witnessing. See Timothy K. Beougher, *Overcoming Walls to Witnessing* (Charlotte, NC: Billy Graham Evangelistic Association, 1993), 13-15.

provide additional rationale for treatment of the subject. Further, a true understanding of the meaning and application of evangelistic boldness can assist individual believers in overcoming their greatest hindrance to sharing their faith which is fear.[2] Unless believers find a way to overcome their fear of sharing their faith with others, they will never obey the mandate of Christ to fulfill the Great Commission.[3] Also, this teaching can serve to correct a misunderstanding of what boldness in evangelism actually is. A faulty understanding and practice of "so called" boldness in evangelism observed by some believers actually may have become a hindrance for them to share their faith with others. In addition, this study can help to counteract the "pushback" against any type of evangelistic efforts in today's culture in any manner whether "bland or bold" from some even within the church, particularly the millennial generation.[4] By contrast, with three-fourths of the churches in the United Sates are plateaued or declining and because baptismal statistics have trended downward for decades in most denominations, the church does not need to "back away" or retreat from bold evangelism but needs to "charge ahead" and advance with even more boldness in declaring the Gospel today to those without Christ who are running faster and further away from God and the truth that they need to hear! "If anything is needed in Christian witness today, it is boldness. We don't need bigger music ministries, longer prayer walks or nicer church foyers. We need boldness—wise boldness, gracious boldness, boldness

---

[2] Because of his attempts to train seminary students as well as members of the local church in personal witnessing, this writer's observation causes him to concur with the assertion of Dr. Will McRaney that "…fear is the number-one barrier to personal evangelism." Will McRaney Jr., *The Art of Personal Evangelism: Sharing Jesus in a Changing Culture* (Nashville: Broadman & Holman, 2003), 191. See also Stiles, *Marks of the Messenger,* 113.

[3] For a discussion of areas of fear in personal evangelism including fear of rejection, fear of failure, and fear of the unknown, as well as how to respond to those fears, see McRaney, 192-194. See also Matt Queen, *Everyday Evangelism* (Fort Worth: Seminary Hill Press, 2014), 33-38 and Beougher, 9-17.

[4] See the disturbing report by the Barna Group which indicates that almost half of practicing Christian Millennials (47%) believe that evangelism, that is, attempting to share the Gospel in order to lead non-Christians to faith in Christ, is wrong. "Almost Half of Practicing Christian Millennials Say Evangelism Wrong," Barna Group, February 5, 2019, https://www.barna.com/research/millennials-oppose-evangelism/.

rooted in the hope that we have in the gospel, boldness mixed with love, but boldness nonetheless."[5]

The Meaning and Usage of the Word Boldness

The word in the New Testament translated boldness in English is the Greek word *parrhēsia*. Very literally, the word originally meant "to say everything" that needed to be said.[6] In the ancient Greek world the word was part of the political vocabulary of the Greek city state. Every free citizen in the democratic city state had the right to express his opinion before the governing assembly. The right of a free citizen to exercise *parrhēsia* or boldness in communicating publically his views in the democratic city state was highly valued in the Greek culture. The word *parrhēsia* crossed over from the political arena into usage in the realm of personal relationships as well in ancient Greece. The word denoted that friends were able to speak the truth freely to one another without insincerity concerning one's self or flattery toward the other person. In both the political and personal spheres of communication *parrhēsia* became associated with the ideas of truth and candor. Simply put, *parrhēsia* or boldness to the Greek was "freedom of speech" with the intent to speak the truth with all honesty and frankness.[7]

In the New Testament and in particular in the book of Acts, both the noun *parrhēsia* and verb form *parrhēsiazomai* were related to the public proclamation of the Gospel by the Apostles.[8] The usage of the words by the Apostle Paul in his writings also was in the context of the preaching of the Gospel message. The employment of *parrhēsia* and *parrhēsiazomai* in the book of Acts as well as in the writings of Paul reflected the meaning of the words from both the political and personal realms as understood in the Greek

---

[5] Stiles, *Marks of the Messenger*, 83.

[6] Marrow, *Speaking the Word*, 20. For other shades of meaning of the word, see Walter Bauer, *"parrhēsia"* in *A Greek-English Lexicon of the New Testament and Other Early Christian Literature*, 2nd ed., revised and augmented by F. Wilbur Gingrich and Frederick W. Danker (Chicago: The University of Chicago Press, 1979), 630-31.

[7] Marrow, *Speaking the Word Fearlessly*, 20-21.

[8] For examples of usage of both the noun and verb forms of boldness combined with other verbs and verbal nouns in evangelism contexts in the New Testament, see Thomas P. Johnston, *Evangelizology*, vol. 1, *Introduction and Definition* (Liberty, MO: Evangelism Unlimited, 2019), 418, 451-53.

culture. However, *parrhēsia* as recorded in the New Testament received "its true meaning in the context of salvation in Christ Jesus."[9] The term *parrhēsia* was applied to the proclamation of the Gospel and became so closely associated with the proclamation of the message of the Gospel that it became "almost synonymous with preaching itself."[10] After his dramatic conversion, Paul "had spoken out boldly in the name of Jesus" in Damascus (Acts 9:27).[11] Later, in the city of Jerusalem, Paul was "speaking out boldly in the name of the Lord" (Acts 9:28). On his first Missionary Journey, while spending a considerable amount of time in Iconium, Paul was "speaking boldly with reliance upon the Lord" (Acts 14:3). On his third Missionary Journey, Paul entered the synagogue in Ephesus and "continued speaking out boldly for three months, reasoning and persuading them about the kingdom of God" (Acts 19:8).

However, *parrhēsia* was not applied exclusively to Paul and the other Apostles and their public proclamation of the Gospel in the book of Acts. Peter and John were arrested by the Jewish authorities after they had been instrumental in the miraculous healing of a lame beggar at the gate called Beautiful outside the Jewish temple in Jerusalem. Peter seized the opportunity to preach the Gospel to the crowd of people who gathered in amazement at the miraculous healing of the lame man and at least two thousand men responded to Peter's message by placing their faith in the Lord Jesus Christ. Following their interrogation by the Jewish leaders and their subsequent release from jail, Peter and John returned to the group of fellow believers and reported to them how they had been threatened by the Jewish authorities if they spoke any more in the name of Jesus. The group of believers began to cry out to God in fervent prayer specifically asking the Lord to "take note of their threats and grant that your bond-servants may speak your word with all confidence" (Acts 4:29). The Bible revealed, "When they had prayed, the place where they had gathered together was shaken, and they were all filled with the Holy Spirit and began to speak the word of God with boldness" (Acts 4:31). The Apostles were not the only ones filled with the Spirit nor the only ones who

---

[9] Marrow, *Speaking the Word*, 28.

[10] Marrow, *Speaking the Word*, 28.

[11] All Scripture references will be from the New American Standard Bible unless otherwise noted.

shared the saving Gospel of Jesus following the powerful prayer meeting in which they had participated. The Scripture recorded that all of the believers in the place of prayer were filled with the Holy Spirit and that all of them began to share the truth of the Gospel with *parrhēsia* or boldness with people around them. Boldness not only accompanied the public proclamation of the Gospel by the Apostles but also boldness characterized the individual proclamation or personal witness of the common follower of Jesus Christ filled by the Holy Spirit.

As indicated above, the Apostle Paul employed the words *parrhēsia* and *parrhēsiazomai* in his writings in relation to the preaching of the Gospel. In his first letter to the believers in Thessalonica, the Apostle Paul reminded them after he and his companions "had already suffered and been mistreated in Philippi" that they "had the boldness in our God to speak to you the Gospel of God amid much oppression" (1 Thess. 2:2). He requested of the Ephesian believers that they pray on his behalf "that utterance may be given to me in the opening of my mouth to make known with boldness the mystery of the Gospel, for which I am in chains; that in proclaiming it I may speak boldly as I ought to speak" (Ephesians 6:19-20). Paul made a similar appeal to the believers at the church in Colossae when he asked them to pray "that God would open up to us a door for the word, so that I may speak forth the mystery of Christ…that I may make it clear in the way I ought to speak" (Colossians 4:3-4)). Although in the last passage cited Paul did not include the actual word for boldness, taken together, these verses from the writings of Paul as well as the previous verses from the book of Acts that described his preaching reveal that the primary focus of his ministry was the proclamation of the saving Gospel of Jesus Christ. Further, he wanted to make certain that he proclaimed the truth of the Gospel both with such clarity of speech as well as boldness of speech from the Holy Spirit in order that those who heard it could understand the message of salvation and be compelled to respond to it with repentance and faith.

Other New Testament Examples
of Evangelistic Boldness

Although the previous section dealt with the meaning and usage of the word *parrhēsia* or boldness historically and biblically, the Scripture references provided examples of boldness in the New Testament, particularly in the ministry of the Apostle Paul. However, several other instances of bold proclamation of the truth of the Gospel are present in the New Testament even though the word boldness itself does not appear in the descriptive narrative. During His earthly ministry, Jesus Himself was very bold in His declaration of the truth as to how a person could come into a right relationship with the Father. In fact, Jesus began His public ministry of proclamation in a very similar vein of His forerunner, the bold preacher of repentance from the Judean wilderness, John the Baptist. Mark recorded in his Gospel account that "Jesus came into Galilee, preaching the Gospel of God, and saying, 'The time is fulfilled, and the kingdom of God is at hand; repent and believe the Gospel' "(Mark 1:14-15). When Nicodemus came to Jesus at night to visit with Him concerning spiritual matters, Jesus was very bold and direct with the highly respected religious teacher in Israel. In fact, the initial response of Jesus to Nicodemus was somewhat abrupt.[12] Rather than entertain questions or engage in discussion on matters of religion, Jesus boldly declared to Nicodemus, "Truly, truly, I say to you, unless one is born again he cannot see the kingdom of God" (John 3:3). When the rich young ruler inquired about what he needed to do in order to inherit eternal life, he addressed Jesus as "Good Teacher." Jesus responded by asking him, "Why do you call Me good? No one is good except God alone" (Luke 18:18-19). Jesus then boldly demanded that the wealthy young man sell all his possessions and give the proceeds to the poor and follow Him if he wanted to obtain eternal life (Luke 18:22). In His interaction with the Samaritan woman Jesus encountered at Jacob's well, He was very direct with her about her immoral lifestyle and her misunderstanding of the nature of genuine worship of the one true God (John 4:16-24). Jesus boldly confronted the demon possessed man who lived among the tombs in the country of the Gerasenes. Jesus cast out the legion of demons from the man and delivered him from the domain of darkness into the kingdom of light (Mark 5:1-20). Jesus spoke boldly and directly to Matthew who was sitting at his tax collector's booth and commanded him to "Follow Me!" (Matthew 9:9). Jesus told

---

[12] In an excellent work describing how Jesus dealt with individuals and particular groups of people attempting to lead them to place their faith in Himself as Messiah, Dr. Robert Coleman indicated the boldness of Jesus in dealing with Nicodemus who was a member of the religious elite of his day. "Jesus brushes aside the nice talk and gets right to the point." Robert E. Coleman, *The Master's Way of Personal Evangelism* (Wheaton, IL: Crossway Books, 1997), 31.

another tax collector named Zaccheus to come down out of the tree that he had climbed in order to get a glimpse of Jesus passing by because Jesus boldly invited Himself to come to the house of Zaccheus (Luke 19:5). Jesus was so bold and direct as to ask a very sick man at the pool of Bethesda whether or not he really wanted to get well (John 5:6). Jesus then miraculously healed him both physically and spiritually (John 5:7-15).

Other examples of evangelistic boldness are given in the book of Acts which do not include the word boldness itself in the biblical narrative. On the day of Pentecost, the Apostle Peter boldly preached the message of salvation in Jesus Christ and three thousand people responded in repentance and faith and were baptized that very day (Acts 2:14-41). As mentioned previously, Peter boldly preached to the crowd that had gathered around the temple upon hearing of the miraculous healing of the lame beggar outside the gate called Beautiful and another two thousand souls were birthed into the kingdom of God. Later Peter was called upon to preach to the Gentile household of the Roman centurion Cornelius in Caesarea. Peter boldly presented the claims of Christ to the relatives and friends of Cornelius who were converted to Christ (Acts 10: 24-48). Additional instances of the Apostle Paul boldly proclaiming the Gospel were recorded in the book of Acts. Paul and Silas were imprisoned in Philippi, beaten, and placed in stocks. About midnight Paul and Silas were praying and singing hymns of praise to God and the Lord sent an earthquake which caused all the prison doors to open and the chains to be unfastened. Because he thought all of his prisoners had escaped, the jailer was going to commit suicide. Paul cried out to him not to harm himself because all of the prisoners still were in the jail. When the jailer fell down before Paul and Silas asked them what he needed to do in order to be saved, they boldly declared to him, "Believe in the Lord Jesus, and you will be saved, you and your household" (Acts 16:31). Paul and Silas then had the opportunity to speak the word of the Lord to the rest of the Philippian jailer's household and all of them came to faith in Christ and were baptized (Acts 16:32-33). The Apostle Paul boldly preached Christ on Mars Hill to the skeptical Athenians (Acts 17:16-34). Paul also boldly shared his personal conversion testimony before a hostile crowd in Jerusalem (Acts 22) and before King Agrippa and the entire court of Governor Festus in Caesarea (Acts 26). One of the most dramatic examples of the bold preaching of the Gospel by

Paul was in the cities of Lystra and Derbe. Paul and Barnabas preached the Gospel to the people of Lystra following a miraculous healing of a lame man. Jews from Antioch and Iconium who opposed the preaching of the Gospel traveled to Lystra and influenced the crowd to stone Paul for his preaching. The crowd then dragged him outside the city supposing that he was dead. While the disciples stood around him, Paul got up and entered the city. The very next day Paul and Barnabas traveled to Derbe. They boldly preached the Gospel there and many came to faith in Christ (Acts 14:8-23).

An illustration of boldness in a personal witnessing encounter provides a very significant and applicable example of evangelistic boldness in the book of Acts. The witnessing encounter occurred between Philip the evangelist and an Ethiopian eunuch on a desert road descending from Jerusalem to Gaza. While Philip was experiencing a successful evangelistic campaign in Samaria, an angel of the Lord told him to go south to the desert road where he encountered the Ethiopian eunuch along with his entourage who was returning to his homeland after traveling to Jerusalem on a religious pilgrimage. Philip obeyed the direction of the Holy Spirit and ran up to the eunuch's chariot. Philip heard him reading from the scroll of Isaiah and boldly asked this important official in the court of Candice, the queen of Ethiopia, if he understood what he was reading. The official indicated that he needed someone to instruct him and invited Philip to sit with him in his chariot. The eunuch had been reading a Messianic passage about the Suffering Servant from Isaiah 53. When he asked of whom the prophet was speaking, about himself or someone else, Philip very boldly preached Jesus to him beginning from that passage of Scripture. The eunuch believed in Jesus and when they came upon an oasis in the desert, Philip baptized him. (Acts 8:4-40).

My Practical Definition of Evangelistic Boldness

According to the historical and biblical background of the usage of the word *parrhēsia* or boldness, the word originally meant having the freedom to speak what needed to be said in a particular context with all truthfulness and frankness. The biblical examples of evangelistic boldness revealed that those who shared the Gospel with boldness did so by taking the initiative in any given situation and by speaking the truth with conviction and without compromise. From a grammatical understanding of the background of the word *parrhēsia* or boldness, from a study of the examples of those who publicly as well as personally shared their faith with boldness as recorded in the New Testament, and from my own experience of sharing the Gospel for many years in many different contexts along with my attempts to equip and train others to share their faith in the local church and in the seminary classroom, I developed a definition of boldness that I call the "practical, working" definition of boldness in personal evangelism. ***My definition of boldness in personal evangelism is going one step beyond your comfort level as you attempt to share your faith with another person.*** My definition calls for the witness to get outside of his or her comfort zone if necessary in order to share the Gospel fully which includes initiating a Gospel conversation, presenting the Gospel itself, and calling for response to the Gospel.[13]

All people are different. People have different personalities. Some are introverts while some are extroverts. Some are timid while some are confident. Some struggle with meeting new people while some "have never met a stranger." Some have trouble starting and carrying on a conversation while some can talk to anybody about anything at any time. Some are scared to death to share their faith with others while some cannot wait to tell somebody about Jesus! Also, people have different levels and kinds of experience in evangelism. Some never or rarely ever have shared their faith with anyone while others have shared their faith multiple times in various contexts with very many people. Some never have seen a person come to Christ through their personal witness while others have seen many souls saved through their personal witness. Some have had bad experiences sharing their faith while others have had wonderful experiences sharing their faith. However, neither a person's personality type whether an introvert or extrovert nor a person's experience in evangelism whether good or bad "gives him a pass" on personal evangelism. All believers are commanded to share their faith with others. All believers are obligated to share their faith with others. All believers need some level of boldness in order to share their faith with others.

---

[13] Simply understood, my practical definition of boldness assists a believer wanting to be a personal witness in obedience to the Great Commission. Rev. Bob Harrington, former Chaplain of Bourbon Street, taught "that boldness as a witness comes from obedience not the absence of fear." See Charles S. Kelley Jr., *Fuel the Fire: Lessons from the History of Southern Baptist Evangelism* (Nashville: B&H Academic, 2018), xi. See also Stiles, *Marks of the Messenger,* 87-89.

Here is where my definition of boldness in personal evangelism is helpful for any believer of any personality type with any level or kind of experience in personal evangelism who attempts to share his or her faith with others. For those who struggle with meeting new people, the start of boldness in evangelism for them is going one step beyond their comfort level to meet a lost person who needs to hear the Gospel. For those who have trouble starting and carrying on a conversation, boldness in evangelism for them is going one step beyond their comfort level by pushing past the reluctance to talk with lost people and by being willing to engage them in a Gospel conversation. At this point is when those attempting to share their faith with others are in real need of boldness. Many will begin a conversation but have a difficult time getting to the Gospel. The boldness needed at that time is for them to go one step beyond their comfort level by introducing spiritual matters as well as by bringing the truths of the Gospel into the conversation. If the Gospel is not shared, the exchange is not a Gospel conversation but simply a personal conversation. Boldness is necessary to begin to talk about Jesus and to share what the Bible requires for salvation in a witnessing encounter.

Although some struggle with having enough boldness to get to the Gospel in the conversation and communicating the need for repentance and faith in order for a person to come into a right relationship with God, the place where boldness is needed the most in personal evangelism is in calling for a response to the Gospel that has been shared. Many can meet a stranger, begin a Gospel conversation, and even share the truth of the Gospel and the biblical requirements for a person to be saved but then fail to call that person to respond to the Gospel message.[14] Most believers need a "boost of boldness" at this critical point to go one step beyond their comfort level to call for those with whom they have shared the Gospel to respond by repenting of their sin and placing their faith in the Lord Jesus. A certain amount of boldness is required to ask a person to call on the name of the Lord in prayer for salvation immediately at the conclusion of a presentation of the Gospel. "Drawing the net" or calling for an immediate deci-

---

[14] Greg Laurie, *Tell Someone: You Can Share the Good News* (Nashville: B&H Publishing Group, 2016), 103-07. "We tend to hate putting people on the spot, but the gospel is not really the gospel without letting people know a response is required." Stiles, *Marks of the Messenger,* 89.

sion usually causes the most fear, presents the greatest challenge, and requires the most boldness for believers sharing their faith with others.

What my students in my evangelism classes have told me is that recalling my "practical, working" definition of boldness in personal evangelism helps them to overcome their fear and to proceed forward with their witness despite their natural hesitation as they attempt to share their faith with others. They have indicated that they pray for the Lord to give them boldness and then say to themselves at the different stages of their witness, "I need to be bold and go one step beyond my comfort level and introduce myself to this lost person. I need to be bold and to go one step beyond my comfort level and begin a Gospel conversation with this person. I need to be bold and to go one step beyond my comfort level and actually share the Gospel with this person and what the Bible requires for salvation. I need to be bold and to go one step beyond my comfort level and call for this person to respond to the Gospel in repentance and faith right now and lead this person in a prayer to receive Jesus as Savior and Lord." Not every student has to tell himself or herself to go one step beyond his or her comfort level at every stage of the witnessing encounter. The definition of boldness simply assists the students to continue forward in the witnessing encounter by reminding them to be bold at each stage of their attempt to lead a person to faith in Christ.

How to Obtain Evangelistic Boldness

As mentioned previously, some believers have been reluctant to share their faith because they have observed those with a faulty understanding of boldness in evangelism whose "so called" boldness in witnessing has "turned off" lost people to the Gospel while at the same time has "turned off" the saved people watching from intentional personal evangelism. Boldness in personal evangelism does not mean being brash, overbearing, rude, or "pushy" when sharing the Gospel. ***Boldness in personal evangelism is simply going one step beyond your comfort level as a witness.*** Boldness is taking the initiative to engage someone with the Gospel, having the freedom to speak the truth of the Gospel, and inviting the person to respond to the Gospel.

As helpful and encouraging as my practical definition of boldness can be to those who desire to share their faith with others, boldness in evangelism does not come simply from knowing and reflecting on a definition of the word. Boldness in evangelism in actuality comes from the Holy Spirit of God. He is the One Who supplies a believer with boldness to share his faith with others.[15] The Bible records that the Apostle Paul requested that others pray for him that he would "make known with boldness the mystery of the Gospel" (Ephesians 6:20). The Bible also records that when the believers "prayed, the place where they had gathered together was shaken, and they were all filled with the Holy Spirit and began to speak the word of God with boldness" (Acts 4:31). These verses indicate that in order to be a bold witness for Christ a believer should pray for boldness and seek the filling of the Holy Spirit.[16] Ultimately the Holy Spirit is the only One Who can convince the mind, convict the heart, and convert the soul of a lost sinner in need of a Savior. "Without the Holy Spirit, all evangelism is powerless to win the lost."[17] Evangelism is a spiritual work that requires spiritual power that comes only from fervent prayer[18] and the filling of the Holy Spirit.[19]

In order to obtain evangelistic boldness, a believer should pray and ask for holy boldness from the Lord and the empowerment of the Holy Spirit in order that the unholy sinner can hear the Holy

---

[15] For a fuller discussion of the role that the Holy Spirit plays in evangelism, see McRaney, 27-34. See also Wm. Craig Price and Mario Melendez, "The Role of the Holy Spirit in Evangelism: Aspects of Lukan Pneumatology," in *Engage: Tools for Contemporary Evangelism*, gen. ed. Wm. Craig Price (Birmingham, AL: NOBTS Press, an imprint of Iron Stream Media, 2019), 15-32.

[16] Beougher, 14-15. See also D. Scott Hildreth and Steven A. McKinion, *Sharing Jesus without Freaking Out: Evangelism the Way You Were Born to Do It*, 2nd ed. (B&H Academic, 2020), 128. In the section on "Prayer and Evangelism," the authors admonish those who desire to be faithful witnesses to "pray for boldness," and include my practical definition of boldness in evangelism.

[17] Price and Melendez, "The Role of the Holy Spirit," 26-27.

[18] For instruction on the necessity and practice of prayer for effective evangelism, see Jeffrey C. Farmer, "The Role of Prayer in Evangelism," in *Engage: Tools for Contemporary Evangelism*, gen. ed. Wm. Craig Price (Birmingham, AL: NOBTS Press, an imprint of Iron Stream Media, 2019), 225-40. See also John Mark Terry, *Church Evangelism: Creating a Culture for Growth in Your Congregation* (Nashville: Broadman & Holman Publishers, 1997), 15-27. "Christians should pray for power to carry out the Great Commission, and they should pray for guidance as they obey that divine command." Terry, *Church Evangelism*, 26-27.

[19] See Acts 1:8. For insight concerning the filling of the Holy Spirit for effective evangelism, see Appendix C: How You Can Walk in the Spirit in Bill Bright, *Witnessing without Fear: How to Share Your Faith with Confidence* (Orlando: NewLife Publications, 2003), 207-12.

Word of God, and be convinced, convicted and converted by the Holy Spirit of God. As a result, the unholy sinner can become a holy man or woman of God, that is, a saint, through repentance and faith in Christ and enter into right relationship with the Holy God of the universe! Why not take a moment right now and ask the Lord to give you boldness to overcome the fear that holds you back from being the consistent personal witness you know that you need to be and that you really want to be? Then take at least one step beyond your comfort level and allow the Holy Spirit to use you as a bold personal witness for the eternal good of the person who hears and responds to the message of the Gospel from your lips and ultimately for the glory of God that will be exhibited through your life.

The greatest thing about evangelism is that we get to do it—you and me. Somehow the great Creator God allows us—protoplasmic specks in the universe—to partner with him in his grand design. It's a wonder and a mystery. To be healthy—really healthy—not just in evangelism, but in all of our spiritual life, is to have just a glimpse of what it means to take hold of that privilege in faith, with truth, through love, and in boldness and faithfulness to the praise of his glorious grace.[20]

Go ahead and take that one step beyond your comfort level and become a bold and courageous witness for Christ today!

---

[20] Stiles, *Marks of the Messenger*, 122.

JBTM 18.1 (Spring 2021): 119–89

Book Reviews

Hearers & Doers: A Pastor's Guide to Making Disciples through Scripture and Doctrine. By Kevin J. Vanhoozer. Bellingham,WA: Lexham, 2019. Xxviii + 259 pages. Hardcover, $19.99.

Kevin Vanhoozer is Research Professor of Systematic Theology at Trinity Evangelical Divinity School in Deerfield, IL. He is perhaps best known for his *The Drama of Doctrine: A Canonical-Linguistic Approach to Christian Theology* (Louisville, KY: Westminster, John Knox, 2005). Vanhoozer earned his PhD from Cambridge University, studying under the Roman Catholic scholar Nicholas Lash. From 1990-2019 he wrote nine books, co-authored two others, and also edited ten books. Therefore, his academic repertoire is quite extensive. This review will discuss the aim of *Hearers & Doers*, provide a chapter-by-chapter overview, and discuss several plot points of the book.

Hearers & Doers is the newest of Vanhoozer's books. In this work he appears to fill out the last two chapters of his *Drama of Doctrine* which consider the gospel, conversion, and the Great Commission. His aim for *Hearers & Doers* may best be expressed in Chapter Six, "The Company of the Gospel":

> The true end of theology, its final purpose, is not an orthodox compendium of doctrine but an orthodox community of disciples who embody the mind of Jesus Christ everywhere, to everyone, at all times. The church, says Bonhoeffer, is God's "new will and purpose for humanity." (127-28)

The reason for this book is to assist pastors in re-envisioning their congregants to see themselves as "the new humanity in Christ" (124). Pastors act as "eye doctors" helping churches to be "a city of God" as Augustine wrote, "a heavenly city marked by love of God rather than the self-love that characterizes citizens of the earthly city" (65).

Vanhoozer divided *Hearers & Doers* into two parts: "Warming Up: Why Discipleship Matters" and "Working Out: How Discipleship Happens." Each part is made up of four chapters. In Chapter One, Vanhoozer discussed the fact that all people are being discipled by someone. Therefore, it is important for the pastor to properly leverage that discipleship. He wrote, "secular culture is itself a powerful disciple-making force that pastor-theologians need to understand and, if need be, call out" (xxv-xxvi). Chapter Two focused on the need for spiritual fitness, using the analogy of our culture's infatuation with physical fitness. In Chapter Three, Vanhoozer addressed the need to be both hearers and doers of the word of God. Chapter Four addressed the purpose for this fitness exercise, that is, for Christians to be discipled as suitable citizens of the world and of the heavenly city, that is the church. Vanhoozer wrote, "Making disciples through Scripture and doctrine is a matter of following the words that lead to Christ in order to live lives worthy of our citizenship of the gospel of Jesus Christ" (69-70).

In Part Two, Vanhoozer changed gears to "explore further how to make disciples by casting a vision of what the Bible is and is for, complete with concrete proposals designed to improve the church's spiritual fitness, especially by strengthening its God-centered social imaginary" (86). Chapter Five described the Protestant Reformation as in some way "unfinished." Vanhoozer redefined *sola Scriptura* away from implying individual interpretation and towards using "the early ecumenical councils, as well as other means, like biblical commentaries, to deepen the church's understanding of the word" (97). Using the dual interpretive grid of doctrine and tradition, guided by an adept shepherd, the church will then grow into the new humanity on earth:

> "It is in this people, this holy nation, that God reigns. The church is the local embassy and living parable of the kingdom of God.... . We begin to see how the church is the new Israel, the new Jerusalem, and the temple at the center: the place where Christ dwells with humanity and heaven comes to earth." (112)

Chapter Six explains that the pastor's role is to guide the "social imaginary" of his congregation to properly "perform the gospel." "The church, says Bonhoeffer, is 'God's new will and purpose for humanity'" (128). Hence, the church is called to perform the resurrection and martyrdom as a theatrical spectacle for the world to see. According to Vanhoozer, liturgy becomes especially important in living out the gospel: "we learn to get real by living liturgically" (144). Chapter Six concludes with admonitions to live compassionately while also identifying with those, like Peter, within the church who are specifically charged to tell others about Jesus.

Chapter Seven was for this reviewer the most strategic chapter in the book. It was almost as if the author became autobiographical about how he once viewed and now views the interpretation of Scripture. In his section titled "Doctrinal Forks in the Disciple's Road," Vanhoozer described how "Interpretive pluralism provokes a crisis in discipleship" (165). In this chapter, he strongly argued against Protestant and Evangelical individualism in biblical interpretation. Rather, he reasoned for a "catholic" (whole church) interpretation. Vanhoozer explained that a catholicity in interpretation becomes a challenge to some of his students:

> "I regularly have students in my seminary classes who either have not grown up in a confessional tradition or who did but are then shocked to discover that there are other traditions, each of which may claim the mantle 'Protestant' or 'evangelical' or, simply, 'biblical'" (169).

Therefore, in Chapter Seven, Vanhoozer calls for a "consensus" reading and interpretation of the Bible:

> "The problem with thinking that individuals interpret the Bible alone—that is, by and for themselves, in isolation from the church and tradition—is not only the lack of checks and balances on their readings, but the inevitable ensuing neglect of the gifts the Spirit has provided. In particular, *sola Scriptura* denies the importance of reading in communion with the saints. We are now in a better position to see how the church catholic—by which I am thinking in particular of the consensus tradition preserved in the ancient creeds—is the context in which an individual's reading of the biblical text makes sense (thanks to the illumination of the Spirit) and exercise of its authority." (180)

> "What God has therefore joined together—canonicity and catholicity—let no one (especially Reformation Protestants or evangelicals!) put asunder." (181)

> "Tradition is our best Philip—the Spirit's provision of community to aid us in our reading. Scripture *alone* is the supreme authority, yet God in his grace decided that it is not good for Scripture to be alone. He thus authorized tradition so that, when he saw it, he said, 'This at last is norm of my norm and light of my light; she shall be called postapostolic testimony, because she was taken out of apostolic testimony.'" (181)

Hence, it appears that Vanhoozer's greatest assistance in Christian discipleship in Chapter Seven is to excise the individualistic approach to interpretation from church members—which he sees as a counterproductive byproduct of *sola Scriptura*. He posits an alternative wholistic catholicity in biblical interpretation.

Chapter Eight then approaches spiritual disciplines for making disciples and spiritual formation within the local church. The author recommends three exercises for making disciples: Exercise 1: "Take/Read; Come/See"; Exercise 2: "Take Up Your Cross"; and Exercise 3: "Practice Death (and Resurrection)." In the end, Christians will be prepared to meet the complications of life ahead of them:

> "Teaching Scripture and doctrine involves more than theory. The proper end of reading Scripture and doing theology is to help disciples mature into men and women who are ready for solid food (1 Cor 3:2; Heb 5:12-14), a long walk, and the rough and tumble of daily life." (235)

In his conclusion to *Hearers & Doers*, Vanhoozer appears to caricature individualistic interpretation by twice repeating a cultural phrase:

> "'I did it my way' is hardly a fitting thing for a disciple to sing, or say." (242)

> "*Not* 'I did it my way,' but rather, 'I did it his way, through him who strengthens me.'" (245)

By way of commendation and critique, this review will highlight several main plot points. For the pastor looking for concrete ideas to implement discipleship in his church, this is not the book to achieve that end. While it is titled, a "guide to making disciples," it appears to be more of a theoretical framework. My analysis will be limited to three areas: multiform interpretation, sufficiency of Scripture, and biblical material.

Multiform Interpretation: While the ideal of interpreting Scripture with an ecumenical catholicity from ages past is appealing, the law of non-contradiction renders that interpretive model logically impossible. With multitudinous contradictory doctrinal disagreements over the last two millennia, one is left choosing one "catholicity" over another. At best a true consensus approach becomes a lowest common denominator approach.

Sufficiency of Scripture: How can the sufficiency of Scripture be believed if certain language groups of unspecified persons are needed to provide its proper interpretive grid? In answer to a perceived vacuum of doctrinal clarity in Scripture, Vanhoozer appealed to a Eurocentric Manifest Destiny, in which various European state-churches provide a "Spirit-led" interpretive grid, called "catholic," for the rest of the world. While also falling prey to the law of non-contradiction, as noted above, this approach appears to fly in the face of Christ's own words in which it is "the few," not "the many," that are on the road to salvation (Matt 7:13-14). Further, as to a sufficient closed canon, Revelation 22:18-19 speaks directly to the dangers of adding or subtracting from the prophecies in the book. For in doing either one or the other, questions are reframed and foreign Central Interpretive Motifs can be introduced into biblical interpretation.

Biblical Material: As far as conversion, evangelism, the gospel, and the Great Commission, for this reviewer, being a lecturer on such themes, the void on these concepts was truly disheartening. Conversion-language was couched in liturgy (e.g. Baptism and the Eucharist), "doing" the gospel, and following Christ. He made clear: "Making disciples, then, involves more than converting souls" (6). Evangelizing was likewise relegated to several snippets: "The Great Commission clearly involves more than evangelism" (xx). "This exercise is all about learning to see oneself as a beam of the gospel light (truth) by identifying with those, like Peter, who are charged to tell others about Jesus, the light of the world" (160).

The gospel, briefly mentioned several times, omitted the outright committing of sin, preferring Augustine's view of sin as a negation (e.g., xxiv-xxv). As far as the Great Commission, only Matthew's commission was mentioned, and that in cursory fashion. A study of "teaching to observe" may have assisted Vanhoozer in his emphasis on disciples being "doers." But in this case, Jesus put a direct limitation on that study, that being only his own commands: "teaching them to observe all things that I have commanded you" (Matt 28:20). Thus Jesus himself did not include historical-theological studies in his prescribed plan for discipleship.

For any who have read Vanhoozer's *Drama of Doctrine* and desired greater clarity on Chapters 11 and 12 in that book, *Hearers & Doers* may prove a helpful read. For any interested in strong arguments against Protestant or Evangelical "individualistic interpretation," Chapter Seven in *Hearers & Doers* provides potent discussion, albeit one-sided. The pastor seeking to move his congregation toward increased ecumenical dialogue and political activism will find in this book an excellent theoretical basis for so doing. However, the pastor seeking biblical principles of discipleship will likely not find that for which he is looking in *Hearers & Doers*.

Thomas P. Johnston,
Midwestern Baptist Theological Seminary,
Kansas City, Missouri

God on the Brain: What Cognitive Science Does (and Does Not) Tell Us about Faith, Human Nature, and the Divine. By Bradley L. Sickler. Wheaton, IL: Crossway, 2020. 208 Pages. Paperback, $19.99.

As Charles Taylor has argued, people are living in contested spaces where there are many competing ways of viewing and being in the world that are informed by various worldviews or social imaginaries.[1] One of the most pervasive worldviews competing for people's attention is "Scientism."[2] This worldview is encapsulated in the idea that "science has displaced religion by answering questions through natural explanations, whereas religious people answer those same questions by invoking God out of ignorance" (39). It is argued that science has subtracted religious belief and spiritual superstition away from society and has paved the way for scientific objectivity. In this understanding, people of religious faith are left with having to employ "god-of-the-gaps" arguments in order to remain on land that is steadily shrinking or sinking.

The situation, Sickler argues, is far more complex than it is generally presented at the popular level and his work in *God on the Brain* is an attempt to show people that the debates between science and religion are often presented in a way that does capture the full picture of what is going on. Sickler focuses on cognitive neuroscience because of its close proximity to the subject of theological anthropology. Sickler's hope is to provide Christians with a resource to help them navigate the question of who they are when they are receiving so many, often conflicting, arguments from scientists, philosophers, and preachers.

Sickler constructs a theological anthropology centered around the axiom that "humanity is made by God the Creator in his own

---

[1] Taylor, Charles, *A Secular Age*. Harvard University Press. 2007, p. 558.

[2] Moreland, *J. P. Scientism and Secularism: Learning to Respond to a Dangerous Ideology*. Crossway, 2018, pp 25-27.

image" and the corollaries (1) that we have souls, (2) we are meant to know God, and (3) we are wired for morality. Sickler clarifies and unpacks these corollaries by emphasizing that "the soul is a basic, unified, continuing, property-bearing immaterial existent with causal powers" that cannot be reduced to something simpler because the soul is "a metaphysically fundamental entity" (19). Sickler argues that humans have a dualistic nature of both soul and body but is less clear when discussing the *relationship* between the soul and the body. From the definition above, it appears his position could be Thomistic (although Sickler never mentions Thomism). However, in other places his explanation appears more Cartesian with the body and soul being: linked but ultimately separable, distinct from and independent of one another, and with the soul taking causal primacy over the body (138-40).

Regarding the relationship between science and religion, Sickler argues that "when there are conflicts between scientific and religious communities, there is nearly always an underlying central issue: the explanation of data. The debate is not usually over what the data *are* but what they *mean*" (42). The real debate is not about facts but about how people's pretheoretical dispositions, their worldview, influences their interpretation of everything, data included because of people's background beliefs. In doing this, Sickler moves past caricatures of historical moments that people point to in reference to the so-called science versus religion argument by addressing what really went on in several famous controversies such as the debate between the Catholic Church and proponents of heliocentrism, Copernicus and Galileo.

In examining research into "religious experiences," Sickler highlights that in most of these studies the experiences people are researching are not generally what Christians view as typical religious experiences. Rather, these researches are looking at dreams and visions brought about by meditative states which are not normative experiences for Christian life. Additionally, Sickler highlights the philosophical issue with arguing that if you "can generate a model of the brain states of dreams and visions, it simply would not follow that those experiences were not of God" no more than the existence of a giraffe is explained away by mapping the brain state of a human's response to seeing or thinking about a giraffe would. (121).

Sickler also addresses how cognitive neuroscience and religion interact on the subjects of human freedom, reason and morality, and how Reformed Epistemology relates to the naturalness of religious belief. In terms of human freedom, Sickler looks as solutions to the perceived problem of God's absolute sovereignty and humanity's apparent freedom and demonstrates that, regardless of which stance cognitive neuroscientists take–mechanical determinism or libertarian freedom–" the brain sciences pose no threat to...Christianity"(159). He reaches this conclusion by arguing that compatibilism is perfectly acceptable to orthodox Christianity and has been the view of freedom by some of the traditions most important thinkers…. On the other hand, if compatibilism is flawed and fails to capture what we really mean by freedom, then libertarianism is the right framework" (159). Sickler clarifies this saying that libertarianism can only function within a theological framework if people reject materialism and "embrace some form of substance dualism to allow for real causal power and counterfactual freedom" (159).

Sickler's concluding argument that people can pick either one, compatibilism or a qualified libertarianism, does not provide assurance as to which Sickler endorses and, more pertinent, how readers should make sense of the issue at hand. Readers would benefit from Sickler standing his ground on one of the options. It seems that this vague conclusion is due in part to the loose definition or description of the soul and the body constructed at the start of the book. If Sickler were to more explicitly align his thoughts with Cartesian dualism, he may have been more able to endorse compatibilism more easily; if he had endorsed some variation of hylomorphism, then he may have been more able to wholeheartedly embraced libertarian free will from a more unified anthropology.

Overall, Sickler's treatment of the relationship between science and religion provides readers with a helpful framework that they can apply not just to cognitive neuroscience and psychology, but to other fields and systems as well. For the two chapters addressing this topic alone I would recommend this book to anyone seeking to make sense of the deluge of scientific arguments against the existence of God or of souls. Despite a few areas where Sickler could have been more direct or clear about where he stands, the book has no real glaring weaknesses that would make it an ineffectual read for anyone seeking understanding in a complex and contested society.

Alex R. Wendel is the Associate Director of the Leeke Magee Christian Counseling Center and a PhD student in Counselor Education and Supervision at the New Orleans Baptist Theological Seminary. He attends Lakeshore Community Church where he sometimes plays drums too loudly on the worship ministry team.

Beyond Authority and Submission: Women and Men in Marriage, Church, and Society. By Rachel Green Miller. Phillipsburg, NJ: P&R, 2019. 280 pages. Paperback, $17.99.

Rachel Green Miller blogs at rachelgreenmiller.com and is a member of the Orthodox Presbyterian Church. In *Beyond Authority and Submission,* Miller has two overarching goals. First, she desires to convince complementarian Christians that their views on men and women come more from the Greeks, Romans, and Victorians than from the Bible. "My goal in this book has been to give you a new or greater awareness of the unbiblical and extra-biblical beliefs that need to be peeled back" concerning men and women (258). Second, she wants these complementarians to temper their views on authority and submission in favor of a focus on unity, interdependence and service, because "the hyper-focus on authority and submission has done considerable damage to relationships between men and women in the home, in the church, and in our societies (257)." Miller no longer refers to herself as a complementarian and, in part, this book is her attempt to demonstrate shortcomings in the modern complementarian movement.

In Part 2 of her book, Miller examines four eras of history: the Greco-Roman period, the Victorian era, first-wave feminism, and later feminism. She claims that modern complementarian views are based more on the Greeks, Romans, and Victorians than the Bible, and she sees modern complementarianism as an overreaction to radical feminism. She believes, "We've inherited a mixture of good and bad beliefs—particularly about women and men. As we consider our cultural inheritance, we need to be willing to get rid of the parts of it that aren't consistent with Scripture" (257). So in Part 3, she examines four issues: the nature of women and men, women and men in marriage, women and men in the church, and women and men in society. She presents what she claims are the prevalent views of complementarians on each of these issues before offering what she sees as a more biblical perceptive.

Miller is certainly correct that we should derive our views on men and women from the Bible and not from the culture. We should also be willing to test all of our views against Scripture. But this claim leads to the first of four reasons Miller might fail to convince many complementarians: she offers little explanation of biblical passages that complementarians use to support their views. To give a few examples, she calls into question the idea that 1 Peter 3:7 teaches that "women's weakness is simply part of God's design" (109), but she offers no positive understanding of what the verse means. Miller offers very little explanation of Paul's discussion of men and women in 1 Corinthians 11:1–16. She is adamant that 1 Timothy 2:11–15 does not teach that women are more easily deceived than men (223–25), but she does not fully explain why Paul appealed to the creation order to justify what she believes is a command that women cannot be pastors. Miller argues that complementarians are getting their ideas more from history than the Bible, but presumably, the complementarians she cites believe their ideas are biblical. Consequently, she is unlikely to convince these complementarians they are wrong with such thin treatments of the key biblical passages relevant to this debate.

The second reason she is unlikely to convince many complementarians is that she has not always accurately represented the claims they make.[3] Early in the book, Miller cites a blog by Emily Jenson. According to Miller, Jenson taught that if a husband "wants his wife to get up early and make him breakfast, she should submit to his desire to do so" (27). Interestingly, Jenson never used the word submission in her article, but instead, she claimed,

> Insofar as you can manage, honor the way he likes to do things. Not because he's always right, but because God's word calls us to look out for the interests of others. Loving your neighbor and your spouse are really one in the same – both include laying down your life for the sake of another. Godly love seeks to satisfy another's preferences as strongly as they preserve their own.[4]

---

[3] Some of the authors she regularly references in her book have contended that she has not accurately represented their arguments. See for example, https://mereorthodoxy.com/book-review-beyond-authority-and-submission/.

[4] https://cbmw.org/2015/11/13/wives-honor-your-husbands-preferences/

What Jenson actually wrote sounds a lot more like unity, interdependence, and service than a hyper-focus on authority and submission.

Third, Miller offers no compelling description of the differences between men and women. She is adamantly against unbiblical stereotypes, and rightly so. She is also adamant that there are differences between men and women. She says, "It is not my intention here to flatten out the distinctions between the sexes. God created us, male and female, in His image" (147). But aside from Miller's claims that wives should submit to their husbands and that only men can be pastors, readers will be hard-pressed to find what she thinks these biblical distinctions between the sexes are. She argues, "The Scriptures give us a much greater range of feminine behavior and actions than the prevalent complementarian definition of femininity does" (136), and she opposes placing unbiblical restrictions on men or women. But because Miller is primarily reacting against the complementarian view, and because she fails to offer her view on the appropriate distinctions between men and women, readers are left without a compelling, biblical portrait of what it means to be male and female.

This leads to the fourth reason she might fail to convince many complementarians and the most concerning issue for Southern Baptists. She effectively pits two biblical concepts against each other in a way that prompts her readers to choose one and reject the other. She says, "By emphasizing unity, interdependence, and service in marriage, we can move beyond authority and submission as the lens through which we understand the relationship between husband and wife" (176). But in choosing the lens of unity, interdependence, and service, she effectively eliminates any meaningful concept of biblical submission. She writes that "a servant leader isn't so much a leader who learns to serve but a servant who learns to lead through service" (24). But if, as the Baptist Faith and Message states, "A wife is to submit herself graciously to the servant leadership of her husband,"[5] then both words matter, servant and leader. To set these two ideas in opposition is ultimately to choose one and reject the other. Miller rightly rejects abuses of authority and submission, but she has offered no explanation of what submission looks like in the context of a marriage.

---

[5] See Article XVIII of the Baptist Faith and Message, "The Family," http://www.sbc.net/bfm2000/bfm2000.asp.

In the end, it's hard to see how moving beyond authority and submission is anything other than a rejection of authority and submission.

Miller begins with the noble goal of examining all facets of life in light of Scripture to be as biblical as possible. But in the end, *Beyond Authority and Submission* fails to achieve Miller's goals because she has failed to do just that. She has failed to demonstrate from Scripture why she is right and why complementarians are wrong. Consequently, she leaves this complementarian unconvinced that she has presented a better, more biblical model.

Charles A. Ray III,
New Orleans Baptist Theological Seminary,
New Orleans, Louisiana

Stewards of Eden: What Scripture Says About the Environment and Why It Matters. By Sandra L. Richter. Downers Grove, Ill.: InterVarsity Press, 2020. ix+158 pages. Paperback. $22.00.

The biblical text gives explicit attention to the natural world. Humankind is created and placed in a garden, clearly tasked as guards and workers of the land God gave them to inhabit. The biblical narrative is replete with references to agricultural practices and animal husbandry. The prophets proclaim the words of the LORD in part by using imagery centered on the restoration of the natural world. Jesus's parables are likewise often centered on agricultural themes. For all of the focus on the natural world in the Bible, Christians in general and evangelicals Christians in particular often fail to have a uniquely biblical understanding of the relationship between humanity and the rest of creation. This dissonance between the biblical witness and Christian concern is the driving force behind Sandra Richter's recent work *Stewards of Eden*.

In *Stewards of Eden*, Richter builds upon some of the material in her work *The Epic of Eden* (InterVarsity Press, 2008) by exploring how the Bible presents a theology of environmental stewardship in both the Old and New Testaments. Her brief work challenges Christians to understand the biblical mandate for creation care and apply it to their world and lives.

Richter begins her book by discussing how the creation narrative of Genesis 1–2 provides a foundational understanding of the role of humanity (*'ādām*) in caring for the environment. Next, Richter demonstrates how the OT presents Israel as a vassal nation who has the LORD as their covenant landlord. In other words, their land is not their own, they are to care for it as obedient servants of the LORD. The next four chapters explore how Israel as a covenant nation is to apply environmental ethics in various areas of life—to domestic creatures, to wild creature, to their enemies, and to widows and orphans. The final major chapter of *Stewards of Eden* details how the NT continues the emphasis of environmental care for the people of God by promising a renewed creation. Richter closes her work with a concluding chapter and an appendix, which offers resources for Christians who wish to be more active in environmental stewardship.

Stewards of Eden is divided between biblical theology and vignettes about environmental atrocities Richter labels "case studies." Richter is not satisfied by merely arguing for a biblical view of environmental justice; she is determined to demonstrate to her readers how current environmental practices run horribly afoul of the biblical ideal. For example, in her chapter on the treatment of domestic animals, Richter follows a brief survey of OT Law and historical agriculture practices with a more detailed description of some of the more brutal practices of factory farming.

The focus on contemporary examples of environmental injustice is not accidental. Richter wants her readers to *do* something with the information in *Stewards of Eden*. To this end, she closes the book with a list of seventeen recommendations for how Christians and churches can take action on environmental issues. Richter's recommendations run from suggestions such as learning how to recycle responsibly (115) to "voting your informed conscience" (114). The clear narratives in the case studies she presents and the clarion call to action throughout the work come together to create a powerful challenge to readers.

Richter's acumen as a biblical scholar is well known and there are flashes of such scholarship in *Stewards of Eden*. She does an exceptional job showing her readers how several of the OT Laws speak directly to environmental ethics. Her discussion of how the NT continues to promote an environmental ethic is likewise impressive, especially in her discussion of Romans 8 (100–103). While Richter's exegetical work is insightful, there are times that she seems to abandon the broader biblical presentation of a topic in an effort not to distract from her vision for Christian environmental activism.

The primary shortcoming of Richter's exegesis is her one-sided discussion of how the initial mandate given to humankind at creation informs a Christian environmental ethic. Richter states that Gen 1:28 is a command for human beings to "'take possession of' (Hebrew: *kābaš*), and 'rule' (Hebrew: *rādâ*) all of the previously named habitats and inhabitants of his amazing ecosphere" (9). Richter's translation of the Hebrew word *kābaš* as "taking possession of" is unusual as the verb is typically translated as "subdue" (see CSB, ESV, NASB, NIV, NRSV). Richter's translation is even more curious due to the fact that *kābaš* typically connotes the violent conquest of land (see Num 32:22, 29; Josh 18:1; 2 Sam 8:11). Richter does not hide this information from her readers as she gives a broader discussion of the translation of *kābaš* in an endnote (119 n.4), but she never mentions how the notion of *subduing* land must also figure into a Christian ethic of environment. Richter's inattention to how God's mandate to Eden's stewards to subject the land leads to her condemning industrial agriculture in Punjab India—the result of Norman Borlaug's Nobel prize winning innovation—without consideration to how these practices could be understood as the result of the subjugation of land which has delivered three generations of image-bearers from starvation.

Despite the shortcomings of *Stewards of Eden*, the work stands as a welcome and needed challenge to Evangelical Christians to obey God's command to care for his creation. Richter understands Christian environmental action as gospel action. She closes her work with a powerful reminder "Like all fallout of Eden, the only true solution to our dilemma is the gospel—the message of transformed lives, living in alliance with God's strategic plan" (112).

Cory Barnes,
Shorter University

Authentic Human Sexuality: An Integrated Christian Approach. By Judith K. Balswick and Jack O. Balswick. Downers Grove, IL: Intervarsity Press, 2019. 304 pages. Paperback, $35.00. 3rd Edition.

Judith and Jack Balswick are both professors at Fuller Theological Seminary. They are also licensed family therapists and have written on a plethora of topics related to human sexuality, marriage, and the family. Together they have authored *The Dual-Earner*

Marriage (1995), *The Two Pay-Check Family* (1995), *A Model for Marriage* (2013), and *The Family* (2014, 4th ed.). Beyond their academic accomplishments, they have raised two children, counseled hundreds of couples, and been married for over fifty years! Each of these factors plays a role in understanding the third edition of *Authentic Human Sexuality*.

The Balswicks have divided this book into four parts. In part one, they define the foundation of human sexuality as having a "divine intention," which is to "draw us into meaningful, person-centered relationships" (3). Because of this view of sexuality, the Balswicks begin this part with an overview of Gen 1–3. From here, they discuss various sociocultural, historical, and biological factors that have shaped their understanding of sexuality. They conclude this section by stating that because all fall short of God's design, even the LGBTQ community should be allowed into the "Christian community" so that they can rest "in the fact that God is at work in those who love and desire their Lord" (85).

Part two diverges further into the nature of authentic sexuality. The Balswicks argue that each human has a "God-ordained longing for emotional connection" (89) that should lead one towards living a life of God-like "commitment, grace, empowerment, and intimacy" (101). As such, the Balswicks identify a committed monogamous relationship as "the ideal context for authentic sexuality" (161).

In part three, the Balswicks explain that any sexual contact outside of a covenant commitment is inauthentic. This sort of contact includes sexual harassment, abuse, rape, pornography, and various kinds of sexual addition. The Balswicks provide advice for dealing with these forms of inauthentic sexuality and overwhelmingly affirm that God can heal any form of sexual brokenness. In part four, the Balswicks conclude by giving some practical steps for enacting the principles laid out in the rest of the book.

In all, the Balswicks provide their readers with a plethora of helpful information. While laying the foundation for authentic sexuality, the Balswicks offer a compelling case for why someone cannot "die to oneself" unless they already have a "clear sense of self" (7). The individual desire for self-worth in American culture can be seen in the growing number of books written on this topic. As the Balswicks explain, this desire would be met if Americans would first accept God's design and then develop "significant relationships" by recognizing and accepting others (7).

One of the many ways that an individual can lose their sense of self is via the viewing of pornography. The Balswicks survey how researchers initially believed that pornography was helpful. However, further investigation has demonstrated the exact opposite (see 232–34). Pornography is "*always* dehumanizing," but this does not mean that "anything that is sexually stimulating" is pornographic (225, italics original). Thus, the Balswicks distinguish between pornography and erotica.

Erotica consists of sexually stimulating content that also points someone towards a committed covenant relationship. Such a distinction is helpful since the single Christian is often embarrassed to admit or experience sexual stimulation. Instead, as the Balswicks advise, the unmarried Christian should have a "conscious awareness of" their sexuality and should not merely repress these desires (109). Knowing that certain situations are stimulating allows for one to place proper boundaries around their actions and attitudes. More so, this allows for a single Christian to evaluate their fantasies "in light of God's intention for authentic sexuality," keeping themselves "grounded and accountable" (127). These same principles can be applied to married believers as well.

Many more examples could be discussed here. Still, this does not mean that this book is without its faults. For traditional/conservative Christians, probably one of the most important is the Balswicks' stance on homosexual Christian relationships. As the Balswicks state, "In our view, Scripture seems consistently to refer to marriage as a covenant between a man and a woman, leading us to uphold the heterosexual union as God's originally intended design for humankind.... Yet we support our gay friends and family members who choose to commit themselves to a lifelong, monogamous marital union in the belief that this is God's best for them" (84). In light of statements like this, one must remember that the Balswicks are not biblical scholars. Instead, most of the book is focused on social science research and its relationship to human sexuality (see IX). Furthermore, the Balswicks are also responding to their own life experiences as mentioned their introduction.

As such, this book cannot be recommended on its own. Coupling *Authentic Human Sexuality* with a book like *Real Questions, Real Answers about Sex* (2004) by Louis and Melissa McBurney would make for a compelling course on human sexuality. While the McBurneys' book might be lacking in some of the current social science research, it does offer a defense of the traditionalist view of sexuality. Together, these books would allow a student to be exposed to both sides of this modern debate. In the end, the Balswicks' work offers enough valuable content worthy of being discussed as we await our redeemed sexual bodies.

Ron Lindo,
New Orleans Theological Seminary,
New Orleans, Louisiana

Reenchanting Humanity: A Theology of Mankind. By Owen Strachan. Geanies House, Fearn, Ross-shire, Great Britain: Mentor, 2019. 432 pages. Hardcover, $39.99.

Owen Strachan serves as associate professor of Christian theology, director of the Center for Public Theology, and director of the residential PhD program at Midwestern Baptist Theological Seminary in Kansas City, Missouri. Central to Strachan's research interests is the topic of theological anthropology. In his latest work *Reenchanting Humanity*, Strachan provides Christians with a contemporary presentation of the doctrine of mankind.

At the forefront of his arguments lies the idea of enchantment. The average person in the Western world instinctively adopts a naturalistic worldview and sees human beings as the results of mere chance within a chaotic universe, accidental machines without purpose, design, or end. Scripture starkly contrasts this bleak perspective with its presentation of human beings as God's capstone creation, made in God's image with deeply embedded meaning and purpose. Juxtaposed to the secularism's natural man, Christians who draw truth concerning human beings from Scripture undergo the process of reenchantment, restoring the Christian's vision to glorious spiritual and theological realities that inform human experience. Strachan writes, "The Lord is not in the business of merely engaging humanity, as if he wishes to offer us a slightly better mode of existence. The Father has initiated the project of anthropological reenchantment, making us a new humanity in Christ through the power of the Spirit" (378).

Strachan's book explores nine dimensions of anthropology. He argues that Christians regain their enchanted vision of humanity by knowing what Scripture teaches concerning the ontological, hamartiological, vocational, sexual, unitive, creaturely, ethical, contingent, and teleological aspects of anthropology. The first two anthropological aspects—the ontological and hamartiological aspects—tie human nature to redemptive history. Strachan shows how the existence of God and the reality of God's spoken word allows for sound ontological knowledge concerning human nature. Reenchantment begins with image bearers receiving God's Word, which informs the composition of every human being. While recognizing humanity's divinely implanted ontology, Strachan also acknowledges how human experience is also deeply compromised by sin. God's good creation has been marred. Like Adam, every human dies judicially, spiritually, physically, and eternally (78–83). Strachan's final anthropological aspect—the teleological aspect—completes humanity's redemptive narrative as Christ's work of redemption restores the image of God within Christians.

Strachan uses this redemptive-historical approach to frame his exploration of various anthropological themes. In chapter 3, Strachan traces Scripture's teaching on vocation and work. He shows how Scripture exhorts believers to pursue "the magnification of God by every moment of our existence" (101). Since humans will spend most of their waking hours working, Christians learn to reenchant vocation and rest by submitting everything unto the glory of God (130). Next, Strachan examines biblical teaching on human sexuality in light of recent moral transformations within Western culture. This section presents a modern polemic against those defending gender transitioning and homosexual practices, giving Christians accessible language for challenging Western civilization's moral regression into ethical neopaganism. Chapter 5 evaluates the phenomenon of races and cultures within humanity. Reflecting upon God's goal of uniting people from every nation into a new humanity, Christians engage in racial reconciliation within the context of the local church as a sociological application of the Gospel.

Christians should consider Strachan's arguments in chapter 6 as he evaluates the role of technology within society. Furthermore, Christians must understand the implications of posthumanism and transhumanism since both philosophies test the boundaries between human beings and the rest of creation (271–81). While the former desires to subsume humanity's uniqueness within creation, the latter seeks to overcome mortality and bodily limitations through technology. Next, Strachan engages contemporary debates over justice, situating Christian justice within the context of Calvary and divine justice for sin. In chapter 8, he explores Scripture's teaching on death and contingency, reminding Christians of the inevitability of death and the hope of the bodily resurrection.

For the work of a systematician, this volume's prose is quite accessible to the average reader. Strachan skillfully utilizes weighty theological and philosophical ideas to present a robust biblical anthropology for modern readers. Yet, he interweaves theological analysis with literary anecdotes, newspaper clippings, and current events. At times, his language is overly poetic, such as when he comments upon the secular worldview by saying, "Because of our godless origin, we have no greater body of ethics, no summons to a certain code of conduct. We are here; we die; we dissolve into nothingness. Nothingness is whence we came; nothingness is whither we go" (9–10). He is not afraid to use first and second-person pronouns and verb forms. While many readers will appreciate the readability of this volume, others will find this volume's prose distracting or improper, especially when compared to other single-volume treatments of theological loci, such as Crossway's *Foundations for Evangelical Theology* series.

Many times throughout church history, theological controversy presented Christians with opportunities to deepen their understanding of Scripture's teaching on contested subjects and to sharpen their doctrinal systems. No subject stands as contested today as the study of humanity. Secular thinkers are revolutionizing the modern conscience's understanding of human nature, morality, sexuality, work, technology, and death. The troubled spirits of many Christians will find peace in seeing theologians like Owen Strachan confronting these modern challenges with robust application of theological truths to complex contemporary issues. *Reenchanting Humanity* stands as an example of biblical fidelity and courage, encouraging Christians to continue the work of reenchanting the human spirit in the years to come.

Jared Poulton,
The Southern Baptist Theological Seminary,
Louisville, Kentucky

God has Chosen: The Doctrine of Election through Christian History. By Mark R. Lindsay. Downers Grove: IVP Academic, 2020. 235 Pages. Softcover, $22.49.

Mark Lindsay is Professor of Historical Theology at Trinity College Theological School at the University of Divinity in Melbourne, Australia. He is an historical theologian, professor, and Anglican priest with research interests and expertise in the historical development and intersection of ecclesiology and election, eschatology, the Holocaust, and the theology of Karl Barth. As a Barthian scholar, Lindsay has written several books and articles and in this new book offers a unique approach to election history that diverges from the often-bifurcated discussions on the subject in Baptist circles. Lindsay does not have a dog in that fight.

The author admits right away that this book is not in any way a comprehensive treatment, or a genealogy of the doctrine, but instead, offers a few "snapshots-in-time" of ways in which notable theologs framed election from Scripture, tradition, and their own unique context. He shows points of similarity and sometimes radical departure from the norm. Lindsay begins by briefly surveying a handful of key OT and NT texts that have shaped election thought. Chapter two begins with election in the Patristic period from the Apostolic fathers to Augustine, stopping along the way to give snapshots from Irenaeus, Origen, and Cyprian. The focus is on the relationship of election to the developing ecclesiology of these early Christians.

Chapter three covers the Middle Ages and concerns two men with two very different ideas of election: Thomas Aquinas and Duns Scotus. The Dark Ages, aptly named, sees a complete blurring of the distinction between church and state. Election finds its home in the visible established church/state, with Jews and Muslims playing the role of the reprobates. In chapter four, the violent rending of the established church wrought by the Reformation and Post-Reformation feuds is surveyed through the agitators of the period: Luther, Calvin, Arminius, and their theological offspring. Election and the nature of justification come into laser focus. Chapter five jumps to the nineteenth century with the radically divergent election of Friedrich Schleiermacher with his refusal to accept the established *order of decrees* framework. Next, he moves interestingly to John Nelson Darby. Darby usually comes up in arguments over Dispensational and Covenant theologies but rarely when discussing election. His sharp distinction between the election of Israel and the election of the church is highlighted.

Chapter six consists entirely of Karl Barth's reconsideration of election. Barth sees Christ as the electing God and the elected man. Barth brings a Christocentric and corporate view of election back to the forefront of election thought. Barth sees all men as elected in Christ, and men need only to realize their election. Many contend that this view leads to universalist sympathies, which Barth seems neither to deny nor affirm clearly.

Though unintentional perhaps, Barth's theology flew in the face of Nazism which leads to the interesting last chapter of the book. Chapter seven turns to another interest of Lindsay, namely the idea of the "chosenness" of the Jewish people in view of the Holocaust. Christian views of the role of Israel as the chosen of God takes many forms throughout history, most are unfavorable. He turns the discussion to show how Jewish scholars understood their election over time. He then shifts the focus back on Christianity, showing the Catholic Church's official change of heart regarding the Jewish people that had long been a schizophrenic message of love for the world while harboring a robust anti-Semitism. The regathering of Israel and the shock of the Holocaust forces the world to reassess the role of the Jewish People in God's economy. Lindsay concludes the book by encouraging readers to resist their urge to form tribal groups and refuse to see election as a bifurcation of who is in and who is out, elect and reprobate. Instead, Christians should humbly recognize that they cannot fully know the mind of God regarding the vexing concept of election; they have come to the edge of that knowability.

There is value in Lindsay's brief survey of election. First, he offers a perspective from outside conservative, evangelical, or Baptist circles. His views stem from a true Barthian vision of election that is foreign to most conservatives. While the Neo-Orthodox Barth is sometimes vilified, often deservedly so, he brings a Christ-Centered and corporate view of election back to the forefront of modern theology, despite the strange directions he takes the doctrine. Lindsay steers the discussion of the history of election through the lane of the views of Barth. Hence, he is concerned with how those of that past viewed election christologically and ecclesiologically. It is in some ways a refreshing approach as the author avoids the usual vitriol that comes from election discussions.

While there is benefit in the book for those interested in election, some criticisms are worthy of note. First, while Lindsay offers a fresh perspective, his approach is restrictive and myopic. He only approaches issues of election through his lenses of preunderstanding, which he admits. This is done to the neglect of some of the major issues in the history of theology. He speaks of Augustine's elective views as they relate to the visible church, while avoiding the monumental paradigm shift from the views of the Patristics to a deterministic individual election launched by Augustine. This shift abruptly changed the course of Christian theology, as did many Augustinian concoctions. Second, Lindsay continues through the Reformation giving less space to Calvin, Luther, and Arminius, than he did later with Karl Barth who has his own chapter. The book is saturated with Barth whom the author references in almost every chapter. He ends the book by challenging readers to shake off traditional dogma, and view election as only positive and (actually, not potentially) inclusive of all people, following suit with Barth that all people are elect and only need to realize it. This view of election lends itself to inclusivism and universalism and will be unpalatable to conservative readers. Finally, the chapter on the Holocaust seems somewhat out of place in a historical theology book.

Mark Lindsay offers fresh perspectives on election in Christian History through the eyes of a Neo-Orthodox Barthian theologian and Anglican priest. Notwithstanding, those who are interested in historical theology, or in gaining insight into how the past informs the present conflict on election and adjacent issues among conservatives and Baptists, are encouraged to look elsewhere.

Sean Burleson
Louisiana Baptist University and Seminary,
Shreveport, Louisiana

Ecclesiastes, Song of Songs. By George Athas. Grand Rapids, MI: Zondervan, 2020. 400 pages. Hardcover, $39.99.

This commentary is a part of a series known as *The Story of God Bible Commentary*. This series seeks to interpret the Old Testament "in light of the death and resurrection of Jesus" (15). As such, each commentator examines Old Testament passages according to three main "angles" (15). First, the text of the pericope will be displayed for the reader. This section—entitled "Listen to the Story"—is mostly a reproduction of the NIV translation with a few quick comments about how this passage relates to other texts and ancient ideas. Second, the commentator provides an exegesis of the passage in a section entitled Explain the Story. Third, the task of the final section, entitled Live the Story, is to present readers with a way that they *could* preach Christ from the passage being examined. In all, the editors hope that each commentary in this series "will encourage clergy to preach from the Old Testament and laypeople to study this wonderful, yet often strange, portion of God's Word" (16). In light of this objective, George Athas has authored *Ecclesiastes, Song of Songs.*

Athas is the Director of Postgraduate Studies at Moore College in Sydney, Australia. He is also a visiting professor for George Whitefield College in Cape Town, South Africa. Athas has written several books on the nature of Biblical Hebrew and is a co-editor of *Biblia Hebraica Stuttgartensia: A Reader's Edition* (2014). Lastly, it is worth noting that Athas is also an ordained deacon in the Anglican Church.

Athas begins by noting that both Ecclesiastes and the Song are among the most "unusual and controversial books of the entire Bible" (19) and are "likely to raise eyebrows" (249). Even a simple survey of the history of interpretation demonstrates the variety of explanations given to each. Ecclesiastes has been interpreted as representing "traditional biblical wisdom" on the one hand, and as "a radically unorthodox manifesto" on the other (35). Similarly, the Song has been interpreted through a plethora of allegorical lens as well as "overtly erotic" literature (260). As such, scholars interpreting these books have often presented readers with contrastive viewpoints.

According to Athas, at least one reason for this situation is a lack of awareness of each book's historical and cultural milieu. As Athas states, "Knowing the [historical] context… saves us from needing to perform acrobatic exegesis" (34). Generally, evangelicals have utilized historical information as only a fraction of their overall hermeneutical method. At least one common method of interpretation found in the evangelical tradition revolves around three main factors: 1) the plain meaning of the pericope, 2) the theological contribution of the passage in light of other scriptures, and 3) the author's historical context as best can be recovered. In other words, the level of authority moves from the text to a theological tradition and finally to historical circumstances as can be speculatively reconstructed from internal and external data.

However, Athas's hermeneutical method flips this authority upside down. For him, the highest authority is found in the historical circumstances, then the text, and lastly, one *might* consider a theological tradition. Athas argues for this hermeneutical perspective because each biblical writer "was not writing into the ether but was impacted by his specific historical context" (35). For Athas, he is confident that the writer of Ecclesiastes was a descendent of David living during the "reign of Ptolemy III Euergetes" (28) and that the author of the Song lived during the "Antiochene persecution and the subsequent Maccabean Revolt" (252). This dating designation conveniently places the providence of both books within the 3rd to 2nd century B.C.

Athas will probably explain more of his hermeneutical method, in his forthcoming book entitled *Bridging the Testaments* scheduled to be published by Zondervan. Still, at this moment, his interpretive approach has more problems than solutions. Only one example of the limitations of this hermeneutical method will be provided here.

In Eccl 11:9, the author warns a young man that "God will bring" him "into judgment" for the actions he performs. Athas argues that this verse should be translated as "God *might* bring…into judgment" the youth's actions. The only evidence Athas provides for this translation is that Qohelet probably did not believe in a future judgment (211) and that the *yiqtol* form of the Hebrew verb sometimes has a modal sense (212). However, the phrase used in Eccl 11:9 (*ki…yebiaka*) is also found in Exod 13:5, Deut 6:10, 7:1, and 11:29. None of these verses suggests that God *might* bring the Israelites into the promised land but that He *will* do it! As such, Athas is only arguing that this phrase cannot mean this in Eccl 11:9 simply because he is convinced that Qohelet's theology must be different from the theology found elsewhere in the Hebrew Bible (see 35–36). While this is an intriguing thought, it requires more evidence to be persuasive.

As a final note, I would like to return to the following statement within this series introduction: "Authors are given the freedom to explain the text as they read it, though you will not be surprised to find occasional listings of other options for reading the text" (15). Given that the editors have taken such a stance, one should not expect each commentary to provide the reader with a consistent theological position. In other words, this statement allows for some commentaries within this series to be "orthodox," while others may not be.

Therefore, within this series, readers might find themselves encountering several different hermeneutical perspectives as they move from one commentary to the next. This situation will create a scenario where Southern Baptists will find some commentaries to be more helpful than others. As such, even though I would not recommend this commentary, I would recommend reading reviews of each commentary within this series before deciding whether to purchase any of them.

Ron Lindo,
New Orleans Theological Seminary,
New Orleans, Louisiana

Paul's Idea of Community: Spirit and Culture in Early House Churches, Third Edition, Robert J. Banks, Grand Rapids, MI: Baker Academic, 2020 (ISBN 9781540961754), xvii +222 pp., Pb $26.99

Robert J. Banks is a native of Sydney, Australia. He was educated at Moore Theological College, King's College at the University of London, and Clare College Cambridge University. He holds a Ph.D. in New Testament. Banks has taught all over the world in different evangelical institutions.

The third edition of *Paul's Idea of Community* represents a "thoroughly revised and updated version of the original edition that appeared forty years ago" (vii). By Banks' own admission, "This is not a technical book, nor a popular one either" (xi). Banks wrote, "I have written this for those who find themselves caught in the middle—seeking a comprehensive account of what Paul said, yet in terms they can understand" (xi). Even so, Banks' work is "based on a thorough investigation of the relevant primary and secondary sources, and suggests a number of new interpretations of the material involved" (xii). For eighteen chapters and two appendices, Banks wrote with clarity and concision.

Banks began by covering issues related to the "sociocultural and religious settings" in which the apostle Paul wrote for his churches. In chapter 2, Banks attempted to define Paul's gospel of freedom, which "consists of three main components: independence, dependence, and interdependence" (23). Whether or not one agrees with Banks' idea of the gospel as being centered on "freedom," his proposed components are thoroughly orthodox and evangelical. With chapters 3 and 4, Banks addressed what one could call "the space" inhabited by the church. Chapter 3 dealt with the presence of church meetings in "family business residences." Chapter 4 considered how the church is simultaneously a present, heavenly reality, and a locally organized entity.

In chapters 5 and 6, Banks looked at some of the more familiar images that Paul used to describe the Christian community, focusing on household and body imagery. In chapter 7, Paul's aim for his communities is discussed with Banks explaining the community's role in forming each member's maturity. Banks continues in chapter 8 with how the sacraments and liturgy worked in the church's context to build it up according to the aim of maturity. Chapters 9 and 10 flow out of this discussion, considering how the Spirit's gifts also functioned in a compatible manner with Paul's vision of his communities.

In chapters eleven through fifteen, Banks addressed the people in Paul's communities. Banks noted that "Paul's thinking does not begin with differences that separate people from one another but with those that divide all people from God. He describes the Christian community as uniting all who acknowledge they believe in and live by the gospel, irrespective of nationality, social position, and gender" (96). Among the many commendable aspects of Banks' work, these chapters represent some of the most helpful and most challenging perspectives on Paul's view of the Christian community. On diversity in the church, I find that Banks' work is not only right but sorely need in our day and age. As for Banks' perspective on the role of women in the church's preaching ministry, I find his argument plausible, even if I do not find it compelling.

As Banks addressed the question of the role of women in Paul's communities, he rightly noted that Paul permitted one of the highest roles (public prayer and prophecy) to women, while explaining that he viewed the instructions in 1 Corinthians 14 that "commanded women to keep silent" as primarily in "reference to a particular situation." For the person who asks, "What about 1 Timothy 2?", Banks, while acknowledging the benefit and canonical status of the pastoral epistles, is skeptical of the works being written by the apostle Paul, referring to the "drift of the pastoral epistles." While I find this reasoning troubling, it is not out of sorts with many other Pauline scholars. For Banks, as with others, his issue is not merely with the question of women in church leadership, but rather, the more formalized nature of the church's structure in the pastoral epistles. Interestingly enough, this question has not simply been a matter of academic inquiry, but also personal ministry. Banks himself resigned from his post in the

Anglican Church, at least partly on the grounds of the church's distinction between the clergy and the laity.[6]

With chapters sixteen through eighteen, Banks closed by looking at the relationship of the mission of Christ with the church of Christ and the work of the apostle Paul. These chapters bring the volume to a fitting conclusion. The appendices address the question of the pastorals (as mentioned above) and provide a creative narrative exegesis of "going to church in the first century."

In conclusion, while Banks readily admitted that his work was neither a scholarly work nor a popular work, I would commend the book as a helpful bridge between the two worlds of the academy and the laity. Whether or not one agrees with Banks' reconstructions of Paul's idea of community is not the debate. Instead, Banks provides a plausible and thoroughly documented account of the similarities and differences between Paul's view of the Christian community and those within his cultural surroundings. For those looking for a work that summarily addresses Paul's view of community without getting bogged down in the details of secondary debates, I highly recommend Banks' book. For those looking to become familiar with the various opinions regarding Paul's view of community, I would recommend they either look elsewhere or supplement Banks' work with a more critical assessment.

Casey Hough,
Luther Rice College & Seminary,
Lithonia, Georgia

Cultural Engagement: A Crash Course in Contemporary Issues. By Joshua D. Chatraw and Karen Swallow Prior Chatraw. Grand Rapids, MI: Zondervan Academic, 2019. 368 pages. Hardcover, $29.99.

Joshua D. Chatraw and Karen Swallow Prior, a theologian and an English professor, respectively (13), offer an incredibly helpful resource in their book *Cultural Engagement: A Crash Course in Contemporary Issues.* In this book, they not only address several important cultural issues currently facing Christians; they also introduce readers to a variety of perspectives on those topics by col-

---

[6] For those interested in more details about the life and ministry of Robert Banks, see *The Bible and the Business of Life: Essays in Honour of Robert J. Banks' Sixty-Fifth Birthday*, ATF Press, 2004.

lecting essays from proponents of varying positions. *Cultural Engagement*, then, serves as a good starting point and overview of many present concerns.

Chatraw and Prior recognize the daunting task set before anyone wishing to understand better cultural issues, a task that is daunting both in scope and in volume due to the large number of issues to consider and resources to consult. Their aim for their book, in their own words, is "to provide a panoramic view of the forest of Christian responses to the most pressing issues," a "crash course" as they call it (15). In so doing, they hope to equip Christians to engage issues faithfully and thoughtfully.

The authors divide their work into three parts. In part one, they introduce and clarify the work of cultural engagement, focusing on culture, Christian history, and virtue. In part two, they provide brief introductions to nine topics: sexuality; gender roles; human life and reproductive technology; immigration and race; creation and creature care; politics; work; arts; and war, weapons, and capital punishment. In each chapter, they include short essays from a diverse body of contributors, showing the variety of positions professing Christians hold on each issue. In part three, Chatraw and Prior offer a look at how the gospel affects Christian cultural engagement before Andy Crouch considers healthy and unhealthy postures toward culture.

What is culture, and what does culture do? Chatraw and Prior address these questions in chapter one, clarifying that culture encompasses beliefs, assumptions, and practices while also communicating meaning, shaping sensibilities, and replicating itself (21–31). The authors next consider the ways Christians have sought to understand their relationships with the cultures in which they live, highlighting the nuance necessary for engaging complex cultural issues as well as the needed influence of the gospel for healthy cultural engagement (32–52). The authors then argue for the importance of virtue in cultural engagement, highlighting diligence, humility, integrity, and wisdom (53–60). They conclude, "Ultimately, engaging in culture is nothing more—and nothing less—than seeking the truth in order to love with a godly love" (60).

After doing the foundational work of the first three chapters, Chatraw and Prior transition to part two, in which the nine cultural issues are addressed from multiple perspectives. In their introductory notes on each chapter, the authors discuss the importance and relevance of each subject, drawing on Scripture, history, and other relevant sources to set the stage for the following essays. They then allow each contributing author to speak for himself or herself. The essays, then, range from personal testimonies to data-filled studies, from biblical studies to historical examples. As essays address complex subjects such as racism, immigration, sexuality, reproductive technology, politics, pacifism, and the role of art in the world, each contributing author brings a fresh perspective to the discussion at hand, adding to the value of the book as a whole.

Though such an approach often results in contradictory positions appearing next to one another, Chatraw and Prior see such juxtaposition as a benefit. "By placing these different pieces side by side," they write, "we are not implying they are all equally true or valid" (16). Rather, "The competing views in this book are important to be observed together for the simple reason that they are part of the panoramic landscape of the church's engagement with today's world. And learning to become good listeners (and readers!) Is one of the first steps in engaging culture with grace and truth" (16). Readers are challenged, then, to consider all positions carefully, evaluating them in light of one another and, ultimately, in light of the Bible and theology. Readers should not expect to agree with every contributor but should be willing to listen well to engage the issue at hand more faithfully. Chatraw and Prior provide discussion questions at the close of each chapter in part two to facilitate such critical thought.

One major benefit of this book is its scope. Readers will likely approach this book with a familiarity of some topics and ignorance of others. Because each topic is addressed by multiple authors from varying positions, however, readers will likely encounter fresh perspectives on issues with which they are already familiar, equipping them for deeper engagement. The multiple contributor approach also provides readers helpful introductions to issues they have not yet engaged. Thus, this book will likely offer something new to every reader.

The aim of this work is not to tell readers what to think but rather to teach readers how to think. The use of discussion questions at the end of each chapter in part two serves this aim well, challenging readers to wrestle with the tensions present among the differing positions. The essays are short and are easily accessible, written for "nonspecialists and designed to allow readers to see the contours of the big picture, before diving into more detail through independent or collaborative studies" (16). Readers of *Cultural Engagement* who desire further study in a specific area should be able to move fairly easily into the wider body of literature by looking up the contributing authors and their sources. This book is thus a valuable resource for thoughtful study.

Joe Waller,
New Orleans Baptist Theological Seminary,
New Orleans, Louisiana

Who Is the Holy Spirit? Biblical Insights into His Divine Person. By Malcolm B. Yarnell III. Nashville, TN: B&H Academic, 2019. 137 pages. Hardcover. $ 19.99.

Malcolm Yarnell currently serves as Research Professor of systematic theology at Southwestern Baptist Theological Seminary. He earned his Ph.D. at Oxford University. He has written, co-authored, and edited numerous books and articles. He was invited to contribute this volume on pneumatology to the "Hobbs College Library," edited by Heath Thomas, now President of Oklahoma Baptist University. This series of books is named for Herschel Hobbs, legendary pastor-theologian of the mid-twentieth century and namesake for OBU's Hobbs College of Theology and Ministry. Yarnell mentions his personal relation to Hobbs in the Preface (xviii).

Yarnell states his purpose in writing this book in several ways. He describes the book as an example of biblical theology or theological interpretation of the Bible (xvi). Having noticed a tendency of previous books on the Holy Spirit to focus on the work or activities of the Holy Spirit, he writes to accent the nature, person, and identity of the third person of the Trinity. Although Yarnell has often written scholarly books, his intended audience here includes preachers, teachers, and "the average Christian in the pew" (3). His ultimate purpose, however, is to encourage worship, not satisfy intellectual curiosity (3).

Given the aims of this work, Yarnell discusses key biblical texts that highlight the person of the Holy Spirit. At times he points to historic and contemporary debates, but his primary focus is biblical interpretation. He occasionally directs the reader to his more academic work for more details. These include his chapter on "The Doctrine of the Holy Spirit: The Person and Work of the

Holy Spirit" in *A Theology for the Church*, edited by Daniel L. Akin, and his *God the Trinity: Biblical Portraits*.

After a brief Introduction, Yarnell devotes three chapters to Old Testament perspectives. Chapter 1 focuses on insights from the Book of Genesis, especially chapter one. This chapter, as well as the others, includes a clear outline, often with alliterative points. Here, for instance, he notes how God's Spirit is mysterious, the mover, and mighty (6). He includes helpful cross-references to other texts and explains Hebrew terms and word pictures.

Chapter 2 deals with the nature of the Spirit in the stories of Saul and David in 1 Samuel 10-19. Reviewing a larger block of historical material, he treats the period of the judges briefly and the emergence of monarchy in Hebrew history. He stresses the deity of the Spirit. He notes there is a clear dialectical relation between Spirit and God in these narratives (31).

Psalm 51 is the focus of Chapter 3. This psalm is one of only three texts in the Old Testament that actually refers to the "Holy Spirit" in most English translations. Although the psalm is primarily David's confession of his sin of adultery, Yarnell highlights the nature of the Holy Spirit as well.

Yarnell then dedicates three chapters to the New Testament, again focusing key texts. Chapter 4 treats the Gospel of Matthew. One of Yarnell's key points again is the deity of the Spirit. He also notes the emergence of an explicitly trinitarian conception of God (71-75).

Chapter 5 moves to the Gospel of John, which includes Jesus' significant teaching on the Spirit as Paraclete. Although Yarnell's primary focus is biblical teaching, he briefly notes the debate in Christian history over John 15:26 and the procession of the Spirit. The *filioque* debate contributed to the split between the Eastern and Western branches of the church (87-88). Yarnell's chapter summary includes *"The personal nature of God the Holy Spirit means that he is concerned with you, not merely from the frightening perspective of the transcendent otherness, but from the comforting perspective of his intimate nearness"* (95).

Out of the wealth of material in Paul's letters, Yarnell dedicates Chapter 6 to a study of Romans 8. He briefly discusses the Spirit's relation to life, adoption, and intercession.

Yarnell's "Conclusion" includes brief discussions of what we cannot know or say about the Spirit ("negative theology") and what we can affirm about the Spirit ("positive theology"). His final exhortation to the reader concerns worship.

Yarnell's study is concise but not at all oversimplified. His inclusion of key Old Testament texts reminds us that God's eternal Spirit is present and acknowledged throughout the Bible. His work is readable and accessible. He includes sound exegetical insights, informative word studies, and acknowledgement of exegetical controversies. The book concludes with a short list of suggested resources and indexes of names, subjects, and the Bible citations. In the mid-twentieth century, many scholars described the Holy Spirit as the "Cinderella" of Christian theology, meaning he was the neglected member of the Trinity. Yarnell and others have contributed to a healthy recovery of pneumatology to Christian thought and life.

Overall, this book would be a valuable resource for many readers of this journal. Students, church lay leaders, and church staff members could benefit in different ways. Pastors and Bible study leaders, for instance, could find suggestions here for a sermon series or small group discussions. Yarnell often addresses the reader directly, noting the relevance of pneumatology to the believer's personal life.

Warren McWilliams,
Senior Professor of Theology,
Oklahoma Baptist University (retired)

Joshua. By Lissa M. Wray Beal. The Story of God Bible Commentary. Grand Rapids: Zondervan, 2019, 640 pages, $49.99

Joshua is a recent installment of The Story of God Bible Commentary series. The series preface identifies its target audience as "clergy and laypeople" (13). The series approaches the text by dividing the analysis of each passage into three sections: listen to the story, explain the story, and live the story. The sections guide the reader through analysis of the text to application for the contemporary Christian life. The commentary does not neglect the historical context of the Ancient Near East (ANE) in its analysis but the ultimate goal is for the readers to understand the text and also live or teach the application (15). Wray Beal identifies her reading as a "churchly reading" (20). This type of reading engages the history the of the church's creeds and affirmations that look to the story of Christ. Therefore, the reading "engages Joshua to ask how it prepares for Christ and informs the Church." (20) Wray Beal's commentary follows the overall series pattern and does not shy away from the more controversial passage of Joshua.

One of the more well known issues with the text of Joshua is the entrance into and seizing of the promised land by military force under the command of God. Wray Beal acknowledges that the text is a narrative told in theological historiography. Therefore, the text does not match the modern expectations of historical writing which presents the facts in a chronological order. There is also the influence of ANE hyperbolic language in the total destruction and defeat of the Canaanites (26-9). This type of hyperbolic language reveals the power of the victorious deity and also alleviates some of the tension with the reality that the book acknowledges multiple people who are left and lands yet to be controlled by Israel (30). The ANE comparative texts reveal similar language and results in other nations (130-32). The author additionally takes the stance that *herem* in Joshua, is focused on cities rather than the entire land (38). The author's approach to this conflict is not new but does show a helpful way for her audience to understand the implications and move forward to a modern context without supporting poor colonial applications of Joshua that have occurred throughout history (43-5, 141-44). Therefore, God showed himself as the one true and powerful God who owned the land. He removed a sinful people and established a people based on covenant relationship, not ethnicity. Thus, the modern church or nations cannot claim to be God's people in the way he commanded Israel with Rahab as an early example (44-5).

The churchly reading employed by Wray Beal could at times seem uncomfortable to those clergy trained strictly in the historical-grammatical approach of interpretation, However, it is helpful and often enlightening to integrate historical interpretations and practices with the evaluation of Old Testament texts. One example from the book is the comparison of the parceling of the land in Joshua 21 that reveals an incomplete occupation of the entire promised land. The application portion includes a connection to the concept of God's kingdom being both here and now, but also not yet. Further the concept is connected to the practice of celebrating Advent in the church liturgical calendar (371-72). The incorporation of regular Christian practices with realities of the Israelites can be engaging for many who rarely teach or preach from the Old Testament.

A major strength of Wray Beal's work is consistent writing that fits her audience. The target of audience of the series is clergy and lay persons in the church. While many lay people would be stretched by the commentary, clergy and more studied lay persons would find the text readable and helpful. She includes the ANE contextual issues, along with other church historical readings in a manner that is both explanatory and helpful at the level of educated readers. The majority would not find her explanations to dense to grasp nor off subject. One example is the inheritance of the three daughters in Joshua 17. Wray Beal acknowledges the know practices of women inheriting land both within the Old Testament text and the larger ANE culture. The section is two paragraphs and gives a clear explanation of the regular use of such inheritance. The reader will find this helpful but not overly wordy (317-18). Therefore, the consistent writing style fits the goals and audience of the commentary series.

Wray Beal's contribution of *Joshua* to The Story of God Bible Commentary Series is a useful addition to a pastor's library. The text addresses Joshua both comprehensibly and at an appropriately level for use by clergy. Controversial texts are addressed but with an eye to application and teaching rather than just academic debate. However, she does include adequate references for those who desire to dig further into the debated issues. Her "churchly reading" truly falls in line with the desire to aid clergy in interpreting Joshua. The work should encourage clergy to properly preach and interpret the book of Joshua in their ministry contexts.

Ben Hutchison,
Colorado Christian University,
Lakewood, Colorado

Faith Wins: Overcoming a Crisis of Doubt By Adam Groza. Birmingham, AL: New Hope Publishers, $15.99. 2020. 175 pages. Paperback, $15.99

Readers familiar with popular evangelical publishing may recall Rob Bell's *Love Wins: A Book about Heaven, Hell, and the Fate of Every Person Who Ever Lived* (2011), in which the Emergent Church paragon-turned New Age guru, made a 21st century case for universal salvation. By casting aspersions on the traditional understanding of hell as eternal torment, Bell's work provocatively employed doubt as a catalyst away from orthodox Christianity.

In *Faith Wins: Overcoming a Crisis of Belief,* Adam Groza, professor of philosophy of religion at Gateway Seminary of the Southern Baptist Convention argues that the existence of doubt in the Christian life can be leveraged towards, rather than against, faith. Drawing on the metaphor of a hiking trail as a symbol of existential decision, Groza writes, "You can either go back in the direction you came from or go forward in the direction you intended to go" (10).

Groza defines a crisis of faith as "a time of spiritual doubt, anxiety or despair," and further qualifies: "In such a time, doubt *exceeds* (author's emphasis) faith" (11). *Faith Wins* is a book that seeks to strengthen the professing believer's existing faith, which the author likens to a "dimming switch." Thus, its primary focus is sanctification. The book divides into eight chapters, seven of which employ a biblical character as an object lesson for faith and doubt. Groza's conversational style, interspersed with an array of philosophical, literary, and cultural references, quotations and personal anecdotes, make the reader feel they are listening to discrete sermons on a single subject. This appears intentional, for Groza is, in fact, speaking to the person in the pew.

Paradox is a recurring theme in *Faith Wins*. Groza cites the work of G. K. Chesterton, the early twentieth-century journalist, author, and lay apologist, who was coined "the prince of paradox." For example, Groza notes that the Bible itself is the "source" as well as the "solution" of doubt (33), and while it is true that, "…God preserves the Bible," Christians can forget that the Bible, in fact, "preserves us" (88). A memorable remark from the final chapter reads, "In one sense, it is hard to keep believing when you are suffering. In another sense, it is harder to stop believing" (168).

Like a sermon series, themes and applications emerge and recur throughout. In chapter four, "Peter: To whom Else Shall We Go?" Groza distinguishes three kinds of doubt, "experiential, intellectual, and emotional," (72) thereby navigating a troubled Christian in the confusing inner maze of uncertainty where all three "can be separate and… unique but can overlap, merge, and combine" (73). At various junctures Groza offers rational guidance in the vein of Blaise Pascal. Citing Peter's words in John 6:68 "Lord to whom shall we go?" the author challenges his readers to "consider the alternatives," to the Christian faith (79–80) which are, of course, far from appealing.

Faith Wins wisely accounts for the communal dimension of an individual's spiritual struggles. Overcoming doubts is not a task for the solitary and Groza advises intimate participation in the local church (61, 96, 137, 147, 155). On the individual level, self-deception is at work in doubt. "'I don't know if I believe,'" can in fact mean, 'I don't know if I want to obey'" (147). In chapter seven, the author considers occasions when reason threatens to supplant revelation by noting that a crisis of faith is frequently experienced "at the crossroads of trust and demand" (134–35). The very act of choosing is spiritual warfare (142).

While admission of paradox implies explanatory limitations, *Faith Wins* does appear to equivocate on the nature of doubt in some places. For example, Groza suggests that "doubt is faith looking for answers," (42) an apparent positive judgment. Fifteen pages later, however, we read, "the point is not that we should doubt, but that we should believe" (57). If doubt coexists with faith by nature, defining their relationship would bring helpful clarity. In chapter eight, Groza does explain that doubt has "instrumental" though not "intrinsic goodness" (165). Distinguishing between intrinsic and instrumental goodness may have fit better at the book's beginning, rather than its end.

Without dismissing the supernatural work of the Holy Spirit, *Faith Wins* places personal responsibility at the forefront of a spiritual struggle. The tendency among Christians to treat doubt as inscrutable and irresistible is countered by simple measures such as a daily *routine*, which do in fact, shape one's beliefs (154–55). A reader may recall the wisdom of Medieval patterns of worship framed by canonical hours.

In the epilogue, "Practical Steps for Dealing with Doubt," Groza provides eleven concrete applications for his readers, reiterations of earlier themes—confession, prayer, repentance, corporate worship, and even enjoying beauty (174–80)—a reminder that the substance of *Faith Wins* is meant to be lived out. As a work of devotional apologetics, the book possesses the pastoral warmth necessary to assist a Christian experiencing what the 16th century mystic St. John of the Cross famously called the *dark night of the soul*. With defections and deconversions increasing in American churches, Adam Groza provides timely counsel for clergy and laity alike.

Ryan Rindels,
Gateway Seminary,

Ontario, California;
First Baptist Church, Sonoma, California

Paul and the Hope of Glory: an Exegetical and Theological Study. By Constantine R. Campbell. Grand Rapids: Zondervan, 2020, 503 pages. Paperback, $22.99

Paul and the Hope of Glory is the second of an intended series, evocative of NT Wright's serial publications. The first volume was *Paul and Union with Christ* (2012). These two volumes explore the mysticism and eschatology of Paul. The present volume on eschatology offers passage-by-passage exegesis taken in canonical order presuming the canonical Paul using key word topics. This methodology feels like extended, self-contained word studies focused on one author. The book's three parts cover introductory matters, exegetical study, and theological study. The target audience is mixed, appealing to Pauline scholars but with an eye on church readers. All translations are given in English as well as Greek.

The first part addresses methodology first, which is word study focused. The accepted data is the canonical Pauline corpus. This choice obviously necessitates reconciling distinct perspectives expressed elsewhere (Ephesians, Colossians, 2 Thessalonians, 1–2 Timothy, Titus). While some will find commendable Campbell's canonical Paul route, others, obviously, will find fault and express concern about distorting the "historical" Paul. Campbell is fully aware of these issues but justifies the effort on the basis of producing a more "canonical" view of Paul, leaning in a Brevard Childs direction as a necessary constituent for consummating the full task of exegesis. The point of Pauline corpus is rather moot, however, since the theological impact on understanding the specific topic at hand, Pauline eschatology, is not significant for the main conclusions of the study. When Campbell quotes text, he does so with entire paragraphs. While this "fuller extent" of quotation methodology emphasizes the importance of context, the physical space consumed by providing both Greek and English text some might find distracting and certainly inflates the book's length, perhaps unnecessarily.

The second introductory chapter provides a summary of interpretive history of Pauline eschatology from Schweitzer on. This summary is a well written and concise. Philosophers, who have a lot to say on some of the issues discussed in the next two parts of

Campbell's own book, are not engaged. Exclusive New Testament scholar focus might be said to be in line with an "exegetical study." However, Campbell dives down into philosophical matters such as anthropology, intermediate state, eternal torment, annihilationism, and so forth. Paul himself admittedly does not directly deal with such matters (only implicitly at best), which Campbell points out. And that is the point. Since these parts of the discussion are not, in fact, "exegetical," they either should not have been taken up at all, or, if taken up, should have been under obligation to engage the more relevant conversations offered by philosophers on these very issues—at a minimum at least Christian philosophers. The point becomes acute, for example, when Campbell expresses a surprising opinion on the issue of cremation, but without engaging any philosophical sophistication on the matter. Philosophy can inform theology at this point.

Part two is the exegetical study. The primary topics covered are two ages, parousia, last day, judgment, resurrection, eternal life, inheritance, new creation, Israel, glory, and hope. Each topic has a thorough discussion. Campbell's exegetical contribution is in his succinct summary of pertinent issues. He needs to be heard particularly when issues of translation and Greek language come into play, as they often do in Pauline study, as this area is his core strength. His argument that eschatology is essential to understanding Paul is beautifully worked out in these pages. He unsuccessfully tries to disassociate himself from "center of Paul" discussion that has preoccupied Pauline scholars ever since Schweitzer and Wrede, but only substitutes terminology, offering "pervasive" instead of "center" (453). The argument falls flat. A rose by any other name is still a rose. Campbell is arguing for what is the "center of Paul" no matter what you call that rose. Still, he does an effective job lobbying for the eschatology camp as the center of Paul.

Part three is the theological study. The topics are christocentric eschatology, apocalyptic eschatology, age to come, and present age. The effort is to synthesize the exegesis, taking up many of the same topics from part two again, but intentionally more theologically focused to compose an integrative restatement and summary. Unfortunately, this part inevitably becomes repetitive, at times word for word repeating previous comments. While the integrative discussion enhances exegesis material by showing the place of each topic within the whole of Pauline eschatology, other parts of the discussion simply repeat previous exegetical comments and feel awkwardly redundant. The impression is left of a book longer than really necessary. This synthetic integration discussion, minus the recapitulative exegetical material, perhaps could have been achieved at the end of each chapter in the previous part for a more concise discussion with more punch so as not to exhaust the reader trying faithfully to hang with the author to the end.

Glory is the key integrating concept. Divine glory is inherent to God, suffuses the created order, establishes fundamentally what being fully human is, and defines the *telos* of where everything is going for humanity and creation after the tragedy of the fall, whose premier consequence was loss of God's glory with its inevitable futility of created purpose. Eschatology is that story, whose reality of consummation is unlocked in the incarnation that inaugurates the historical point in time when the recreative forces and power of God to achieve the end are set loose through the death, resurrection, and ascension of Jesus. Creation will be renewed not dissolved. Two ages of fall and fullness overlap in the meantime, creating the present tension of to be or not to be. Groaning for the final consummation through resurrection, grieved by the present struggle with evil, empowered by the union with Christ in the Spirit and its spiritual resurrection already, believers move forward in hope. Life must be lived, indeed, can be lived, expectantly, in this hope of glory centered and facilitated by Christ. This eschatology is Jewish apocalyptic, but the two ages now overlap in tension. Covenantal and historical elements as emphasized by Wright can be accommodated, but Douglas Campbell's exclusive focus on apocalyptic in Paul as a "vertical" intervention of God only is rejected (379).

Of course the discussion invites critique. We are limited to a few examples. Campbell tries unsuccessfully to scrub all "imminence" thinking from Pauline eschatology, perhaps fearing the shadow of Schweitzer. His functional collapse, however, of the meaning of "imminent" into only "possible" has to ignore the *prima facie* evidence of Rom 13:1–14 (367), and is undercut by his own "since the day is near" language (457). Ultimately he is unpersuasive that Paul, though apocalyptic, has no sense of imminence. Campbell also seems to use "law" somewhat indiscriminately, making Torah the universal plight of all humanity: "Death, sin, and the law work in concert as a formidable triumvirate that, unchallenged, spells the end of human life" (340). Being loose on law causes the exegesis to stumble on the argument about Gentiles in Romans 1–2. For example, arguing Rom 2:14–16 is "cryptically about Christian gentiles" (137n3) confusingly inserts a New Aeon category into an Old Aeon discussion and obfuscates the point. Major push back should be expected on Campbell's exegesis of Romans 9–11. His conclusion that "all Israel" equals only remnant Israel is less than satisfying, not only playing into the hands of supersessionism, but theologically meaning God, even though he gained Gentiles, lost his gambit on Israelites—which, lest we forget, is where the discussion started (Rom 9:4). Neither Romans 9:6–13 nor 11:26 should be interpreted in such a way as to ignore the whole burden of the discussion. That is, Paul never expressed a wish to be anathema for the sake of Gentiles. Campbell likewise infelicitously uses the expression "true Israel," which, we must point out, is not actually Pauline (250, 426). Finally, the exegesis of *apo* in 2 Thess 1:9 (157–58) is out of step with 1 Thess 4:8, and undercut by statements to the opposite effect in comments on God's wrath expressed as "apart from him" later (393).

The title is almost perfect for giving the essence of the book. I could have wished for the subtitle: "A Study of Eschatology," to identify spot on the centering thought. (We already could guess the discussion would offer exegesis and theology.) New Testament students, with or without language skills, would profit richly from this book for its solid theological synthesis of a major area of Pauline study, controversial elements here and there notwithstanding.

Gerald L. Stevens,
Distinguished Professor of New Testament and Greek,
New Orleans Baptist Theological Seminary

Pastors and Their Critics: A Guide to Coping with Criticism in the Ministry. By Joel R. Beeke and Nick Thompson. Phillipsburg: P&R, 2020. 169 pages. Softcover, $15.99.

Children at the playground chant a familiar children's rhyme: "Sticks and stones may break my bones, but words shall never hurt me." However, at some point, most parents understand they will have to console their children who have been on the receiving end of the words we taught them would never hurt. Those children grow up and feel the truth about what God says about our speech: "Death and life are in the power of the tongue," and, "No human being can tame the tongue. It is a restless evil, full of deadly poison" (Prov. 18:21; Jam. 3:5–12). Many of us vividly remember at least a time or two when someone used their words to inflict deep wounds. Pastors are by no means immune to being on the receiving end of hurtful words, frequently resulting in "exasperation, insomnia, cynicism, burnout, and even despair" (15).

Joel R. Beeke and Nick Thompson partner to write a timely book about coping with criticism, something all pastors face. Beeke is the president and professor of systematic theology and homiletics at Puritan Reformed Theological Seminary (PRTS), a pastor at the Heritage Reformed Congregation in Grand Rapids, and an author of over a hundred books. With a doctorate in Reformation and Post-Reformation theology from Westminster Theological Seminary in Philadelphia and over forty years of pastoral experience, he is qualified to write on this topic. Thompson, a graduate of PRTS, ably assists Beeke—especially in the appendix—to deal "comprehensively with the various dimensions of criticism in the Christian ministry from a biblical and Reformed perspective" (16).

The book divides into four parts with an appendix. In part one, the authors lay a biblical theology for coping with criticism. They say, "Unjust criticism is woven like a black thread throughout covenant history" (20). God, the only One who has nothing worthy of criticism, was the first target of unjust, verbal abuse in the Garden, as Satan questioned the truthfulness of God's Word and subtly twisted it. The authors trace out the way Moses, David, and Nehemiah handled criticism in the Old Testament before pointing the reader to the ultimate model of responding to criticism in godliness, our Lord Jesus Christ. They say, "Christ's death not only purchased redemption, but also provided a pattern for His disciples to follow" (36). To endure criticism, pastors must keep their eyes focused on Jesus, who, in gentle meekness, showed great strength to "rule his own spirit under such provocation" (40).

Part two comprises the largest part of the book. Here, Beeke and Thompson provide several helpful principles for coping with criticism in the ministry. They say, "Verbal critique is unavoidable because of the tragic reality of sin, the destructive schemes of Satan, and the sanctifying purposes of God" (52). They encourage pastors to receive criticism realistically and humbly and respond to it with sober judgment and grace.

Part three offers some practical principles for creating a healthy culture of giving and receiving constructive criticism in the church. It is not only essential to learn to accept criticism but also to provide constructive criticism to others. While many pastors focus on the *logos*—what needs to be said—Beeke and Thompson recommend pastors think equally about the aspects of *ethos* and *pathos* related to criticism. Daniel Akin, the seminary president at Southeastern Baptist Theological Seminary, has a phrase he regularly repeats: "What you say is more important than how you say it, but how you say it has never been more important." Pastors must be men of integrity and aim to reach their listeners' ears through their affections (113).

In part four, the authors put forward a theological vision for coping with criticism in ministry. Beeke and Thompson invite readers to adjust their focus for ministry so they will be able to receive and give criticism in a godly way. The vision they articulate centers around the glory of God, the edification of the church, the rapidly approaching last day, and our eternal home. Finally, in the appendix, Thompson takes center stage to discuss how students can use seminary to prepare for inevitable criticism to come while serving the Lord in a fallen world.

There are three reasons both seminary students and seasoned pastors should pick up this book. First, Beeke draws on his over forty years of ministry experience by using lived stories to help readers understand the principles he is setting forth. Personally, one of my favorite parts of seminary education was spending time with my professors, especially ones with years in the trenches of pastoral ministry. When Ligon Duncan would step to the side of the lectern and take off his glasses during class, students knew he was moving away from his well-prepared notes to speak to our hearts and share pastoral wisdom worth its weight in gold. In this book, Beeke—himself an effective preacher—illustrates the joys and pains of ministry through story after story gleaned from the school of hard knocks. His expertise in the reformed tradition is evident in this book, and he directs readers to further reading that will complement these stories from his personal experience. Young preachers need men they can look up to for advice. Beeke offers to be such an older brother to counsel them through difficult days.

Second, Beeke helps readers shift their gaze off their present circumstances toward their Savior who loves them, especially in chapter two, "Christological Foundations for Coping with Criticism." Pastors going through a difficult season tend to suffer from myopia. In other words, it feels as if the intensity of the situation they are in does not allow them to see anything else. Many times, they consider quitting. Where will pastors turn when they have had the wind knocked out of them through harsh criticism? Beeke and Thompson remind pastors of their tender Savior who identified with them in every way and became a faithful and merciful High Priest. Jesus is willing and able to help them in their distress (Heb. 2:17–18). Additionally, pastors need to realize afresh that Jesus is our pattern for discipleship. The authors say, "Let us walk in the footsteps of the crucified Messiah, trusting in the Father as He did, and lean on His Spirit so that His death and life may be exhibited in us for the watching world to see" (46).

Third, pastors need to have a theological vision to sustain criticism, and Beeke and Thompson offer an excellent one in chapter nine, "Reorient Your Perspective." This chapter will help pastors keep the main things the main things. They say, "These God-breathed bifocals shift our focus away from ourselves to God, His church, judgment day, and eternity. With these truths enveloping our sight, criticism is put in its rightful place" (133). The heartfelt charge at the end will encourage pastors not only to cope but to persevere amid verbal shrapnel until their faith becomes sight. In the meantime, pastor, this book will be a worthy investment for you as you lead God's church during difficult days.

Scott Lucky,
Parkway Baptist Church, Clinton, MS

Preaching with Cultural Intelligence: Understanding the People Who Hear Our Sermons. By Matthew D. Kim. Grand Rapids, MI: Baker Academic, 2017. 269 pages. Paperback, $14.99

Matthew Kim serves as the associate professor of preaching and ministry at Gordon Conwell Theological Seminary. In his book, *Preaching with Cultural Intelligence: Understanding the People Who Hear Our Sermons,* Kim seeks to provide a helpful rubric for preachers as they craft sermons with cultural intelligence (xiii). He develops a theoretical framework and a preaching template that will help the reader increase their preaching effectiveness with cultural outsiders (xv).

Kim divides his book into two parts: cultural intelligence in theory and cultural intelligence in practice (vii). In the first section, Kim seeks to introduce the concept of cultural intelligence to demonstrate its value to the preacher. He borrows a definition of cultural intelligence from two business professors, P. Christopher Early and Soon Ang. They define cultural intelligence as "the capability to deal effectively with other people with whom the person does not share a common cultural background and understanding" (5). He uses this conceptual framework to propose a homiletical process designed to increase cultural intelligence within the preacher. In the second section, Kim identifies five cultural contexts in which the preacher may apply this new "homiletical template" (xv).

In chapter 1, Kim seeks to define culture and to describe the synergetic relationship between preaching and cultural intelligence. He devotes significant space to explaining the four stages of cultural quotient theory (CQ). Kim says that his homiletical framework relies heavily on subsets of CQ called CQ Knowledge and CQ Action (3-12). He uses this conceptual framework to propose a three-stage homiletical template that integrates cultural intelligence. Kim's first stage focuses on the interpretation of the biblical text and context. The second stage centers on the idea of building a homiletical bridge. The third stage focuses on sermon delivery that utilizes cultural intelligence (13-30).

Kim's homiletical template finds roots in preaching traditions that are familiar to many evangelicals. He views much of his work as an extension of the research conducted by preachers such as Haddon Robinson and John Stott (3, 35-36). Notably, Kim does not seek to overhaul traditional hermeneutics and homiletics. Concerning his interpretive model, Kim stands firmly within the evangelical tradition with his commitment to prioritizing authorial intent. He aims to illuminate the value of cultural exegesis as a means of identifying authorial intent more clearly.

Kim rounds out the first section of the book by focusing on hermeneutics and self-exegesis. In chapter 3, he proposes a hermeneutical model that emphasizes the biblical author's central idea in the pericope while also highlighting the cultural background of the author. He suggests that consistently exposing the listener to the biblical context will help them more accurately negotiate points of congruence and discontinuity with their own culture (44). In chapter 4, Kim highlights the need for the preacher to engage in self-exegesis. He writes, "our goal in cultural intelligence is to grow in empathy and begin to embrace cultural differences so that we can fully function as the body of Christ" (49). Kim believes that the practice of self-exegesis will help the preacher build the requisite competence and empathy necessary to exegete the culture of others (60-61).

In the second section of the book, Kim examines five cultural contexts: denominations, ethnicities, genders, locations, and religions. He uses the same format for chapters 5-9. At the beginning of each chapter, Kim introduces the complexities associated with each culture and casts a vision for why they are relevant to the preacher. Then, he utilizes his three-stage homiletical template to structure each of the remaining chapters. His goal is to demonstrate the efficacy of a homiletical template that integrates cultural intelligence into the preparation and delivery of sermons (xv). Kim concludes by saying that "preaching with cultural intelligence involves such a heart and approach to life. Cultural intelligence in preaching is another way to demonstrate our love for God and for people" (216). In other words, he views this homiletical approach as an essential tool for the preacher to live out the Great Commandment.

Kim's book has two clear strengths. The first strength of this book is the practice exercises in the appendices. Kim did not write this book to propose an unapproachable academic theory. He provides useful templates in the appendices that will aid preachers as they integrate cultural intelligence into their sermons. The second major strength of Kim's book is his emphasis on self-exegesis. He suggests that many preachers would benefit from critical reflection about their cultural background. The work of self-exegesis inherently makes the preacher a more empathetic interpreter of other cultures. Preachers who develop this skill will be able to communicate the truth of Scripture to all cultures with compassionate precision.

Kim's goal in writing this book is to provide preachers with the requisite tools to preach with cultural intelligence. However, he cautions his reader to approach his book as an entryway to further study on preaching with cultural intelligence. The net effect he wants to achieve is to spur on further dialogue. Kim hopes that this book encourages his reader to commit to a lifelong study on preaching with cultural intelligence.

Stape Patterson,
Northbrook Baptist Church, Cullman, AL.
Midwestern Baptist Theological Seminary, Kansas City, MO.

Visual Theology Study Guide: Seeing and Understanding the Truth About God. By Tim Challies and Josh Byers. Grand Rapids, MI: Zondervan, 2018. 112 pages. Paperback, $10.99.

Tim Challies has cultivated a large foothold online. Through his blog and numerous books, Challies engages pastors and laymen with truths of the Christian faith. In the *Visual Theology Study Guide* (VTSG), Josh Byers joins Challies to provide a study guide that they hope will help believers "grow in godliness by practicing" the lessons taught in the *Visual Theology* book, which must not be confused with VTSG (7). Challies and Byers have organized VTSG in a way conducive to personal and small group study sessions.

Each chapter in VTSG follows a set pattern. The authors begin with what they call the "Big Picture" in which they summarize the content of the chapter with a quote from the *Visual Theology* book. Next, the authors provide key terms for understanding the content of the chapter. Unfortunately, the key terms are explained only by references to the *Visual Theology* book and Bible verses. For example, "preach" is a key term in chapter one; however, the only definition offered for "preach" is "*VT*, 21; Romans 1:8-16; 1 Timothy 1:12-17" (11). Next, the authors provide a list of questions to help students unpack the content of the chapter. These questions are one of the strongest points of the study guide and could lead to fruitful discussions in a small group setting. The authors then use a paragraph, a biblical passage, and a diagram to help learners gain a deeper appreciation of the topic presented in the chapter. Since the title of the book contains the word "visual," readers may be interested in the graphics provided in the book. While the graphics are often insightful, they could be more visually appealing if Zondervan had used color instead of grayscale. The chapter concludes with an invitation to personal reflection and a blank page on which the authors invite readers to design their own graphic to depict the content of the chapter.

The primary focus of VTSG is discipleship of individuals who already identify as conservative Christians. VTSG has no chapter on the authority of Scripture, nor does the study guide contain a discussion on the nature of God. Instead, the authors assume that their audience already values the Bible and believes God exists. This is not a weakness of the book. Indeed, assuming an evangelical paradigm allows Challies and Byers to move quickly because they do not have to do worldview building. In a church setting comprised of committed Christians, VTSG could be an effective study tool. However, this book is not designed for apologetic purposes or to assuage doubts.

Challies and Byers aim to change their readers' lifestyles by helping readers understand their identity in Christ. Too often, pastors, Sunday school teachers, and lay leaders promote biblical ethics in a way more consistent with the Old Testament Law than with Jesus's commands. Instead of giving his disciples a long list of actions to do and not do, Jesus famously told his disciples to focus on loving God and one's neighbor. Jesus sought to change lifestyles by first changing a person's focus. Challies and Byers follow a similar route. Instead of discussing lists of actions indicative of a mature Christian, the authors begin VTSG by discussing the believer's identity in Christ before moving to the believer's role as an actor in the drama of redemption. Due to believers' identity in Christ, the authors encourage Christians to put off their old ways and put on new ways in line with the gospel of Christ. Only after establishing believers' identity in Christ do Challies and Byers move toward ethical implications. They conclude the book by encouraging believers to live for Christ in their vocations, relationships, and stewardship.

VTSG is a helpful book for pastors and church leaders to guide Christians to a deeper understanding of the Christian life. Perhaps the greatest strength of VTSG is its biblical methodology. By helping Christians understand who they are in Christ, the authors promote lasting lifestyle change. However, for VTSG to be as beneficial as possible, pastors and church leaders will need to purchase the *Visual Theology* book which is widely available at an affordable price. After all, VTSG is merely a study guide to the larger work of the *Visual Theology* book.

Nicholas Maricle,
New Orleans Baptist Theological Seminary,
New Orleans, Louisiana

Analyzing Doctrine: Toward a Systematic Theology. By Oliver D. Crisp. Waco, Texas: Baylor University Press, 2019. Pp. 270. $39.95, hardcover.

Oliver D. Crisp is Professor of Analytic Theology at the Logos Institute for Analytic and Exegetical Theology, St. Mary's College, the University of St Andrews and a monumental figure in the analytic theology movement. He has authored numerous books in the fields of systematic, historical, and analytic theology including *Divinity and Humanity: The Incarnation Reconsidered*, *Deviant Calvinism: Broadening Reformed Theology*, and *Retrieving Doctrine: Essays in Reformed Theology*. He has edited and co-edited several volumes including *Analytic Theology: New Essays in the Philosophy of Theology* (with Michael C. Rea); co-founded the Los Angeles Theology Conference (with Fred Sanders) and the *Journal of Analytic Theology* (with Michael C. Rea), and published dozens of journal articles and book chapters.

Analyzing Doctrine, according to Crisp, is "an attempt to provide something like a dogmatic sketch of some of the main load-bearing structures around which a systematic theology would be built" (2). Crisp argues that analytic theology *"can (and should) be practiced as a species of systematic theology"* (17, emphasis his), and *Analyzing Doctrine* is the systematizing of his work in analytic theology. Crisp focuses on "the theological core of the Christian faith—namely, the doctrine of God, of Christ, and of the nature of salvation" (2-3).

Crisp devotes the first chapter to theological method and demonstrates how analytic theology can be a species of systematic theology. He argues that analytic theology fits within the bounds of what he calls the 'Shared Task of systematic theology;' namely:

> Commitment to an intellectual undertaking that involves (though it may not comprise) explicating the conceptual content of the Christian tradition (with the expectation that this is normally done from a position within the tradition, as an adherent of that tradition), using particular religious texts that are part of the Christian tradition, including sacred Scripture, as well as human reason, reflection, and praxis (particularly religious practices), as sources for theological judgments. (22)

He argues that "at its best analytic theology as systematic theology is a way of doing systematic theology that utilizes the tools and methods of contemporary analytic philosophy for the purposes of constructive Christian theology, paying attention to the Christian tradition and development of doctrine" (32, emphasis his).

The next three chapters concern the doctrine of God. Crisp argues, in chapter 2, for what he calls 'chastened theism' which he considers to be a "theologically realist near neighbor of classical theism and alternative to theistic personalism," (34). God is a real, mind-independent being. God is knowable but incomprehensible. Crisp's theism is *chastened* because it appeals to biblical and ecclesiastical tradition and "is an approach to the theological task that is cognizant of the fact that any attempt to articulate a systematic account of Christian doctrine must begin from the admission that this is just one partial, flawed, incomplete, and fragile attempt to articulate the great things of the gospel" (49). His following chapters on divine simplicity and the Trinity demonstrate how his chastened theism plays out in two "central components of a full-orbed doctrine of God" (50). In chapter 3, he presents his chastened theistic model of simplicity which he calls 'the parsimonious doctrine.' God is a concrete, necessary, and immaterial person. "On this view God is thought of as being metaphysically simple but not absolutely mereologically simple" (66). That is, God is metaphysically primitive: "not composed of more fundamental [concrete] components" (66). Crisp's model rejects the notion that God is pure act, affirms that God exemplifies distinct attributes, and leaves open the possibility that the three persons of the Trinity are more than mere subsisting relations. In chapter 4, he rejects Latin, social, and constitution views of the Trinity in favor of a position he calls 'chastened Trinitarian mysterianism.' He argues that "no model of the Trinity is adequate because God is fundamentally mysterious and beyond our ken," therefore, "we might be better off acknowledging that we do not have a single account of the doctrine that makes complete sense, and that our various models of the Trinity are at best piecemeal attempts to grasp something beyond our comprehension" (9).

Chapters 5 and 6 are about God's purpose for the world. Crisp argues for a version of the "incarnation anyway" doctrine called the 'christological union account.' Had humanity never sinned, the incarnation would have happened anyway because one (or *the*) fundamental end for which God created the world is for divinity and humanity to be united in the life of God.

In the seventh chapter, Crisp explains how his views on original sin have changed from his previous works. He takes a moderate Reformed position and no longer holds to original guilt. Even though all humans after the primal sin possess original sin, they are guilty neither of the primal sin nor of their being generated in this condition. Original sin is a corruption of nature that inevitably leads to sin; and humans become guilty for their actual sins. Nevertheless, "Possession of original sin leads to death and separation from God irrespective of actual sin" (153).

Chapters 8 through 11 discuss key issues intersecting the doctrines of Christ and salvation. Chapter 8 is devoted to the virgin birth. He maintains that Christians should retain the traditional dogma of the virgin birth despite several biblical and theological objections posed by Andrew Lincoln. In the next chapter, Crisp deals with the number of Christ's wills. He favors dyothelitism (two wills) over monothelitism (one will). Crisp tackles the interrelationship of theosis and participation in the tenth chapter. On his view, "participation in the divine involves exemplifying certain qualities had by the glorified human nature of Christ that are not currently enjoyed by fallen human beings. But it also involves a relation of intimate union with Christ, though one that ... stops short of hypostatic union" (203). In the final constructive chapter, Crisp offers an account of the bodily resurrection that leans heavily (but not uncritically) upon Robert Jenson's work supplemented with the hyperspace metaphysics of Hud Hudson.

Analyzing Doctrine is commendable for a number of reasons. First, it is not only readable and accessible but also interesting and enjoyable. Crisp writes in clear prose that is not bogged down with symbolic logic (a common feature in analytic philosophy and theology). For this reason, analytic and non-analytic theologians and philosophers can easily follow the arguments. Furthermore, the book can be read *in toto* or selectively because the chapters are fairly self-contained. The readability, length, and structure make *Analyzing Doctrine* ideal for upper undergraduate and masters-level students in theology as well as pastors and interested laypersons. Of course, analytic and systematic theologians will be the most interested persons.

Second, *Analyzing Doctrine* is constructive but not revisionist. Crisp attempts to remain within the bounds of historical orthodoxy as set by the major creeds and confessions of faith. This commitment to orthodoxy is especially clear in his chapters on divine simplicity, the Trinity, the virgin birth, and Christ's two wills. Those who are familiar with Crisp's work will not be surprised by many of the positions taken in *Analyzing Doctrine*, but that is not to say that he has merely republished old material. Crisp engages new ideas and interlocutors, provides fresh insight, and shows the structure and interrelationships of the core theological loci.

The following are a few of the weaknesses of *Analyzing Doctrine*. First, despite its intentional brevity, the book should have devoted at least one chapter to the doctrine of the atonement. Crisp provides only a one-page outline of his union account of atonement and directs the reader elsewhere in a footnote. The doctrine of atonement, along with the Trinity and the incarnation, is one of the central uniquely Christian doctrines, and, as such, deserves to be treated adequately.

Second, in his chapter on incarnation, Crisp argues against the Edwardsian view "that God's goal in creation is, in the final analysis, to bring himself glory," (135). Crisp worries "that the Edwardsian obsession with divine self-glorification as the ultimate end of all God's creative works makes the creation, including creatures like you and me, merely the instruments by means of which God brings himself glory," (136). For Crisp, christological union must be more fundamental than glorification. Here, I offer a response in favor of the Edwardsian view.

First, there is overwhelming scriptural support for God valuing his own glory above all else. For example, when God says, "I will give you a new heart, and a new spirit I will put within you," (Ezek 36:26, all Scripture from ESV), he prefaces with "It is not for your sake, O house of Israel, that I am about to act, but for the sake of my holy name," (Ezek 36:22). Elsewhere, God says to Pharaoh, whose heart God hardened himself, "But for this purpose I have raised you up, to show you my power, so that my name may be proclaimed in all the earth," (Ex 9:16). So, in both salvation and condemnation, God acts for the sake of his own glory.

Second, contra Crisp's objection, God does, indeed, use human creatures as instruments. For example, God calls Assyria, "the rod of my anger" (Isa 10:5) as he uses Assyria to assault Jerusalem. Then, when Assyria boasts, God says, "Shall the axe boast over him who hews with it, or the saw magnify itself against him who wields it?" (Isa 10:15). Furthermore, Scripture often connects

God's self-glorification with his use of creatures as instruments. Consider Pharaoh in Exodus 9 quoted above. And even more poignantly:

> Has the potter no right over the clay, to make out of the same lump one vessel for honorable use and another for dishonorable use? What if God, desiring to show his wrath and to make known his power, has endured with much patience vessels of wrath prepared for destruction, in order to make known the riches of his glory for vessels of mercy, which he has prepared beforehand for glory — even us whom he has called, not from the Jews only but also from the Gentiles? (Rom 9:22-24)

It seems, then, that Crisp's objection to the Edwardsian view does not sit well with the claims of Scripture.

As a third weakness to *Analyzing Doctrine*, it is regrettable that Crisp abandons the doctrine of original guilt, especially because his previous work on the doctrine was innovative and consistent with his system. Crisp thinks original guilt "is immoral because it is necessarily morally wrong to punish the innocent, and I am innocent of Adam's sin (I did not commit his sin or condone it). It is also immoral because the guilt of one person's sin does not transfer to another (I am not guilty of committing Adam's sin)" (145-146). Moreover, he avers that "The oft-touted Adam Christology of Rom 5:12-19 does not yield anything like a clear and unambiguous doctrine of original guilt" (146).

Rather than repeat the familiar exegetical and theological arguments for the doctrine of original guilt, I shall draw the readers' attention to an apparent inconsistency in Crisp's view. According to Crisp, humans are guilty for neither the primal sin nor their being born into the state of corruption, but, nevertheless, "Possession of original sin leads to death and separation from God irrespective of actual sin" because it "renders the bearer unfit for the presence of God and liable to be disbarred from the goods associated with the life to come in the presence of God" (153). In other words, original sin, even apart from actual sin, leads to condemnation. Crisp doubts, however, that infants and mentally impaired persons, upon their death, are condemned. Rather, Crisp is optimistic that God would elect those who are incapable of faith and acting morally, "so that the possession of original sin, which would normally lead to condemnation without the interposition of the benefits of Christ's saving work, does not lead to this conclusion" (152). Despite his concession about infants and those who are incapable of faith, Crisp is still left with the conclusion that, at least in theory, original sin condemns apart from actual sin. Because humans are condemned for being in their corrupted state, they are punishable for something they neither did nor condoned nor for which they were declared guilty. This conclusion is inconsistent with Crisp's motivation to deny original guilt. Proponents of the doctrine of original guilt can say that the guilty alone are condemned. But on Crisp's view, it seems the innocent are condemned, too.

Analyzing Doctrine turns the attention of analytic theology from the narrow task of clarifying and solving theological problems to the broad task of theological world-building. It examines the core theological loci—the doctrine of God, Christ, and salvation—and gives them a coherent structure. *Analyzing Doctrine* is constructive, clear, concise, readable, and enjoyable. I am, however, at odds with Crisp on a few issues, two of which I highlighted: the ultimate end for which God created the world and original guilt. Nevertheless, we have much in common as he defends an orthodox account of the Christian faith.

Randall K. Johnson
The Southern Baptist Theological Seminary

When Narcissism Comes to Church: Healing Your Community from Emotional and Spiritual Abuse. By Chuck DeGroat. Downer's Grove, IL: InterVarsity Press, 2020. 192 pages. Hardcover, $22.00.

Chuck DeGroat, professor of pastoral care and Christian spirituality at Western Theological Seminary and a licensed therapist and spiritual director, represents that subset of individuals who navigate the integration of theology and psychology. In this book, DeGroat addresses the popular and often misunderstood topic of narcissism and describes its presentation in both individuals and systems. The work is an accessible read, providing a compassionate and responsible understanding of narcissism and its impacts to a lay Christian audience.

DeGroat begins by presenting both descriptive, anecdotal pictures of narcissism and information about narcissism. The anecdotes display the subtleties of narcissism, illustrating why many people have trouble detecting it while demonstrating through story concepts related to narcissism. Through consistent use of such anecdotes, the book maintains a personal rather than clinical feel, aiding its accessibility for a popular audience. From the very beginning of the book, narcissism is addressed in both people and systems, since "systems can be arrogantly convinced of their greatness or, paradoxically, vulnerably narcissistic in a twisted form of self-deprecating self-righteousness" (104).

DeGroat's presentation of narcissism explores concepts foundational to a true understanding of the trait including the differences between grandiose and vulnerable narcissism, the spectrum of narcissism ranging from healthy to toxic, and the relation of narcissism to other similar personality disorders. Most basic premises throughout the book rest on the supposition that narcissism primarily acts as a defense strategy against pathological shame. The research literature on narcissism debates this underlying premise, primarily because it cannot be tested. Many narcissists either do not realize or will not admit to underlying shame. The other possibility, of course, is that the underlying shame was imagined by clinicians to make sense of the disorder (a possibility for grandiose rather than vulnerable narcissism). Nevertheless, several prominent scholars endorse the same view as DeGroat, and practically the idea of underlying shame promotes a compassionate view of narcissists, something that DeGroat emphasizes throughout the book. As much as narcissism has toxic, destructive effects, narcissists are human beings made in the image of God who can experience redemption.

Interestingly, in chapter 3, DeGroat describes each form of narcissism in church members from the framework of each Enneagram type. While helpful for broadening the reader's understanding of various presentations of narcissism, the Enneagram itself has mixed data regarding validity, and a conceptualization of narcissism by Enneagram type certainly does not show up in the research literature. Readers should recognize the use of the Enneagram as a literary tool rather than a representation of accepted clinical categories. DeGroat then describes characteristics of narcissistic pastors and narcissistic systems in chapters 4 through 6. His descriptions serve as helpful templates against which a church member can measure personal experiences. While in no way a diagnostic tool, the chapters can help victims of narcissistic people or systems make sense of their experiences through exploration of several facets of narcissism (impatience, entitlement, inconsistent behavior, etc.). Many people who have been hurt by narcissists wonder if they are crazy, if they are the problem, or if what they experienced was even real. DeGroat's book can bring these trauma victims out of the fog and into a healing journey in which they begin to recognize and name abuse. The final chapters aid this healing by focusing specifically on the emotional and spiritual abuse that occurs in the presence of narcissism along with steps to take toward healing for both the victim(s) and the narcissist(s).

The real strength of the book is DeGroat's application of clinical expertise and descriptions of a complex disorder for a lay Christian audience. The author clearly demonstrates his experience working with narcissism in Christian contexts, and he accurately portrays the damage that can be done when a pastor, church member, or church system displays narcissism. By referencing Christian authors like Eugene Peterson and Henri Nouwen, DeGroat connects with his Christian audience and is able to integrate principles from both theology and psychology. He stays true to the biblical principle of redemption, refusing to give up hope that people and systems can change. This hopefulness provides the safety necessary for narcissistic people and systems to do the painful work of introspection (153). While most of the book holds up against psychology research, readers must still approach it with a critical eye. By mixing scholarly sources with popular sources (peer-reviewed journal articles showing up next to blog posts), DeGroat may cause confusion among readers who do not have the expertise to distinguish the reliability of sources. Readers must not give the same weight to anecdotes or blogs that they give to meta-analyses published in scholarly journals.

Pastors may feel hesitancy regarding this book, fearing the unjust label of "narcissist" for themselves or their ministries. Baptist readers may chafe at some of DeGroat's criticisms of systems and anecdotes describing narcissistic church planters. For instance, DeGroat writes "I am convinced that the missional fervor and rise in church planting we've witnessed since the 1980s can be correlated with the growing prevalence of narcissism" (8). That sentence alone will make some Baptists throw down the book in disgust. However, readers must keep in mind DeGroat's history as a psychological evaluator of church planters to understand his criticisms of narcissistic young planters and the systems that approved them in spite of DeGroat's cautions. Firsthand experience of systemic irresponsibility can leave a particularly bitter taste in the mouths of those who tried to blow the whistle. Further, Baptists must not avoid the opportunity for self-reflection, particularly in a time when glaring problems of racism and sexism (both of which can be related to narcissism) in denominational systems have been exposed. Diane Langberg, a leader in the field of trauma and toxic religious systems, points out that "[w]hen it comes to injustice, silence is not a virtue; it is a vice two times compounded because it contains both indifference to the victims and complicity with the destroyers."[7] To stay complacent and silent in the area of narcissism is to allow evil to continue unchecked and to allow self-deception to reign in our hearts. DeGroat's book is an empathic invitation into the light and onto a healing journey that will help church members and systems better reflect Jesus. The book provides helpful material on narcissism from a pastor/clinician's viewpoint while describing narcissism such that a pastor or church member could recognize it in self, others, and systems. Those who are curious about narcissism will benefit from the information provided. Those who have been hurt by narcissistic persons or systems may be able to, perhaps for the first time, recognize and label the abuse they experienced. Those who have narcissistic tendencies (which is all of us) can see themselves in these pages and engage in a journey of repentance and growth into humble Christlikeness. For these reasons, I would recommend the book to all Christian readers.

Jamie Klemashevich
New Orleans Baptist Theological Seminary
New Orleans, Louisiana

Answering God's Call: Finding, Following, and Fulfilling God's Will for Your Life. By R. Scott Pace. Nashville: B&H Academic, 2020. 144 pages. Hardcover, $19.99.

The story is familiar. One chilly, autumn Lord's Day morning, a young man—a high school senior—is converted as he listens to the pastor enthusiastically press home the words of Jesus: "Those who are well have no need of a physician, but those who are sick. I came not to call the righteous, but sinners" (Mark 2:17). The young man immediately throws himself into following Christ with

---

[7] Diane Langberg, *Suffering and the Heart of God: How Trauma Destroys and Christ Restores* (Greensboro: New Growth Press, 2015), 20.

zeal, devouring books and delighting in service, even in the most mundane and unseen ways. Nevertheless, as he grows in his walk with the Lord, a nagging question haunts him. One day, the eager college-junior approaches his home church pastor and anxiously asks, "What is God's will for my life?"

R. Scott Pace is no stranger to this question and prays his book will be a blueprint to help readers find, follow, and fulfill God's will for their lives (xiii). Formerly serving university students at Oklahoma Baptist University, Pace now splits his time between leading college students as the dean of the College of Southeastern, and preparing future pastors and missionaries as an associate professor of pastoral ministry and preaching at Southeastern Baptist Theological Seminary, holding the Johnny Hunt Chair of Biblical Preaching. His latest book takes its place among two of his previous compact volumes, *Preaching by the Book* (2018) and *Student Ministry by the Book* (2019), adding to the growing Hobbs College Library from OBU, edited by Heath A. Thomas.

Pace divides his book into three parts, each composed of an introduction and two chapters. In part one, "Answering God's Call," readers learn "how the Lord calls an individual, why he calls people to specific tasks, and how we can discern his personal will for our lives as we answer his call" (1–2). Christians have a calling that is both universal and unique. Moving readers away from merely exploring the calling of God mystically, Pace insists all Christians have a call to salvation, service, and surrender (2–3). Regarding uniqueness, Pace says, "The Lord has chosen you to serve him in a particular way, at a specific place and time, with a unique combination of talents and gifts, for his strategic purpose" (4). This part of the book focuses on confirming and clarifying God's call on your life.

Part two, "Assisting the Church," covers God enlisting us in and equipping us for His service. These days, most young Christians do not have a high view of the church. Pace aims to correct this misunderstanding by laying a biblical foundation for the church with three passages from Matthew—the Great Confession, Great Commandment, and Great Commission (Matt. 16:13–18; 22:34–40; 28:18–20). He says, "God has specifically called you to serve his kingdom and has provided you with the necessary gifts to accomplish his purpose for your life" (42). In this section, Pace shows how believers should function within the global and local church and how God's purposes for the church will affect and can determine our callings.

Part three, "Abiding in Christ," details the spiritual disciplines of approaching His throne and applying His truth. Knowing God is eternal life and should be the only boast of a believer (John 17:3; Jer. 9:23-24). Pace says, "If knowing God in a more personal and intimate way is going to become our driving motivation in life, we must devote ourselves to the spiritual disciplines that position us to 'grow in the grace and knowledge of our Lord and Savior Jesus Christ' (2 Pet. 3:18)" (77). I have observed believers tend to find *either* praying or reading the Bible to come more naturally to them while feeling weak—and sometimes defeated—in the other area. Very rarely have I seen someone who was both a tremendous Bible reader *and* a prayer warrior. To my shame, the following quote is accurate: "If you want to humble a man, ask him about his prayer life." In chapters five and six, Pace encourages readers to devote themselves to the basics—prayer and the reading and application of God's Word—and gives them practical steps to take. Finally, Pace concludes his book with some thoughts drawn from Colossians 3:23, insisting what we do, how we do what we do, and why we do what we do all matter to the Lord.

Three strengths of Pace's book deserve mention. First, Pace does a good job walking the fine line of dealing with calling for *both* church members and those who will serve as pastors and missionaries. His current role of working with college students and seminarians helps him uniquely speak to those who will inhabit both the pew and pulpit. He says, "After all, God's calling is not limited to vocational ministry; he uses all types of careers for his kingdom purposes" (7). It is important to remember there is no junior varsity in the kingdom of God—all are equally important and useful to the Lord of the church as members of His body (1 Cor. 12:11–27). However, as pastors seek to develop future ministry leaders, two ditches must be avoided regarding calling. First, pastors occasionally witness people running from a calling to serve the Lord as a pastor or missionary. These people forget Paul's trustworthy saying, "If anyone aspires to the office of overseer, he desires a noble task" (1 Tim. 3:1). Equally detrimental, though, is the person who perceives a calling from the Lord that He never gave. Chapter one will be beneficial for pastors discipling members and for members seeking to determine God's will for their lives.

Second, Pace helps readers discern their call according to Scripture without neglecting the Holy Spirit's work. Much of Baptist life concerning the discernment of God's will for our lives is steeped in an overly mystical—almost Schleiermacherian—subjective experience. Conversely, Pace says, "Our success in every area of life will be determined by our reliance on God's Word. Scripture provides everything we need to succeed for Christ when we allow it to inform and infuse our lives" (98). The reader will appreciate the amount of Scripture woven throughout the pages of his book, culminating in chapter six, "We Must Apply His Truth."

Third, in addition to a focus on biblical truths, Pace is determined to give readers a practical application of the material he presents. In each chapter, readers searching for God's will for their lives will discover the "Living It Out" section relevant and valuable. With my struggle to pray, I found the "Living It Out" section in chapter five, "We Can Approach His Throne," to be practical and beneficial.

Pace's book is recommended as being particularly helpful to university students and seminarians. As an adjunct professor of Christian Worldview and one of the pastors at a local church, younger Christians regularly ask me to help them discern God's will for their lives. I am always looking for helpful ways to counsel these eager inquirers. In addition to *Am I Called?* by Dave Harvey and *Called to the Ministry* by Edmund P. Clowney, I now have an accessible resource to give to students and congregation members.

Scott Lucky,
Parkway Baptist Church,
Clinton, MS

The End of the Timeless God. By R. T. Mullins. Oxford Studies in Analytic Theology. Oxford: Oxford University Press, 2016. 264 pages. Hardcover. $125.00.

R. T. Mullins is University Researcher for the Helsinki Collegium at the University of Helsinki in Finland. He earned his Ph.D. from the University of St. Andrews, and he has held academic posts at Cambridge University, University of St. Andrews, and the University of Edinburgh before taking his current appointment at the University of Helsinki. He has published a number of articles dealing with models of God, philosophy of time, the problem of evil, and disability theology. He has authored two books: *The End of the Timeless God* (2016) and *God and Emotion* (2020).

God's relationship to time has been a concern for both philosophical and systematic theologians since the patristics. From Augustine's *De Trinitate*, to Thomas's *Summa Theologiae*, to the work at hand, Christian thinkers have struggled to tease out this relation. Mullins's thesis is that, though the church has traditionally affirmed the doctrine of divine timelessness, i.e. divine atemporality, there seem to be both biblical and logical inconsistencies with it when one attempts to break it down and analyze its coherence with other doctrinal commitments in Christian theology. Thus, he concludes, the doctrine of divine atemporality is neither consistent with the portrait of God provided in Scripture, nor is it internally coherent with its own program. The primary focus of the book is devoted to teasing out the internal-coherence issues with divine timelessness, though the author does demonstrate concern with the biblical issues as well.

Mullins's argument begins by asking the age-old question most popularly associated with St. Augustine in the *Confessions*: "What is time?" If one aims to understand the relationship between God and time, then they need to know exactly what time itself is. There have been two primary ways of understanding *time*. The first is the *relational* theory of time, which claims that "time exists if and only if change exists. If there is a change there is a time. If no change ever occurred, then time would never occur" (14). This has been the traditional theory of time throughout the history of both theology and philosophy. Major proponents of this view have included Augustine, Boethius, Anselm, and Thomas. The second theory of time is the absolute theory: "On an *absolute* view of time, time can exist without change or movement" (15). Proponents of this theory have included Isaac Newton, Samuel Clarke, and Alan Padgett. Padgett understood absolute time to be "the dimension of the possibility of change" rather than change itself, per the relational theory (16). On the relational theory, time is a creature of God, something he brings into being from nothing. On the absolute theory, according to Newton and Clarke, time is not a creature, nor is it something extrinsic to God's being; rather, it is one of God's attributes, part of his very being. As a result, time never *begins* to exist. It is not created. Instead, it is eternal with God in the same way that love is eternal, namely as one of God's essential attributes. Though Mullins finds the absolute theory of time more plausible, he does not spend much time defending it as it is not essential to his argument against divine atemporality. He proceeds to develop his argument throughout the remainder of the book assuming the relational theory of time (18).

Mullins provides further important definitions concerning time that affect the God-and-time debate. Many contemporary discussions about time tend to use the terms *A-theory of time* and *B-theory of time*. On the *A-theory of time*, "time is held to be dynamic in the sense that it is constantly moving forward. All series of events can be described in terms of having the properties *past, present*, or *future*" (19). This is also known as a tensed theory of time. On the *B-theory of time*, however, time is not dynamic or tensed. It is, rather, static and tenseless. For the B-theorist, change is understood as objects having different properties at different times. Mullins provides the helpful clarification that the discussions surrounding A and B theories have proven quite unhelpful in the majority of philosophy of time discussions. The reason for this is that these theories are not actually theories of time but theories of change, language, and propositions (23–24). For the A-theory, there exists an actual temporal becoming. On the B-theory, this is not the case. Temporal becoming is rather an illusion. Many also have confused *A-theory of time* with the term *presentism*, and *B-theory of time* with *four-dimensional eternalism*, or just *eternalism*. *Presentism* and *eternalism* are particular theories concerning the ontology of time, i.e. what time(s) actually exist. The A and B theories, again, are more so theories of change than they are of time. Since so much confusion surrounds the A and B theories, and since they are not actually theories of time, Mullins rightly chooses to leave them absent for the development of his argument against timelessness. He does, however, return to discuss *presentism* and *eternalism* since these are theories on the ontology of time and are pertinent to his argument. According to *presentism*, only the present time exists. As soon as it comes into existence it passes out of existence. Neither the past nor the future concretely exist, only the present does. On *eternalism*, all moments of time always exist. The past, the present, and the future all concretely exist equally. Many today have assumed, Mullins notes, that divine timelessness entails eternalism, and that divine temporality entails presentism. This, however, is not the case. As he demonstrates in later chapters, the majority of theologians and philosophers throughout the Christian tradition have affirmed both presentism along with timelessness. I will discuss this more below when discussing chapter 4.

In chapter 3, Mullins clarifies the understanding of *eternity* on which he will build his argument. Since his argument ultimately aims to demonstrate the incoherence of divine atemporality, he assumes the traditional view of *eternity* as timeless eternity. Drawing from the protestant scholastic theologian Benedict Pictet, Mullins articulates that the claim that God is timelessly eternal entails the three following propositions:

1. "God exists without beginning.
2. God exists without end.
3. God exists without succession, or successive moments, in His life" (44).

It is at this point that Mullins demonstrates necessary entailments for the divine timeless research project against which he is arguing. In order for God to be timelessly eternal then he must be immutable, i.e. God cannot experience change in any shape, form, or fashion, be it intrinsic change or extrinsic change. If God does not undergo any intrinsic or extrinsic change, then he necessarily is timeless, as well as impassible (47–51). Not only divine immutability, but divine timelessness also entails divine simplicity. Divine simplicity, according to Mullins, entails the following six propositions:

1. "God cannot have any spatial or temporal parts" (52).
2. "God cannot have any accidental properties" (58).
3. "There cannot be any real distinction between one essential property and another in God's nature because God does not have any properties" (54).
4. "There cannot be a real distinction between essence and existence in God" (52).
5. "The divine nature lacks conceptual distinctions" (53).
6. "God is pure act such that God lacks all potential" (58).

Mullins rightly notes that these four doctrines—simplicity, immutability, impassability, and timelessness—all mutually entail one another. If one of these doctrines and their entailed propositions does not obtain, then the others unravel in turn. So, in order for one to have a successful divine timeless research program, they must affirm all four of these doctrines in addition to affirming all other core doctrines to the Christian faith, such as the Trinity, the Incarnation, and Creation *ex nihilo*.

Mullins constructs his argument against the divine timelessness research project in chapters four through seven. In chapter four, he argues that divine timelessness is not consistent with the traditional doctrine of divine omniscience. Per this doctrine, God knows all true propositions, both those necessarily true and contingently true. In order to make this argument, Mullins first demonstrates that presentism has been the ontology of time affirmed throughout the majority of the Christian tradition. Again, *presentism* holds that only the present concretely exists. The past and future do not concretely exist. The presentist also affirms *endurantism*, that concretely existing things *endure* through time, and endurantism has been affirmed as the classical view throughout Christian history as well. Since God is timeless, i.e. has no beginning, no end, and no succession, it is not clear how, or that, God can know what time it is *now*. For example, if I look at my phone, it says that it is 2:30pm, then I know what time it is now. However, when I look at my phone at 2:31pm, then I know that *now* it is 2:31pm. At 2:31pm, the proposition, "It is 2:30pm," becomes false. If a proposition is false, then, by definition, it cannot be *known*. Since I endure through time as time progresses forward, then I am capable of knowing what time it is now. This cannot be the case, however, for a timeless being. If God is timeless, then he experiences no succession whatsoever, i.e. he does not experience temporal change. As a timeless being, God does not endure through time. But suppose God simply perceives creation at 2:30pm; surely, he could know that it is now 2:30pm. But at 2:31pm, the truth value of this proposition would change to false. According to omniscience, God knows all true propositions. Therefore, God cannot know that it is 2:30pm if it is currently 2:31pm since the proposition "It is 2:30pm" would be false. More importantly, since God is immutable, then he cannot experience any intrinsic or extrinsic change whatsoever, including a change in his knowledge, which is identical with himself per divine simplicity. On a presentist ontology of time, which is the classical view, a timeless God could not actually be omniscient since he could not know what time it is now.

Not only is divine timelessness inconsistent with God's omniscience, but it is also inconsistent with the doctrine of creation *ex nihilo*. In chapter 5, Mullins confronts two particular issues that arise for the one who affirms both presentism and divine timelessness: "First, the timeless God cannot create a presentist temporal universe out of nothing. Second, the timeless God cannot sustain a presentist universe in existence" (99). If God creates something out of nothing, then that something *begins* to exist. This beginning, necessarily, is a temporal beginning. So, if God creates time, then time itself *begins* to exist. The problem here is that if time begins to exist, then this presupposes some prior time wherein this newly created time begins to exist, i.e. a time before time, which is incoherent. This is a problem also for the rest of creation. If creation is from nothing, then it begins to exist. There is no way around that. And if something begins to exist, then this means that there has been a *change* in the previous states of affairs. However, this creates a problem for divine immutability, which holds that God experiences no intrinsic or extrinsic change. Again, according to divine timelessness, there is no succession in the life of God. So, per this doctrine, when God creates, there is no succession. However, it is unclear how there is no succession if creation *begins* to exist. There seems to be a clear moment of succession between the creation's non-existence and its existence (101–103). Not only is creation *ex nihilo* a problem for divine timelessness, but so is the claim that God sustains creation. On the classical presentist view, if God always sustains creation, then that means he sustains it at t_1, t_2, t_3, and so on. Again, on presentism, the past and future do not exist. Rather, only the present exists, and it is always becoming into the next successive moment. If God is always sustaining the creation, then that means he is sustaining the creation during each successive moment, at t_1, t_2, t_3, and so on. Again, this seems to be a clear instance of succession in the life of God, if he is sustaining creation at t_1, t_2, t_3, and so on. There are two alternatives here for the divine timelessness research project. First, it could argue that creation is co-eternal with God, which is a direct contradiction to creation *ex nihilo*. Second, it could argue that God does not really relate to creation. Mullins correctly observes that neither of these alternatives are viable for the Christian since both creation *ex nihilo* and that God really relates to the creation are essential Christian doctrines (122–26). To deny that God really relates to creation means to deny that he is *really* creator, redeemer, and Lord, as these are relations he holds to the creation.

In chapter 6, Mullins tackles the issues of divine timelessness and four-dimensional eternalism. Again, according to eternalism, all moments exist simultaneously and equally for all of (timeless) eternity. Many who affirm divine timelessness, such as Katherine

Rogers, forgo presentism in favor of eternalism, which is supposed to help them overcome the issues already mentioned concerning omniscience and creation. Mullins spends the bulk of this chapter primarily addressing Rogers's eternalism and demonstrating that it is still unsuccessful to overcome the issues surrounding God's relation to creation. More specifically, it is still unclear how, on the eternalist view, the timeless God creates from nothing. Rogers invokes the metaphysical theory of theistic idealism, which holds that all of reality exists as God's thoughts. God's thoughts are contingent on God for their existence, but since God never begins to think, they are co-eternal with him. The problem here is that this still denies that creation begins to exist. Moreover, it still denies that creation is from nothing. Mullins then turns his attention to what he perceives to be the foundational doctrine for divine timelessness: divine simplicity (DS).

DS, Mullins argues, ultimately entails a modal collapse (137–43). Modality is a component of philosophical logic that deals with necessity, contingency, and possibility. To say that something is necessary means it could never be otherwise. To say that something exists necessarily means that it could never not exist; it *must* exist. This is *absolute necessity*. God, i.e. a necessary being, necessarily exists and could never not exist. There is also *contingent necessity*. Something is a contingent necessity if it does not exist of itself necessarily but does so because it has been caused to exist. For example, it is not necessary that a mark exist on my white board. However, if I draw a mark on the white board, i.e. cause the mark to exist, then it necessarily exists on the white board. According to DS, God is pure act and has no potential. In other words, everything that could be for God is actual for God, for if it were not actualized then it would be potential, of which God has none. This creates a problem with another essential Christian doctrine: the doctrine of God's freedom. Christians, in affirmation of what is taught in Scripture, affirm that it was not necessary that God create. He could have not created. Creation was his free choice. If God could choose to do otherwise, then this means that God has the potential to do otherwise. But on DS, God does not have potential because he is pure act. If God has created, then, per DS, he was not actually free to not create, because this would imply that God had non-actualized potential. Not only this, but, per DS, God could not have created in such a way that creation could have been different, because this would have been potential in God.

The way creation exists is the way that God had to create it. On DS, everything that exists ultimately exists as an *absolute necessity*. This is what a modal collapse is: the modal reduction of everything to the status of absolute necessity. Everything that exists in creation, including all of the evil therein, on DS, is an absolute necessity, because God is pure act and has no potential. Implied here is that God ultimately was not free to create, but, because he is pure act and could not have done otherwise, had to create, and he had to create the world as it actually is and not in any other way. This is in contradiction to all of those places in Scripture where it depicts God repenting and desiring that things had been otherwise.

The final chapter for Mullins argument addresses the incompatibility of divine timelessness with the incarnation. In summary, the orthodox doctrine of the incarnation, as articulated by the ecumenical councils, namely Chalcedon and Constantinople III, is incompatible with the timeless God. Neither Chalcedonian Christology nor the orthodox doctrine of dyotheletism, i.e. the doctrine that Christ had two minds and wills. Every attempt, Mullins shows, to affirm these views along with divine timelessness results either in Nestorianism or adoptionism, both of which are condemned heresies in the Christian tradition. If the attempt to reconcile timelessness with the orthodox doctrine of the incarnation does not result in these heresies, then it results contradicting either the doctrines of immutability or simplicity. In sum, the incarnation becomes a logical impossibility for the timeless God. Mullins concludes the book with a brief Conclusion chapter wherein he demonstrates the lack of scriptural support for divine timelessness. He closes by suggesting that Christians should dispense with the timeless God in order to remain faithful to Scripture, which depicts a God that is temporal, though he is not a prisoner to time.

Mullins's *The End of the Timeless God* is one of the more important contemporary contributions to the God-and-time discussion. Especially commendable is how articulate he is throughout the book. He does an outstanding job at providing necessary definitions the reader needs to know in order navigate the book, and, due to his use of analytic philosophy, is able to build his argument carefully and methodically without ridding it of perspicuity. Though the intended audience of the book seems to be other professional theologians and philosophers, I would be comfortable in assigning this book to a second or third semester seminary student in one of my classes. Mullins's ability to provide such a clear and accessible treatment of such an erudite and esoteric discussion is highly commendable.

One of the strongest aspects of *The End of the Timeless God* is also what might prevent many readers from accepting its thesis. Throughout, Mullins demonstrates that the doctrine of divine timelessness cannot be separated from the entailed doctrines of simplicity, immutability, and impassability. These four doctrines together serve as the basis for the model of God known as *classical theism*. Indeed, one cannot be a classical theist, at least not in any traditional sense, and reject any of these four doctrines, for to reject one ultimately leads to the rejection of them all. If Mullins's argument is sound, i.e. it has all true premises and is valid in form, then the Christian will not only be dispensing with the timeless God, but the God of classical theism. This very well might be a destination that the reader is not comfortable arriving at. This does not mean that one has to reject the biblical and Christian portrait of God. It very well might be the case, especially in light of Mullins's arguments, that classical theism is not the model of God that best represents the biblical depiction of God, to which all Christians most fundamentally want to hold. Regardless of one's commitments to classical theism, Mullins's arguments in this book deserve to be taken seriously and thought through thoroughly.

The End of the Timeless God is an endeavor in philosophical theology. More specifically, it is an endeavor in analytic theology. Analytic theology is an approach to Christian theology that aims to use the best tools provided by analytic philosophy, i.e. methodic argumentation, logical rigor, and linguistic perspicuity, to articulate and defend Christian doctrine, especially those doctrines essential to the faith, e.g. the Trinity, the Incarnation, etc. Analytic theology has not been spared any detractors. A great many other theologians have been critical of the project, arguing that many analytic theologians ignore the developments of doctrine throughout the Christian tradition and ignore the contributions of historical theology altogether. Mullins's book, however, is not one that can receive that accusation. Throughout the book, he not only dialogues with important patristic and medieval theologians who have contributed to the discussion, but he also interacts with some of the best scholarship on said theologians. In addition to his trenchant analyses of Augustine's and Thomas's work, Mullins also enters into dialogue with well-decorated Augustinian and Thomistic scholars, such as Paul Helm, Katherine Rogers, Eleonore Stump, Norman Kretzmann, and many others. One only need to glance through his exhaustive footnotes to see that the author, to the best of his ability, has dialogued with the great tradition as well as some of the best theologians commenting on the tradition.

The only critique I have with *The End of the Timeless God* is with the tone of the final paragraph of the book, especially the last three sentences: "Divine timelessness has had a long run in Church history, but it is time to bury it and move on. We should not mourn its passing. It shall not be missed" (209). Such comments might be perceived by readers as an arrogant indictment on a doctrine that has been held for the majority of the Christian tradition and by some of the tradition's best theologians. While I do not think this is Mullins's intention here, I could easily sympathize with those who might not offer as charitable of a reading. Though I find Mullins's arguments against divine timelessness to be very persuasive, many readers, for whom classical theism is very close and dear to them, may not be quite ready to dispense with it. And this is understandable. It is very concerning to think that the church might have misunderstood something such as God's relation to time for the majority of its existence. I think Mullins does offer some pastoral comfort for such a person in his insistence that moving beyond divine timelessness and classical theism gives us the opportunity to cultivate a new model of God that will better represent the portraits of God painted in Scripture. Such should always be the task of the church that is *semper reformanda*—always reforming.

In summary, Mullins has written a very challenging and well-argued book that is a must read for anyone interested in the God-and-time discussion, as well as the doctrine of God in general. His arguments are careful and logically consistent, and they provide much for the reader to think on. I would recommend this book primarily to other professional theologians and philosophers interested in the doctrine of God, though I would also recommend it to seminary students and other graduate students of theology and philosophy.

Andrew Hollingsworth,
Brewton-Parker College,
Mt. Vernon, Georgia

David Hume. By James. N. Anderson. Great Thinkers. Edited by Nathan D. Shannon. Phillipsburg, NJ: P&R, 2019. 125 pages. Paperback, $14.99.

Confessional Protestants with interest in apologetics often find themselves overwhelmed at the sheer breadth of writings in the respective western philosophical tradition. Moreover, those who digest the primary sources can struggle to connect a thinker's impact on Christian theology. The Great Thinkers series seeks to bridge this gap.

Great Thinkers is, in many ways, a continuation of the project encapsulated in John Frame's *History of Western Philosophy and Theology* (P&R, 2015). By focusing on single figures in digestible volumes, the series has the potential for greater depth while at the same time increasing readership. As the introduction notes, the publisher seeks to be *academically informed, biblically and theological faithful,* and *accessible* (x).

As a Christian philosopher and ordained minister, James Anderson does academic justice to Hume's thought without lapsing into pedantry. Good apologetic works are able to maintain the razor's edge between intellectual depth and nuance on the one hand, and a compelling polemical style, on the other. *David Hume* is one of these. The book divides into eight concise, encyclopedic chapters that correspond to Anderson's twofold purpose for writing the book, which is "to provide a summary exposition of the major points of Hume's thought" and "to offer a critical assessment of them from a distinctively Reformed perspective" (xxiii).

Apologists and theologians often cite David Hume for his formidable arguments against miracles, yet his impact extends deeper and wider than many realize. After giving a succinct summation of the Scotsman's life, Anderson identifies the nature of Hume's philosophical project and expounds the following salient points: Hume's anti-supernaturalism is methodological, not metaphysical naturalism (10), the idea of causation is a psychological feature of our minds, not a metaphysical feature of our world (19), and that his epistemology is "psychologized" (20–21).

Anderson cites contemporary examples where Hume's thought is applied in various contexts and any inherent problems for orthodox Christians. The author cites Bart Ehrman's *Jesus Interrupted* (HarperCollins, 2009) as exemplary of intentional or unintentional use of Hume's arguments against miracles. Like Hume, Ehrman rejects miracles as a matter of principle, not evidence (63). In discussing Hume's ethics, Anderson explains the philosopher's "sentimentalist" position as one of which the passions have primacy over reason. The implications for this turn are extensive. By locating the origin and existence of justice in public utility, Hume is arguably the father of Utilitarianism. Contemporary ethical trends, such as the defense of animal rights juxtaposed with the advocacy of abortion, can be traced back to Hume's thought where maximizing pleasure and minimizing pain are primary considerations (59).

Identifying holes in Hume's thought, Anderson notes how an exclusively empirical method precludes a mind-independent reality and thus carries the specter of solipsism (80–81). Additionally, his ethical framework cannot account for moral obligations between human beings. Though some aspects of Hume's philosophy are meatier to digest, for instance, the distinction between ideas and impressions, Anderson deftly draws the reader to their implications.

Chapter seven provides a constructive modern alternative to Hume's religious skepticism. Two premises raised by Hume constitute "the evidentialist challenge." Premise 1 asserts that a belief is rationally justified only if it is supported by sufficient evidence, and Premise 2 maintains that Christian beliefs are not supported by sufficient evidence. Apologists today are split over which premise should be attacked. Anderson focuses on the former, drawing from the Reformed philosopher Alvin Plantinga the notion that many beliefs are "properly basic," and thus, rationally justified, a possibility Hume did not entertain (88). According to the author, the presuppositionalism of Cornelius Van Til offers the simple conclusion that Hume's naturalism is inherently incompatible with a Christian worldview.

Anderson locates several places where Hume's empiricism is self-defeating. For example, though Hume claimed to construct a strictly "scientific" understanding of human nature and the world, his arguments against miracles would actually hinder scientific discovery. Anderson writes, "No future observations could be accepted as evidence against a presumptive law of nature… [f]or the consistent Humean, neither relativity theory nor quantum mechanics should have been accepted by physicists" (98). That Hume's skepticism about probabilistic reasoning in his *Enquiry* unintentionally supports the idea of a miracle is a clever observation, for, on the philosopher's own terms, we should never believe that a death will not be followed by a resurrection despite the apparent cause and effect over millennia (102).

Anderson acknowledges that some aspects of Hume's thought are amenable to Reformed Apologetics—e.g., his denial of Natural Theology—and provides support for these claims. Citing apologists who've attempted to apply and harmonize Hume's thought with the Christian faith would have been a helpful addition. In the broader intellectual context, moral psychologist Jonathan Haidt endorsed Hume's sentimentalism in *The Righteous Mind* (Pantheon, 2012). Perhaps a footnote mentioning the appropriation of Hume in contemporary psychology would prove insightful.

Readers with a general knowledge of Christian apologetics and who understand the principle questions raised in western philosophy would benefit the most from reading *David Hume*. For example, Hume's denial of causation is, *prima facie*, absurd to an observer with a common-sense ontological realism. *David Hume* concludes with a poetic and fitting epilogue, contrasting the statue of the empiricist philosopher in Edinburgh with another great Scot of a bygone era: John Knox. The figures symbolize two intellectual paths that continue to battle for the heart and mind of Western Civilization, a battle of which the author is himself consciously engaged.

Ryan Rindels
Gateway Seminary, Ontario, California;
First Baptist Church, Sonoma, California